Helping Students Overcome Social Anxiety

The Guilford Practical Intervention in the Schools Series

Kenneth W. Merrell, *Founding Editor*
T. Chris Riley-Tillman, *Series Editor*

www.guilford.com/practical

This series presents the most reader-friendly resources available in key areas of evidence-based practice in school settings. Practitioners will find trustworthy guides on effective behavioral, mental health, and academic interventions, and assessment and measurement approaches. Covering all aspects of planning, implementing, and evaluating high-quality services for students, books in the series are carefully crafted for everyday utility. Features include ready-to-use reproducibles, lay-flat binding to facilitate photocopying, appealing visual elements, and an oversized format. Recent titles have Web pages where purchasers can download and print the reproducible materials.

Recent Volumes

Helping Students Overcome Social Anxiety

Skills for Academic and Social Success
(SASS)

CARRIE MASIA WARNER
DANIELA COLOGNORI
CHELSEA LYNCH

THE GUILFORD PRESS
New York   London

Copyright © 2018 The Guilford Press
A Division of Guilford Publications, Inc.
370 Seventh Avenue, Suite 1200, New York, NY 10001
www.guilford.com

Printed in Canada

This book is printed on acid-free paper.

Last digit is print number: 9   8   7   6   5   4   3   2   1

Library of Congress Cataloging-in-Publication Data

Names: Masia Warner, Carrie, author.
Title: Helping students overcome social anxiety : skills for academic and social success (SASS) /
    Carrie Masia Warner, Daniela Colognori, and Chelsea Lynch.
Description: New York, NY : The Guilford Press, [2018] | Series: The Guilford practical
    intervention in the schools series
Identifiers: LCCN 2017051990 | ISBN 9781462534609 (paperback : acid-free paper)
Subjects: LCSH: Social phobia in adolescence—Treatment. | Social phobia in children—
    Treatment. | BISAC: PSYCHOLOGY / Psychopathology / Anxieties & Phobias. | EDUCATION /
    Counseling / General. | SOCIAL SCIENCE / Social Work. | PSYCHOLOGY / Psychotherapy /
    Child & Adolescent.
Classification: LCC RJ506.S63 W37 2018 | DDC 618.92/85225—dc23
LC record available at *https://lccn.loc.gov/2017051990*

About the Authors

Carrie Masia Warner, PhD, is Professor of Psychology at Montclair State University in New Jersey, Research Scientist at the Nathan Kline Institute for Psychiatric Research, and Adjunct Associate Professor in the Department of Child and Adolescent Psychiatry at NYU Langone Medical Center. Dr. Masia Warner is an expert in pediatric anxiety disorders and school implementation of evidence-based interventions. She has systematically developed and evaluated interventions for children and adolescents in community settings, with a focus on enhancing the identification and treatment of teenagers with social anxiety and training front-line school professionals. She has published over 65 peer-reviewed articles and book chapters.

Daniela Colognori, PsyD, is Clinical Director of the Tourette Syndrome Clinic at the Graduate School of Applied and Professional Psychology at Rutgers, The State University of New Jersey. She is also a founding partner at Specialized Psychological Services, a private clinical practice, where she provides cognitive-behavioral therapy for individuals with anxiety, mood, tic, and body-focused repetitive behavior disorders. Dr. Colognori's research interests and publications focus on improving access to evidence-based interventions for youth with anxiety and mood disorders through partnerships with schools.

Chelsea Lynch, MA, is a graduate student in the Clinical Psychology Doctoral Program at Florida State University. She worked in the NYU Langone Medical Center's Child Study Center on a randomized clinical trial evaluating the effectiveness of counselor-delivered cognitive-behavioral therapy for social anxiety in schools. Ms. Lynch has also worked in clinical outpatient, residential, and forensic settings. She currently conducts psychological assessments and provides evidence-based psychological treatment to adults and youth in the community as a student therapist in the Florida State University Psychology Clinic. Her research interests include evaluating psychological risk factors that contribute to the development and maintenance of co-occurring psychological disorders.

▼

Acknowledgments

The intervention strategies described in this book are based on the program *Skills for Academic and Social Success* (SASS), a social anxiety treatment specifically designed for school-based delivery with adolescents. We greatly appreciate the contributions of the many school administrators, personnel, counselors, and students with whom we have worked. Grants awarded to Carrie Masia Warner by the National Institute of Mental Health (No. R01 MH081881, K23 MH065373), the Anxiety and Depression Association of America, and the Andrew Kukes Foundation for Social Anxiety provided integral funding for the rigorous evaluation of the school-based intervention for social anxiety.

We wish to thank several esteemed colleagues for their contributions and feedback during various stages of the development and evaluation of SASS. We are grateful to Dr. Deborah C. Beidel for providing us with *Social Effectiveness Therapy for Children* (SET-C) and to Dr. Ronald Rapee for his work on realistic thinking and educating parents about strategies for helping anxious children. Their respective work served as a foundation for the school-based intervention described in this book. We also appreciate feedback from Drs. Anne Marie Albano, Deborah Beidel, and Ronald Rapee on initial versions of the SASS program. Finally, we express our deepest gratitude to Dr. Rachel Klein for her tremendous support and invaluable contributions to the design and execution of the systematic empirical studies evaluating the implementation of SASS in schools.

Contents

PART II. PROMOTING SKILLS FOR ACADEMIC AND SOCIAL SUCCESS (SASS)

PART III. SUPPLEMENTARY STRATEGIES

13. Getting Parents Involved: How Can They Help? 157

14. School Social Events and Peer Assistants 169

PART IV. OTHER PRACTICAL AND CLINICAL CONSIDERATIONS

PART I

RECOGNIZING
AND ADDRESSING
SOCIAL ANXIETY AT SCHOOL

CHAPTER 1

What Is Social Anxiety?

It is common for teenagers to be self-conscious and to care about what others think of them. Adolescence is a time of constant flux, with increasing academic demands, shifts in friendships, and changing physical appearance, all of which present new challenges and insecurities. A focus on peer relationships and worries about fitting in or gaining approval from others are central to this developmental period. Therefore, some nervousness in social situations during this time is typical and expected. However, some teenagers have more significant fears of social and performance situations that cause them to avoid these situations or endure them with great distress. This social anxiety is greater than the well-known social angst of the teenage years because it interferes with quality of life and healthy development. Understanding how social anxiety differs from typical teenage nervousness and recognizing when students require intervention is crucial for fostering academic and social success in teenagers within the school environment and beyond.

SOCIAL ANXIETY DEFINED

Social anxiety disorder is characterized by excessive fear of social and performance situations due to concern about being rejected or humiliated in front of others (American Psychiatric Association, 2013). In essence, social anxiety is an intense fear of negative evaluation or disapproval from others. Students with social anxiety commonly fear situations such as speaking with new or unfamiliar people, answering questions in class, giving verbal presentations, initiating conversations, attending parties or school activities, speaking to teachers or other authority figures, performing in musical and athletic activities, and extending social invitations to others (Mesa, Nieves, & Beidel, 2011; Hofmann et al., 1999). These situations are either endured with intense distress or avoided (e.g., remaining silent rather than initiating conversations with teammates or sharing thoughts in class). Often the avoidance occurs across a wide range of mainstream activities, causing pervasive limitations in social and academic functioning (Wittchen, Stein, & Kessler, 1999).

Social anxiety is conceptualized as involving three systems (Lang, 1968): cognitive, physical, and behavioral. The cognitive or mental component is wrought with worry about poor social performance or negative evaluation both in anticipation of and during social situations. Physical reactions to social events include tachycardia, blushing, shaking, and sweating. Finally, avoidance is the defining feature of the behavioral system. Circumvention of social interactions may be subtle, such as avoiding eye contact or choosing a sports team or school club with minimal interaction (Beidel & Turner, 2007). There is also substantial evidence that teenagers with social anxiety have mild social skills deficits (e.g., difficulty engaging in extended conversations) that may contribute to avoidance of social situations (Beidel, Turner, & Morris, 1999; Kendall, Settipani, & Cummings, 2012; Spence, Donovan, & Brechman-Toussaint, 1999). Understanding these three components is essential for effectively intervening in the anxiety cycle. This three-component model of the cognitive, physical, and behavioral features of social anxiety will be thoroughly described in Chapter 4, with specific guidance on how to explain this system to students.

> **Social anxiety involves three systems: cognitive, physical, and behavioral.**

WHAT DOES SOCIAL ANXIETY LOOK LIKE?

Sean is a quiet 15-year-old sophomore who is easily "lost in the crowd." He had a few close friends in elementary school, but when they entered middle school and joined with other peers, Sean had trouble forming new relationships. He spends very little time with peers outside of school and only invites his long-term close friends to get together. He sits at a lunch table with a group of boys in the cafeteria but says little. Sean is on the track team but mostly keeps to himself during meets unless someone approaches him. He rarely attends track dinners or parties with his teammates, and he refuses to join any school clubs that require more interaction. Sean is compliant and well behaved in class, and his grades are above average. His teachers never have much to say about him because he doesn't often interact with them. On report cards, he has received comments that he should try to participate more, but when encouraged to speak up in class, he becomes extremely uncomfortable or agitated. Does this student sound familiar?

HOW IS SHYNESS DIFFERENT FROM SOCIAL ANXIETY?

We all know shy teenagers who are reserved or initially reluctant to engage with unfamiliar people. Shyness, which is often considered a temperamental or personality trait, is defined as inhibition in interpersonal situations (Henderson & Zimbardo, 1998). While shyness is closely related to social anxiety, there are important distinctions. One essential difference is the degree of functional impairment (Heiser, Turner, Beidel, & Roberson-Nay, 2009; Turner, Beidel, & Townsley, 1990). For many, the experience of feeling shy may be temporary. Shy adolescents typically experience less worry anticipating social interactions and less distress while in social situations. In addition, shy adolescents do not often restrict their social activities due to fear, for instance, by leaving parties or school events prematurely or completely avoiding them to the degree that socially anxious adolescents do. More commonly, shy teenagers may be socially reserved but after a brief time, they become comfortable and readily engage in interactions (Heiser et al., 2009). This is illustrated in the case of Sean described above. If he were merely shy, he may have struggled to make new friends the first few months of ninth grade but would have established some new friendships by his sophomore year. Similarly, a shy teen would have found a way to participate more in class after becoming accustomed to new teachers and especially following constructive feedback on report cards about class participation. Unlike shyness, social anxiety is characterized by persistent worries that consume considerable time and energy and negatively impact the quality of students' lives.

IMPAIRMENT ASSOCIATED WITH SOCIAL ANXIETY

Social anxiety can be damaging in the teenage years and later in life. The social discomfort and avoidance experienced by youngsters with social anxiety disorder can often contribute to limited friendships, restricted school involvement (e.g., school clubs and sports teams), peer victimization (Ranta, Kaltiala-Heino, Fröjd, & Marttunen, 2013; Ranta, Kaltiala-Heino, Pelkonen, & Marttunen, 2009), and difficulty executing class requirements (e.g., verbal presentations, group projects, class participation) (Erath, Flanagan, & Bierman, 2007). In the case of Sean, he experiences significant distress, and his anxiety interferes across many settings, including in extracurricular activities, in the classroom, and socially with peers. Without intervention, Sean will continue to struggle with social anxiety, and his continued anxiety and avoidance put him at greater risk for additional mental health problems. Additional impairments associated with social anxiety disorder include loneliness, low self-esteem, negative self-worth, and depression (Beidel et al., 1999; Grover, Ginsburg, & Ialongo, 2007; Katzelnick et al., 2001; Wittchen et al., 1999). Possibly due to a lack of social support, students with social anxiety disorder are also at increased risk for suicidal ideation and behavior (Nelson et al., 2000). Additionally, research findings consistently point to a connection between social anxiety and later alcohol use (Black et al., 2012) with evidence that social anxiety disorder often occurs first. The use of alcohol to alleviate discomfort in social situations increases the likelihood of problematic alcohol use and increases the risk for alcohol use disorders (Carrigan & Randall, 2003; Thomas, Randall, & Carrigan, 2003).

WON'T THEY GROW OUT OF IT?

Social anxiety is among the most common psychological conditions in adolescents, impacting an estimated 9.1% during their lifetime (Merikangas et al., 2010). Social anxiety disorder may start as early as age 5, with its peak onset around age 12 (Kessler et al., 2005), corresponding with an increased complexity of social demands. With adolescence come new challenges, including separating from family and assuming more responsibilities for establishing and maintaining peer relationships. Unlike in childhood, it is no longer acceptable for parents to schedule playdates. Party invitations also become more selective. Therefore, a socially reticent child who functioned well in elementary school may begin to struggle in middle school when faced with new challenges like transitioning friendships, cliques, romantic connections, and increased expectations from teachers and coaches. From adolescence, social anxiety disorder tends to run a chronic, unremitting course into adulthood (Pine, Cohen, Gurley, Brook, & Ma, 1998), meaning that socially anxious teenagers who do not receive intervention typically continue to struggle with social anxiety as adults. The

> **Social anxiety disorder tends to run a chronic, unremitting course.**

debilitating impairment from social anxiety disorder that persists into young adulthood further contributes to exigent college transitions, underemployment, compromised professional attainment, impaired interpersonal relationships, and continued risk for depression and substance use problems throughout adulthood (Beesdo-Baum et al., 2012; Wittchen et al., 1999).

While there are effective treatment strategies to help these youths, the majority of students with social anxiety disorder do not receive mental health services, partially due to misconceptions that social anxiety is part of an individual's personality, like shyness, or an expected adolescent experience that will be outgrown. Socially anxious students are also overlooked because they do not typically exhibit overt behavior problems (Beidel et al., 1999; Fisher, Masia Warner, & Klein, 2004; Ryan & Masia Warner, 2012). Parents and teachers are therefore less likely to refer socially anxious adolescents to treatment unless teens specifically disclose their anxiety (Colognori et al., 2012). This unmet clinical need has motivated efforts to develop novel treatment models, such as employing the skills of school personnel, to better transport evidence-based interventions into the community (Schoenwald & Hoagwood, 2001).

Fortunately, school practitioners are in a valuable position to increase treatment access and provide clinically meaningful care for students. Equipping front-line school practitioners with effective interventions has the added benefit of providing adolescents with sus-

> **School practitioners can increase treatment access and provide clinically meaningful care for students.**

tained access to these therapeutic resources within the school setting (Masia Warner et al., 2016). This book will explain these interventions and provide guidance on how to implement them with socially anxious students in school.

HOW WILL THIS BOOK HELP?

This book has been written to assist school personnel in recognizing and addressing social anxiety in the school environment using evidence-based strategies (Masia Warner et al., 2016). School professionals, such as school counselors, guidance counselors, school social workers, school psychologists, and student advisers, interact with students every day and are clearly invested in the optimal development of youth. School professionals are in a unique position because they have unparalleled access to students, which allows for further promotion of mental and emotional health through implementation of effective, targeted interventions. The skills outlined in this book, such as realistic thinking, social skills, and gradual exposure, have a long history of demonstrated success reducing social anxiety in clinical settings through intervention programs such as Social Effectiveness Therapy for Children (SET-C; Beidel, Turner, & Morris, 1998, 2000). These skills have been adapted for use with socially anxious adolescents in school and have demonstrated effectiveness when delivered by school personnel (Masia Warner et al., 2016). This book will present these evidence-based skills as specifically designed for use with adolescents in schools. We refer to these strategies as Skills for Academic and Social Success (SASS; Fisher et al., 2004; Masia et al., 1999; Ryan & Masia Warner, 2012).

To illustrate how these skills are utilized in a typical case, we include a description of Lauren, a high school student struggling with social anxiety, as she works with her school counselor, Ms. Hillman, to learn strategies to overcome anxiety. Lauren's story is highlighted at the end of Chapters 3–15 to demonstrate the relevant skills as well as their flexible implementation in school using a combination of individual and group meetings. Our goal is to better equip school professionals, who are on the front lines with adolescents, to address the highly prevalent yet under recognized condition of social anxiety that often interferes with school functioning.

Part I of this book is devoted to helping school practitioners recognize social anxiety disorder in adolescents. It also highlights the importance of intervening with youth in the school environment. Chapter 1 provides a description of social anxiety disorder and its associated impairment. This chapter reviews social anxiety and makes the case for the importance of intervention, which the majority of affected adolescents do not receive. Chapter 2 provides school professionals with a rationale for implementing school groups targeting social anxiety. Treatment delivered in school has the potential to enhance treatment effectiveness and support skill development by allowing students to practice in a naturalistic environment where numerous feared situations occur (Ryan & Masia Warner, 2012). Finally, Chapter 3 explains how to identify students struggling with social anxiety who may benefit from intervention. It includes recommendations for school screening procedures that may be beneficial to school practitioners. This chapter also guides school professionals on how to form groups to begin implementing these intervention strategies in school.

Part II of this book teaches school practitioners and counselors how to implement school-based intervention and explains how to use the school environment to effectively treat social anxiety in adolescents. Part II details SASS strategies (Masia et al., 1999), providing a clear rationale for counselors and students as to why each is important for addressing social anxiety. Each chapter also provides counselors with guidelines for implementing skills training in groups or individually and presents instructions and sample scripts. Reproducible handouts that can be used with students and parents, as well as appendices containing additional informational resources, are provided at the end of each chapter. Finally, common treatment challenges are discussed, and strategies are offered regarding how to troubleshoot these issues.

In Chapter 4, school practitioners learn how to educate students about anxiety, including how thoughts, emotions, physiological responses, and avoidance behaviors all work together to maintain anxiety. Providing teenagers with psychoeducation about anxiety is critical for helping them understand the rationale for the recommended strategies. It increases the likelihood that they will be engaged in treatment and remain committed to practicing skills. Chapters 5 and 6 elaborate on the cognitive component of social anxiety. Adolescents with social anxiety tend to have negative thought patterns, characterized by specific types of thinking errors that contribute to anxious feelings, physiological symptoms, and behavioral avoidance (Weems, Berman, Silverman, & Saavedra, 2001). These chapters explain some of the most common thinking errors or cognitive distortions associated with social anxiety (Chapter 5), and they describe how to teach students to engage in realistic thinking to challenge their anxious thoughts (Chapter 6). Engaging in realistic thinking increases the likelihood that students will approach anxiety-provoking situations rather than avoid them (Rapee, 1998; Rapee & Heimberg, 1997; Rapee, Wignall, Spence, Lyneham, & Cobham, 2008).

Chapters 7–10 focus on social skills training for adolescents with social anxiety. Adolescents with social anxiety often show some social skills deficits due to the interference of anxiety and pervasive avoidance of social situations, which hinders social competence (Beidel et al., 1998, 1999; Beidel & Turner, 2007; Spence et al., 1999). Thus, enhancing social skills is an essential component of this intervention for youth. These chapters teach school professionals how to facilitate the practice of important skills, including initiating conversations (Chapter 7), maintaining conversations (Chapter 8), extending invitations to peers (Chapter 8), attending to conversations with others while managing anxiety interference (Chapter 9), and practicing assertiveness (Chapter 10). When students feel more prepared to interact socially, they often report more confidence and are more likely to enter into social situations.

The last two chapters in Part II, Chapters 11 and 12, illustrate how school personnel can conduct exposures with students in school. Gradual exposure to feared situations disrupts the anxiety cycle and reduces the distress, avoidance, and impairment for students with social anxiety disorder (Beidel et al., 1998, 2000). When students face feared situations they learn firsthand that their negative predictions are unlikely and that any potential negative consequences, like embarrassment or making a mistake, are likely tolerable (Clark et al., 2006). Chapter 11 teaches school personnel how to help students identify social fears and how to collaboratively develop exposure exercises with students to target those fears. Chapter 12 then illustrates how to conduct exposures emphasizing how to capitalize on a group format and the school environment.

Part III provides school personnel with important supplementary strategies that can enhance the effectiveness of this school-based intervention for social anxiety by involving parents, prosocial peer facilitators, and teachers in the program. Chapter 13 presents school professionals with strategies for engaging parents. It includes guidelines and scripts for educating parents about social anxiety, providing a rationale for the interventions, and describing parenting strategies supporting this approach (Rapee et al., 2008). Chapter 14 focuses on how school professionals can include prosocial peer facilitators and out-of-school social events (e.g., bowling, laser tag) to allow students to practice newly acquired skills and gain exposure to unstructured social situations (Beidel et al., 1998). Finally, since teachers spend a significant amount of time with students throughout the school day and are invested in supporting student development, Chapter 15 advises school professionals in engaging teachers to support students' social skills development and exposure practice in classrooms.

The final chapters of the book, in Part IV, are devoted to additional clinical considerations for conducting interventions in school. Chapter 16 addresses technical issues related to conducting sustainable school interventions and ordering sessions to maximize the effectiveness of the intervention. Chapter 17 explains how school providers can apply these skills and therapeutic techniques for social anxiety to other common anxiety problems in students. Multiple anxiety disorders often co-occur (Merikangas & Swanson, 2009), and adolescents with social anxiety may present with additional specific fears or general worries. Understanding how these strategies can be applied to various anxiety concerns can help school personnel flexibly and creatively address numerous student worries. The last chapter of the book, Chapter 18, provides school practitioners with final comments on how to maintain student progress. Even after effective treatment for social anxiety, individuals may experience a resurgence of anxiety or relapse of an anxiety disorder (Yonkers, Bruce, Dyck, & Keller, 2003). This chapter is essential for teaching school professionals how to support students' continued practice of skills to maintain gains that occurred over the course of their work together. By the end of this book, school professionals will possess the knowledge they need to identify social anxiety in their students, and to implement effective intervention strategies that capitalize on the school environment.

CHAPTER SUMMARY

- Social anxiety is an intense and pervasive fear of social and performance situations due to concern about negative evaluation or disapproval by others.

- The social discomfort and avoidance causes significant social and academic impairment including limited friendships, restricted school involvement, peer victimization, and difficulty executing class requirements.

- Commonly avoided situations in school include participating in class, initiating conversations with peers, acting assertively, attending parties or school activities, speaking to teachers or other authority figures, and extending social invitations to others.

- Social anxiety is highly prevalent in adolescence and tends to continue into adulthood when untreated.

- Effective intervention strategies for social anxiety, as detailed in this book, are optimal for use in school settings.

CHAPTER 2

Why Treat Social Anxiety at School?

Adolescents spend large portions of their day interacting with friends, other peers, and familiar adults within school and extracurricular environments. For many, school serves as a comfortable, nonthreatening context where they can express themselves, grow academically, and engage in meaningful relationships. This, however, is often not the case for socially anxious youth, who experience numerous feared situations throughout the school day. The amount of time adolescents spend in school for classes and extracurricular activities puts school personnel in an advantageous position to intervene and influence students' social, emotional, and behavioral functioning, as well as their academic growth. Therefore, schools and school personnel play a central role in addressing unmet mental health needs of youth, and they are especially valuable for addressing challenges specific to treating social anxiety. Providing intervention at school minimizes the considerable burdens associated with obtaining treatment in the community. It enhances access to intervention and supports the generalization of new skills by facilitating practice within students' typical environment. This chapter details why it is essential to implement treatment for social anxiety in schools.

WHY SHOULD SCHOOLS INVEST IN TREATING SOCIAL ANXIETY?

School-based treatment for social anxiety is ideal because schools are where teenagers spend most of their day and where socially anxious adolescents often experience the greatest number of feared situations and incur the most impairment. As mentioned, adolescents with social anxiety experience many difficulties related to academic requirements such as participating in class, asking for help from teachers, working with other students, or delivering classroom presentations. They are also generally less engaged in extracurricular activities (Beidel et al., 1999, 2007; Spence et al., 1999).

> **Students with social anxiety incur significant academic and social impairment.**

Additionally, students with social anxiety are at increased risk for long-term severe academic and vocational impairment including greater rates of school refusal (Van Ameringen, Mancini, & Farvolden, 2003), higher likelihood of failing a grade (Stein & Kean, 2000), higher rates of school dropout (Stein & Kean, 2000; Van Ameringen et al., 2003), decreased likelihood of pursuing advanced education (Kessler, 2003; Kessler, Foster, Saunders, & Stang, 1995), and poorer future employment performance (Kessler, Stang, Wittchen, Stein, & Walters, 1999; Wittchen et al., 1999).

Treating social anxiety early has strong potential to positively affect these crucial educational outcomes. The cognitive-behavioral strategies reviewed in this book are present oriented and emphasize both skill development and practice. These strategies are highly compatible with educational approaches relying on problem solving and repetition to solidify mastery of skills (Christner, Forrest, Morley, & Weinstein, 2007), and they are relevant to current educational reform goals (Sulkowski, Joyce, & Storch, 2012).

Response to Intervention and School-Based Social Anxiety Treatment

School professionals reading this book will likely be familiar with the amended Individuals with Disabilities Education Improvement Act of 2004 (IDEIA, 2004), the national special education law informing funding priorities and interventions within special education and related services. The 2004 Act uses language consistent with a response to intervention (RTI) service delivery model, through which schools are empowered to assess students and deploy evidence-based services for early intervention. Although RTI was designed to promote early academic intervention for learning disabilities, extensions to include students with emotional problems have broad implications for treating mental health issues in school (Sulkowski et al., 2012).

In the RTI paradigm, a school should first deliver evidence-based school interventions according to a three-tiered service delivery framework before classifying a student for special education accommodations. When considering academic interventions, these tiers include (1) evidence-based academic curricula for all students, (2) assessment and targeted interventions (e.g., small-group instruction) for students identified as academically at risk, and (3) intensive intervention and remediation for students at significant risk of failure. Implementation of tiered services is designed to increase prevention and early intervention in an effort to benefit students by improving academic and social functioning quickly rather than waiting for students to fail or develop more severe problems (Sulkowski et al., 2012). We describe below how the RTI framework can be applied to the implementation of mental health services for socially anxious students in schools.

Given the wealth of data suggesting that social anxiety impairs academic performance and achievement, the RTI paradigm of IDEIA (2004) can empower schools to provide socially anxious students with evidence-based strategies across a broad range of school service options (Sulkowski et al., 2012). Tier 1 anxiety services may include providing classroom teachers with information about what anxiety looks like in youth and helping teachers identify and refer students to school counselors. Because anxious students often go unrecognized, when feasible for schools, Tier 1 services should also include school-wide behavioral health screenings for anxiety. We expand on strategies for behavioral health screenings in Chapter 3.

When students exhibit symptoms of social anxiety in school, the RTI model empowers school professionals to intervene and provide students with additional supports. Tier 2 services might include further assessment of anxiety and several individual meetings with school counselors. Depending on a student's difficulties, counselors can flexibly choose to teach particular skills from this book, such as realistic thinking or exposures tailored to the student's challenges. Students with severe social anxiety who are experiencing significant distress and impairment in school may benefit from more intensive intervention consistent with Tier 3 services. Schools might run social anxiety skills groups across several weeks that not only cover the broad spectrum of strategies in this book but allow socially anxious students ample opportunities to practice the skills in realistic contexts with similar peers. Figure 2.1 illustrates one potential option for how schools might choose to employ the RTI framework to provide services for socially anxious students.

Current directions in education increasingly support the delivery of school-based mental health services. This book takes an initial step toward training school personnel by providing evidence-based strategies that can be used flexibly in the school setting to help socially anxious students with varying degrees of distress or impairment. We also provide specific guidance on how to intervene within the school context with students both individually and in groups.

DO SCHOOL-BASED PROGRAMS INCREASE ACCESS TO TREATMENT?

Providing evidence-based services in schools advances the public health goal of increasing access and reducing barriers to mental health treatment in a number of ways. Because people with social anxiety are more fearful of potential negative evaluation that comes with

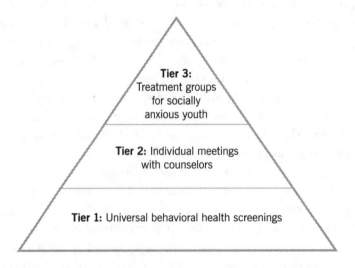

FIGURE 2.1. Employing the RTI framework in social anxiety intervention.

seeking help, they are particularly unlikely to enter treatment on their own (Kessler, 2003; Kessler, Stein, & Berglund, 1998). Therefore, in order to successfully treat adolescents with social anxiety, we first need to identify them through active screening and engagement. Offering services in schools provides opportunities to screen students on a broad scale. It also has the added benefit of helping teachers and other school personnel become more knowledgeable about often overlooked mental disorders like social anxiety. Teacher education about anxiety and knowledge of available intervention programs may facilitate treatment referrals for anxious students who are currently unlikely to be referred (Colognori et al., 2012; Fisher et al., 2004; Ryan & Masia Warner, 2012).

In addition to increased identification of youth requiring services, school-based interventions reduce the financial burden on families by including mental health programs within the range of regularly offered educational services (Weist, Paskewitz, Warner, & Flaherty, 1996).

Providing treatment in school eliminates barriers related to lack of transportation and lack of child care for siblings, and it reduces session cancellation rates by eliminating interference from conflicting parent schedules (Armbruster & Lichtman, 1999; Evans, 1999; Weist et al., 1996). Furthermore, youth utilize available school-based mental health services at higher rates than clinic or hospital-based services (Evans, 1999). Thus, offering school mental health programs supports identification of issues like social anxiety, increases access to care, and reduces barriers to obtaining services for youth who need treatment.

> **School-based programs increase identification of youth in need of services and reduce barriers to treatment.**

WHO SHOULD DELIVER SCHOOL-BASED MENTAL HEALTH PROGRAMS?

Current school-based mental health practices often problematically rely on outside professional clinicians to implement programs. This is costly and unsustainable for most school districts (Herzig-Anderson, Colognori, Fox, Stewart, & Masia Warner, 2012). In order to incorporate interventions into the fabric of schools in a sustainable way, in-house school personnel need to be trained to deliver programs to students. School counselors and guidance counselors occupy the unique role of being responsible for the overall emotional well-being of students and are likely the ideal candidates for implementing such interventions (Herzig-Anderson et al., 2012; Ryan & Masia Warner, 2012). In fact, school counselors routinely express a preference for counseling and guidance tasks related to their professional training, as opposed to other administrative demands such as scheduling, tracking attendance, or overseeing standardized testing that often require their time (Johnson, Rochkind, & Ott, 2010; Moyer, 2011; Reese, 2010). Furthermore, providing these types of services is consistent with national school counseling objectives (American School Counselor Association [ASCA], 2016), which emphasize the importance of maintaining a comprehensive school counseling program (Anctil, Klose Smith, Schenck, & Dahir, 2012; ASCA, 2016; Moyer, 2011; Reese, 2010). In addition to standard career and educational planning services, alcohol and drug abuse prevention, and conflict mediation, comprehensive counseling programs include services for students experiencing emotional and behavioral difficulties (Reese, 2010).

School professionals such as school counselors are the optimal personnel to implement services for social anxiety because they are present and accessible to students on a daily basis, are familiar with the school culture, and are well positioned to develop meaningful therapeutic exercises (i.e., exposures) that capitalize on the school environment (see Chapters 12 and 16 for more detail). Recent research (Masia Warner et al., 2016) has suggested that implementation of services by school counselors may decrease treatment dropout and increase treatment compliance and attendance compared to school-based delivery by outside professionals. In addition, intervention delivered by school personnel, to whom students can have continued access following the termination of treatment, may provide a sustained therapeutic resource (Masia Warner et al., 2016). We recognize that schools employ professionals with a diversity of educational training and degrees to fulfill roles such as those of a school or guidance counselor. Therefore, we use the terms "therapist" or "counselor" interchangeably throughout this book to refer to an internal school professional deemed most appropriate to deliver intervention services based on each individual school's culture and division of responsibilities.

HOW DO SCHOOL SETTINGS ENRICH TREATMENT FOR SOCIAL ANXIETY?

School-based interventions provide opportunities for adolescents with social anxiety to practice skills, challenge beliefs, and enter into commonly avoided situations (e.g., eating in the cafeteria, speaking with school personnel) in realistic contexts where they experience the greatest distress (Fisher et al., 2004; Ryan & Masia Warner, 2012). For instance, classroom exercises can include students answering questions in class, volunteering to complete a problem on the whiteboard or chalkboard, or initiating conversations with peers. Exercises during other times of the school day can involve students asking to join a group of friendly peers in the cafeteria for lunch, greeting friends in the hallway between classes, or using a school bathroom that was previously avoided. Students may also be encouraged to join a club, audition for a play, or perform a musical solo that they have been interested in but too afraid to pursue. Implementing intervention in school also provides opportunities for natural observation as counselors may accompany students during school-based exposure tasks. Direct observation allows counselors to provide additional coaching and adjust intervention strategies to fit individual student needs (Evans, 1999).

In addition, teachers, coaches, and peers with whom socially anxious students routinely interact can support students' progress by participating in exposure tasks and skills practice (Evans, 1999; Ryan & Masia Warner, 2012). Teachers may participate in classroom challenges involving students arriving unprepared or late to class. They might also call on students in class, assign them to groups with unfamiliar peers, or assign leadership roles for group activities. Students can approach club advisers and coaches to discuss joining clubs or teams. Additional exposures can even involve talking with administrative staff in the main office or asking an administrator for assistance. In this way, treatment delivered in school reduces the division between the safe setting in which skills are taught and the naturalistic environment in which they must be implemented. Practicing skills in ecologically valid settings likely enhances treatment effectiveness, as well as generalization of newly acquired skills to situations and environments outside of school (Ryan & Masia Warner, 2012).

HOW DO SCHOOLS SUPPORT TREATMENT IN GROUPS?

School settings also support the implementation of group interventions. Compared to other types of pediatric anxiety (e.g., separation, specific, generalized), social anxiety may be less responsive to individual cognitive-behavioral therapy (CBT) (Ginsburg et al., 2011). Because of the social nature of students' fears, treatment delivered to a group of peers may be more relevant.

Unlike individual treatment, groups provide social exposure and opportunities to confront social fears with similar peers. Groups also allow students to practice social skills and receive feedback to optimize treatment benefits (Beidel et al., 1998; Kendall et al., 2012). In addition to these specific factors, participating in a group of peers with similar struggles can be therapeutic in and of itself. Adolescents with social anxiety are often embarrassed by their discomfort, and believe they are the only ones who worry about rejection and fear social interaction. Hearing their peers express similar thoughts and concerns often makes them feel less alone.

> **Schools enrich treatment for social anxiety and support implementation of group programs.**

Schools have a number of practical advantages over traditional clinical settings that facilitate providing these intervention strategies in a group. Traditional clinical settings often have difficulty forming groups of youth with similar developmental levels and specific clinical difficulties. Coordinating evening or weekend group times also poses a challenge for many community providers. Schools, on the other hand, have greater access to students and can organize groups by grade level to ensure that they include developmentally similar peers. Additionally, school personnel have access to student schedules and can arrange groups to take place during the school day, alternating days and times or scheduling during nonacademic classes to minimize disruption of any one class. Practical strategies for delivering a group intervention in school are further detailed in Chapter 16.

Groups are also a practical delivery method for schools. Schools inherently rely on groups for delivery of instruction, academic assessments, special education services, school activities or clubs, and team sports. Thus, delivery of school-based interventions in group settings could conceivably seem more appropriate or acceptable to students than a treatment relying only on individual therapy with their counselor. It may also be more efficient for school professionals to intervene with multiple students at once rather than meet with each student individually. However, we should note that a group format may not always be possible or desirable. For example, individual meetings may be preferred when students are so anxious or uncomfortable with peers that a group would preclude making progress. Individual meetings may also make it more feasible to accommodate individual student schedules and avoid academic periods, which may be particularly important for a student struggling academically. Furthermore, a combination of group and individual meetings may be beneficial in some circumstances, such as delivering the primary intervention in a group but offering additional support or individualized assessment and feedback in short one-on-one meetings. This book describes basic intervention strategies, followed by practical tips regarding treatment delivery in both groups and individual meetings.

ARE STUDENTS OPEN TO RECEIVING HELP AT SCHOOL?

Worries about stigma (e.g., being labeled as having a "problem") are magnified in socially anxious youth because of their severe sensitivity to negative evaluation. Compared to seeking care at mental health specialty clinics, providing treatment in schools has the potential to normalize student experiences of anxiety and decrease stigma associated with receiving intervention, which makes teacher referrals, parental consent, and student attendance more likely in school-based programs (Weist et al., 1996). This reduced stigma is especially likely when treatment is offered among routine activities or programs provided by schools. Students often miss class for a wide variety of specialized services throughout the day, including in-school delivery of occupational therapy or speech therapy, English-language learning programs, special education services, gifted programs, extracurricular activities such as music or traveling for sports, and routine academic advising meetings. For students with social anxiety, offering an individual or group program within a wide variety of standard school services such as those listed above could increase the acceptability of the program and increase the likelihood that socially anxious students might participate. Additionally, given that students have diverse schedules, interests, and responsibilities that may require them to miss class from time to time, students' participation in school-based intervention programs may not be as obvious to peers as some readers might think.

CHAPTER SUMMARY

- School-based mental health programs can increase identification of youth needing services and reduce barriers to treatment.
- Treatment delivered by school counselors has the potential to decrease treatment dropout and increase treatment compliance and attendance.
- School-based treatment is ideal for social anxiety because schools are where adolescents with social anxiety often incur the most impairment.
- School environments provide a rich context for social exposures and active rehearsal of social skills to decrease avoidance, a key aspect of dysfunction in social anxiety disorder.
- Group treatment may be beneficial and efficient for treating social anxiety, and groups fit well within the school environment.
- School-based mental health treatment has the potential to normalize student experiences and decrease stigma.

CHAPTER 3

Identifying Students Struggling
with Social Anxiety

Despite the negative impact of social anxiety disorder, most adolescents struggling with social anxiety never receive treatment. Recent data estimate that only 12% receive mental health services (Merikangas et al., 2011). One of the main obstacles to treatment access is that social anxiety can be difficult to detect and thus goes largely unidentified by teachers and parents. In contrast to behavior problems like hyperactivity or noncompliance, anxious students are less disruptive, making it more difficult to observe their impairment. Further complicating detection by adults, some socially anxious adolescents intentionally hide their distress because of intense fears of negative evaluation. Teachers or parents may also believe that social reticence is a personality trait or a phase that adolescents will naturally outgrow (Beidel et al., 1999; Fisher et al., 2004; Ryan & Masia Warner, 2012).

For these reasons, it is essential that school professionals be keen observers for signs of social anxiety in students. Although not as overt as disruptive or noncompliant behaviors, there are discernable anxious behaviors associated with social anxiety. Students with social anxiety take an avoidant approach to performance and social situations. This avoidance may be obvious (e.g., refusing to give a verbal report) or subtle (e.g., avoiding eye contact), and can be observed in numerous school settings, including the classroom, cafeteria, hallways, and extracurricular activities. In this chapter we describe what behaviors to look for when attempting to identify socially anxious students. We also include recommendations for self-report scales and school screening procedures to facilitate identification of students struggling with social anxiety.

WHAT DOES SOCIAL ANXIETY
LOOK LIKE IN THE CLASSROOM?

Students with social anxiety are often reluctant to voluntarily answer questions in class due to fears of being the center of attention or fears of negative evaluation. However, some students may push themselves to answer questions aloud when they are certain of the correct response. Students may also avoid asking questions or requesting assistance when they do not understand class material. When verbal presentations are assigned, students may either ask to go first to "get it over with" or last to delay as long as possible (and hope there is an earthquake that will collapse the school on presentation day!). In extreme cases, they may feel too nauseous, for example, to attend school. Interestingly, observers may not notice any visible signs of anxiety when these students present, even though students may report feeling flushed or shaky. Students with social anxiety typically do not volunteer to read aloud and may speak minimally when working in groups. They avoid speaking up assertively or providing their opinions. Students with social anxiety may avoid eye contact with the teacher during class lectures and discussions. They often report distress about arriving late to class because it places them in the spotlight; some will even choose to cut class completely rather than risk having their classmates turn around to face the door. Finally, during unstructured or free time in class (e.g., after finishing an assignment, waiting for the teacher), while most students chat with classmates sitting nearby, socially anxious teenagers may sit quietly or attempt to look occupied (e.g., take out a book or calendar), or may possibly ask to leave the classroom (e.g., go to the bathroom).

> **Students with social anxiety take an avoidant approach to performance and social situations.**

While most socially anxious students show some of these symptoms in classrooms, social anxiety can be context specific. In other words, a student may exhibit more symptoms in a particular class because of difficult content, a demanding teacher, or the presence of many unfamiliar classmates or older peers. At the same time, that student may appear comfortable in other classes. Further, some students who feel academically competent may not experience discomfort in any classes but struggle in other settings like the cafeteria or athletics.

WHAT DOES SOCIAL ANXIETY LOOK LIKE IN OTHER SCHOOL SETTINGS?

Students with social anxiety tend to avoid initiating conversations and interactions with peers, especially unfamiliar ones. Typically, they find it harder to initiate conversations than to respond to peers who approach them. They may be very comfortable with friends they have known for several years but experience distress around less familiar classmates. Therefore, if you observe socially anxious teenagers with their best friends, you might assume social anxiety is not present, but don't be fooled—they would probably appear much quieter and more introverted with less familiar peers. Teenagers with social anxiety may have a few close friends from elementary school or their neighborhood; however, they have difficulty initiating new friendships and will often struggle if their long-term friends move or join other peer groups. They might avoid groups at school with new peers even when close friends are present. Possibly the most intense fear of students with social anxiety is inviting other peers to get together outside of school. This situation heightens their sense of vulnerability due to the possibility of rejection or potential negative evaluation about their preferred activities (e.g., movies, video games).

A common school situation that is difficult for many socially anxious students is eating in the cafeteria. They may sit on the fringes of the group at the lunch table and not say much. In severe cases, they may sit alone or avoid the cafeteria completely, for example, by going to the library during lunch to complete homework instead. While walking in the halls, students with social anxiety often look down or avoid lingering to minimize social interaction. Some have trouble with gym class due to concerns about changing in front of others in the locker room or playing sports in front of others. Students who are very involved in athletics or feel competent in physical activity may not experience as many performance fears when engaged in gym class activities; however, these students may still experience distress when socializing on the sidelines waiting for their team's turn.

Students with social anxiety are often involved in extracurricular activities but gravitate toward those that accommodate their social and performance fears. For example, rather than audition for an individual part in the school play, they may join the stage crew or orchestra. In addition, depending on his particular fears, a socially anxious student may select sports characterized by independent play (e.g., track, swim, or tennis) to reduce worries about negatively affecting teammates' performance (e.g., making a bad pass in soccer). Alternatively, some students prefer team sports to solo activities because they fear being the center of attention and having all eyes on them. Many socially anxious students appear comfortable during structured athletic tasks (e.g., doing a drill) but seem disconnected during unstructured time (e.g., do not speak to teammates on the sidelines or during breaks). In addition, they usually do not speak up during team meetings and tend to go straight home after practices rather than socializing with teammates.

A typical school day presents numerous academic and social demands. Because attention from others makes socially anxious students feel nervous, they attempt to go unnoticed, trying to blend into the background until they are nearly invisible. Being aware of common characteristics is essential to identifying students who may be struggling. School professionals should remember that each student is unique and will not exhibit all of the signs that we have discussed. Rather each student with social anxiety may exhibit some of these behaviors, and different students may experience more or less distress than others across various situations. Table 3.1 summarizes some behavioral signs we have discussed.

HOW CAN I IDENTIFY SOCIALLY ANXIOUS STUDENTS?

Many socially anxious behaviors can be subtle and difficult to observe, especially for school professionals who may only see a student occasionally or for one class period during the day.

Unlike externalizing conditions, which are characterized by disruptive behaviors that are easily observable and interfere with the classroom routine (Owens & Fabiano, 2011), anxiety disorders are not readily detected and may require self-disclosure (Merikangas et al., 2011). Thus, it is understandable that the majority of socially anxious students go uniden-

TABLE 3.1. Common Observable Signs of Social Anxiety in School

- Experiences discomfort talking to peers, especially initiating conversations with unfamiliar peers
- Exhibits physical symptoms that include shaky hands, shaky voice, sweating, or flushed face
- Appears quiet and speaks softly or mumbles, making it difficult to hear
- Avoids eye contact with adults or peers
- Does not raise hand or speak up in class unless called on
- Will not ask a teacher for help or assistance with schoolwork
- Does not take leadership positions during group projects
- Does not talk to others before class or when there is downtime between activities
- Appears particularly nervous during presentations or avoids them altogether (i.e., does behind-the-scenes work in group presentations so others take speaking roles)
- Appears on fringes or outside of group in the cafeteria
- Avoids the cafeteria (e.g., goes to the library to do homework instead)
- Does not socialize with peers in the hallway
- Does not talk to teammates at games or meetings
- Gravitates toward clubs that do not meet or require little participation or is not a part of any extracurricular school activities

tified unless the social anxiety is at the most severe levels (e.g., the student has no friends, refuses to attend school). Therefore, we recommend using validated questionnaires or behavioral rating forms to help assess social anxiety in students. Many students find it easier to endorse anxious feelings on questionnaires than to speak about feelings directly. In addition, when students see standardized instruments with items describing exactly how they feel, they obtain an understanding that many people struggle with social anxiety and that they are not alone. Not only can the use of measures make students more comfortable disclosing anxiety, measures can also assist school professionals in understanding the severity of students' anxiety. Most assessment instruments report scores that are suggestive of clinically meaningful symptoms. These instruments can be used at various points to help school professionals assess whether a student is experiencing social anxiety that warrants intervention.

> **Social anxiety and avoidant behaviors can be subtle and difficult to observe.**

Below, we describe a multi-tiered school screening process for social anxiety consistent with the RTI framework described in Chapter 2. This process includes a universal screening for all students and possibly solicitation of teacher nominations of shy students, followed by targeted multi-method assessment for nominated students or for students who endorse social anxiety on the screener. Similar screening processes have been used successfully in treatment intervention studies (e.g., Masia Warner et al., 2005, 2016; Masia Warner, Fisher, Shrout, Rathor, & Klein, 2007). We discuss questionnaires we have found helpful for identifying social anxiety during school screenings as well as questionnaires that we have found useful during treatment implementation within school settings.

Universal Screenings

For schools interested in taking a preventative approach, we recommend conducting yearly universal behavioral health screenings for all students, consistent with Tier 1 interventions in the RTI framework discussed in Chapter 2.

If your school already conducts routine mental health screenings, which some do, social anxiety self-report forms can easily be included as part of a larger screening battery. Screening measures can be completed during nonacademic class periods that all students must attend, such as a homeroom period, health class, or before gym class. Alternatively, screening tools can be administered individually during regular yearly check-ins with school counselors, perhaps during meetings to schedule classes for the following marking period or semester. Self-report school screenings are very useful for detecting anxiety in students who would not otherwise be identified or treated

> **Self-report measures and school screenings are helpful for identifying socially anxious students.**

(Masia Warner & Fox, 2012; Colognori et al., 2012). We have found the social anxiety subscales of the Multidimensional Anxiety Scale for Children, 2nd Edition (MASC 2), and the Screen for Child Anxiety Related Emotional Disorders (SCARED) to be useful for routine universal school screenings.

The MASC 2–Social Anxiety Subscale

The MASC 2 (March & Parker, 2004; March, Parker, Sullivan, Stallings, & Conners, 1997) assesses the presence of symptoms related to multiple anxiety disorders in youth ages 8–19 years. If a comprehensive assessment of anxiety symptoms is desired, the complete MASC 2 can be administered. The MASC 2 provides scale scores for generalized anxiety disorder, social anxiety, separation anxiety and phobias, obsessions and compulsions, physical symptoms, and harm avoidance. The MASC 2 includes 50-item self (MASC 2–SR) and parent (MASC 2–P) rating forms available for purchase from Multi-Health Systems (MHS) Psychological Assessments and Services (*www.mhs.com*). Both rating forms can be administered using online or paper-and-pencil formats, and both can be scored online using the MHS Online Assessment Center or scoring software. A positive feature of this instrument is that it contains a brief social anxiety subscale that takes only about 10 minutes to administer and can be used for screening social anxiety in large groups to identify students who may benefit from further assessment.

The SCARED–Social Subscale

The SCARED (Birmaher et al., 1997, 1999) is a 41-item inventory for youth ages 9–19 that assesses a broad range of anxiety symptoms including generalized anxiety disorder, separation anxiety disorder, panic disorder, and social anxiety. Like the MASC 2, it has a brief seven-item social anxiety scale that can provide a quick indication of social anxiety. The authors of the instrument suggest that a total score of 8 on the social scale is suggestive of clinically significant social anxiety. Another positive feature of this measure is that it is currently (at time of publication) available for use at no cost through the University of Pittsburgh website (*www.psychiatry.pitt.edu/sites/default/files/Documents/assessments/SCARED%20Child.pdf*).

Teacher Nominations

Because anxious behaviors are subtle and students intentionally try to hide their anxiety, teachers often have difficulty detecting anxious students except in the most severe cases (Fisher et al., 2004; Ryan & Masia Warner, 2012; Sweeney et al., 2015). Most of the students we have worked with in schools have been identified through positive scores on self-report measures rather than from teacher nominations, with only a small fraction of these students also referred by teachers (Sweeney et al., 2015). Therefore, we do not recommended relying on teacher nomination as the primary strategy for identifying social anxiety in students. Rather, teachers can be asked to nominate students who exhibit anxiety in social situations or who seem "shy" as a supplementary approach to student screenings.

Schools implementing this strategy should educate teachers about classroom behaviors that might indicate social anxiety. Counselors can provide teachers with a description of social anxiety and a list of common observable signs of social anxiety, such as those listed in Table 3.1. It is possible that providing teachers with class lists and asking them to circle the names of students who are most reluctant to participate in class or who speak less frequently to peers would improve detection and help ascertain more moderate cases of social anxiety. Teachers' identification skills might also be enhanced by receiving feedback on the accuracy of their referrals on an ongoing basis. Although standardized screenings are necessary for identification, educating teachers and engaging them in the referral process is also critically important for garnering teacher support and engagement in school-based intervention for socially anxious students.

Assessing Students Who Report Anxiety

Once socially anxious students have been identified, possibly through universal screenings, teacher nominations, or some combination of the two, we recommend further assessment to determine whether intervention is warranted and to identify specific targets of treatment (e.g., classroom performance, social interactions, athletic performance). Before meeting with a student individually, counselors can ask the student's teachers to report on anxiety symptoms and avoidant behaviors occurring in the classroom. A counselor might also conduct brief behavioral observations of identified students in academic classrooms or gym classes, or by walking through the lunchroom. The counselor could note any behaviors, such as those listed in Table 3.1, that are consistent or inconsistent with social anxiety. After direct observation, the counselor will likely have a better idea of what each student's anxiety and avoidance behaviors look like in different school settings.

Finally, counselors can discuss students' anxiety and difficulties with them individually. In many schools, students have regular check-ins with guidance counselors or school counselors for class scheduling. During a meeting in the first half of the school year, counselors can initiate a discussion of social anxiety. Because adolescents are not likely to be forthcoming in endorsing anxiety symptoms, counselors can approach this in several ways. Counselors could ask students about any teacher notes on report cards stating a need to speak up or participate in class, or they can ask about anything the student endorsed on the screeners. In addition, counselors may engage the student in a conversation about how she feels and behaves in different school settings, using teacher reports or counselors' behavioral observations to guide the conversation and assess social anxiety symptoms.

We also recommend using two measures—the Liebowitz Social Anxiety Scale for Children and Adolescents (LSAS-CA; Masia Warner, Klein, & Liebowitz, 2003a) or the Social Phobia and Anxiety Inventory for Children (SPAI-C; Beidel, Turner, & Morris, 1995)—to further assess student anxiety and clarify areas of difficulty. The LSAS-CA and SPAI-C may also be used to identify important goals, monitor progress, and evaluate treatment benefits if they are completed during and following intervention. These measures are described below.

The LSAS-CA

The Liebowitz Social Anxiety Scale for Children and Adolescents (LSAS-CA; Masia Warner et al., 2003a) includes 24 situations that children and adolescents with social anxiety may fear and/or avoid. It instructs adolescents to provide separate ratings for how much they fear and avoid each situation on a 0–3 Likert-type scale. Items are divided into social interaction (12 items) and performance (12 items) situations. The LSAS-CA provides a total score and six subscale scores: social anxiety, social avoidance, performance anxiety, performance avoidance, total anxiety, and total avoidance. The LSAS-CA has demonstrated good psychometric properties (Masia Warner et al., 2003b).

A valuable feature for use in schools is that the LSAS-CA assesses eight situations specific to the school environment (e.g., participating in work groups, asking and answering questions in class, joining school clubs). The time required for administering and scoring this measure precludes its use for large school screenings. However, this instrument can be useful in identifying situations to address during intervention, specifically when developing students' fear ladders of their 10 most feared situations (detailed in Chapter 11). You can obtain a free copy of this measure by contacting Dr. Carrie Masia Warner.

The SPAI-C

The Social Phobia and Anxiety Inventory for Children (SPAI-C; Beidel et al., 1995) is a 26-item, self-report instrument that assesses social anxiety in children between the ages of 8 and 14. In school environments, the SPAI-C may detect the existence of social fears related to poor school performance, oppositional behavior, or truancy. This measure provides information on the physical, cognitive, and behavioral aspects of social anxiety and has been validated in both community and clinical samples. It is available for purchase in Spanish and English from MHS (*www.mhs.com*). The SPAI-C takes 20–30 minutes to administer and can be complicated to score due to multiple parts to questions. Both these features may limit its usefulness as a tool for large school screenings, but we recommend its use for more focused assessments. Depending on school size and available resources, the process for mental health screenings may look different across schools. What is most important is that socially anxious students, as well as students struggling with other challenges, be identified and connected with services.

INVITING STUDENTS TO ADDRESS SOCIAL ANXIETY

Students identified as exhibiting elevated social anxiety and associated impairment through self-disclosure or school screenings may benefit from the SASS strategies presented in this book. These students should be provided with feedback about behavioral observations and results of any measures that were administered. Having a conversation about assessment results is important for further identifying key areas of impairment that the student may be most motivated to address. Students will likely respond with a wide range of recognition and willingness. Often, education about social anxiety and a description of what SASS strategies entail are necessary to gain students' commitment to addressing their anxiety. Guidelines for these conversations are provided in Chapter 4.

Communication with parents is recommended when feasible. We recommend using telephone calls or letters to explain students' anxiety in school situations (e.g., classroom, lunchroom), as well as the potential benefits of working with school counselors on strategies that teach SASS. Counselors should explain how the skills focus on helping students overcome challenges and fears, develop confidence, and become more comfortable in social or performance situations. Counselors might also wish to emphasize the academic benefits of exercises relating to public speaking, asking for help, or increasing participation in class. Presenting the everyday, practical benefits of the school intervention strategies may help engage students and parents in the process of treating students' social anxiety. See Chapter 13 for additional tips on talking to parents about social anxiety.

In order to illustrate the school-based intervention strategies described in the next two sections of this book, we have included the case example of Lauren, a student whose social anxiety becomes more impairing as she enters high school. Fortunately, her school counselor, Ms. Hillman, recognizes Lauren's struggle and is able to intervene early in Lauren's high school career. We will present Lauren's initial presentation below and, in subsequent chapters, illustrate how Ms. Hillman utilizes each strategy to help Lauren to overcome her social anxiety.

LAUREN'S STORY

Lauren is a hardworking student who excels in math and science. She enjoys singing and participating in school drama productions. Ms. Hillman, her school counselor, met Lauren at the end of her first semester in ninth grade during a routine meeting to choose second-semester courses. Before every midyear student meeting, Ms. Hillman reviewed the results of behavioral health screenings that students completed as part of their required health class. Ms. Hillman noticed that Lauren had an elevated social anxiety scale on the MASC 2. In looking at Lauren's previous progress reports from middle school, Ms. Hillman also noticed that a few teachers had made comments about how Lauren's lack of participation negatively impacted her grades. During the meeting, Ms. Hillman observed that Lauren was soft-spoken and often responded with one-word answers.

Ms. Hillman spent a little extra time with Lauren to ask about how she had adjusted to high school. Lauren said school was going "okay" and explained that she had a few close friends whom she had known since elementary school. She also shared that she had joined stage crew for the upcoming spring musical production. Following some probing by Ms. Hillman, Lauren acknowledged difficulty making new friends and expressed a desire to be more involved in school events and clubs. When Ms. Hillman further queried about class participation, Lauren became embarrassed and admitted that speaking up was challenging because she worried she would give the wrong answer. Ms. Hillman praised Lauren for sharing her feelings: "I know this must be hard for you, Lauren, but I'm glad you are able to share this with me. I think I might be able to help."

Ms. Hillman then asked Lauren to complete the LSAS-CA, explaining that she wanted to get some more information about how Lauren responds to different school situations. Upon completing the questionnaire, Lauren commented, "That was really me in a nutshell. What is this for?" Ms. Hillman answered that it was a questionnaire about social anxiety, and that from what Lauren described, it seemed she was uncomfortable in situations that required her to perform or interact with others. Lauren was a little confused. "I thought that social anxiety is when you have no friends. Also, I actually like singing onstage, as long as I'm in a chorus with other people." Ms. Hillman addressed some of the common misconceptions about social anxiety described in Chapter 1 and explained that the school counseling department often taught students like Lauren strategies to feel more comfortable in social situations. Ms. Hillman then asked Lauren whether she could contact her mother to discuss some of what Lauren had shared. Lauren agreed, saying that her mother was always nagging her about spending more time with friends and getting more involved in school. Ms. Hillman asked Lauren whether they could talk more after the phone call with Lauren's mother. Lauren agreed and thanked Ms. Hillman for her help.

During Ms. Hillman's phone call with Lauren's mother, she mentioned the teacher comments regarding low class participation and the floodgates opened! Lauren's mother shared concerns that Lauren was not reaching her academic potential. She reported that Lauren avoided talking to her teachers at all costs, even if she needed help or believed she had been graded incorrectly. Her mother also described the significant anxiety Lauren experienced leading up to any type of oral presentation. She told Ms. Hillman how Lauren struggled with group projects because she was unable to assert her opinion unless partnered with one of her best friends. Regarding friendships, Lauren's mother confirmed that Lauren had a small group of good friends with whom she had been close since elementary school but expressed frustration about how Lauren refused to initiate any new friendships. Even with her close friends, she preferred to let others make plans, although she would initiate from time to time. She seemed intimidated by large groups of peers and avoided attending parties or hanging out with anyone other than her close friends. Lauren's mother explained how Lauren's discomfort around unfamiliar peers interfered with involvement in school. She reported that Lauren loved singing, and was quite talented, but often avoided auditioning for select choirs because she was afraid to perform a solo. She avoided auditioning for the school musical for this reason and instead joined stage crew. Throughout this conversation, Lauren's mother became upset, expressing how concerned she was that Lauren's anxiety was holding her back. "I try to encourage her to push herself, but she just gets angry. I hate to see her like that." Ms. Hillman praised Lauren's mother for her insight into her daughter's struggles and normalized her concerns. Ms. Hillman then spent a few minutes presenting a brief overview of some of the techniques described in this book and asked Lauren's mother if she would be interested in having Lauren work on some of these difficulties with her over the next few months. Lauren's mother seemed relieved and offered to come in for a parent meeting at a later date.

After students have been identified and agree to engage in intervention, it is time to begin the hard but rewarding work of addressing social anxiety in school. Part II of this book details therapeutic strategies for addressing social anxiety in school and teaches school counselors how to provide effective treatment to socially anxious students individually and in groups. We will follow Lauren as she confronts her anxiety and builds confidence in school.

CHAPTER SUMMARY

- Social anxiety in adolescents is difficult to detect.

- It is essential that school professionals be keen observers of signs of social anxiety in students, some of which can be subtle.

- Common behaviors are discomfort initiating conversations with unfamiliar peers, refraining from speaking up in class, talking minimally to teammates or in other group situations, avoiding eye contact, and appearing on the fringes or outside of groups.

- A multi-tiered assessment strategy including rating scales, soliciting teacher nominations, and behavioral observations of students can help to identify students struggling with social anxiety who might benefit from school-based treatment.

PART II

PROMOTING SKILLS FOR ACADEMIC AND SOCIAL SUCCESS (SASS)

CHAPTER 4

Educating Teenagers about Social Anxiety

Part I provided readers with a rationale for school-based social anxiety intervention and introduced assessment strategies for identifying and inviting students to participate in school programs. In this part of the book, Chapters 4–12 detail therapeutic strategies for addressing social anxiety in school. These chapters guide school practitioners in implementing individual and group sessions in school. We recommend beginning any anxiety intervention program by teaching students about anxiety, including how emotions, physiological responses, thoughts, and avoidance behaviors work together to maintain anxiety. Providing teenagers with a thorough explanation of anxiety is critical for helping them understand the rationale for recommended intervention strategies. Students who appreciate the reasons behind treatment are more likely to be engaged, complete difficult tasks, and practice skills both in session and on their own. This chapter defines the key components of social anxiety (i.e., emotions, physical feelings, thoughts, and behaviors) and describes their interconnectedness and role in fueling anxiety. School practitioners can learn how to educate students about anxiety in a way that empowers students to engage with treatment toward the goal of reducing their anxiety and avoidance.

EVERYONE EXPERIENCES ANXIETY! WHY?

Presenting anxiety as a universal, normal biological process can help reduce students' fear and discomfort about experiencing anxiety or distress (Donker, Griffiths, Cuijpers, & Christensen, 2009). More specifically, we have found it valuable to use the instinctive response of "fight or flight" to present anxiety from a scientific perspective. The "fight-or-flight" response is controlled by the sympathetic nervous system, a branch of the autonomic nervous system responsible for regulating the body's energy levels and preparation for action.

When we perceive threats from the environment, our fight-or-flight process is activated via the sympathetic nervous system. Activation includes the release of adrenaline and other neurotransmitters. These chemical messengers trigger a series of rapid physical changes (e.g., heart racing, sweating, pupil dilation) that prepare the body to address threat by fleeing or fighting (Stratakis & Chrousos, 1995).

When explaining the fight-or-flight response to teenagers, we recommend introducing this concept with an example. If a car came racing toward us while we were crossing the street, our heart rate would increase, providing increased blood flow to our limbs to help us run to the sidewalk quickly. When the car is first perceived, anxiety and its accompanying physiological sensations produce the cognitive and physical conditions that increase our chances of survival in this dangerous situation. This evolutionary perspective helps normalize anxiety because it demonstrates how anxiety can serve a protective function by increasing our ability to detect and avoid danger.

> **Explaining the body's "fight-or-flight" response helps normalize anxiety for students.**

WHAT IS SOCIAL ANXIETY?

While everyone experiences anxiety in unsafe situations, individuals with social anxiety often perceive threat in the absence of physical danger (i.e., in social and performance situations), which triggers the anxious response similar to when actual danger is present. Based on the CBT model of anxiety (Beck & Emery, 1985), anxiety is comprised of three components: (1) emotions and their physiological components, (2) thoughts, and (3) behaviors.

Emotions and Physical Symptoms

Emotions are natural human states that can be described as moods, feelings, attitudes, or sensations one feels in the body. Teenagers with social anxiety typically report feeling nervous, scared, anxious, embarrassed, ashamed, self-conscious, or reserved. Many of these emotions are accompanied by uncomfortable physical symptoms and arousal (Beidel, Turner, & Dancu, 1985), such as a racing heart, heart palpitations, heavy breathing, shortness of breath, blushing, sweating, butterflies in the stomach, stomach pain, frequent urination, headaches, dizziness, shakiness, muscle tension, and dry mouth. Socially anxious adolescents experience these emotional and physical sensations as negative and unwanted (Anderson & Hope, 2009), and thus try to eliminate them. This can lead to avoidance of situations that produce these feelings. As we will discuss further, avoidance is a key factor in maintaining anxiety.

Thoughts

Thoughts, or cognitions, are what we say to ourselves, often referred to as self-talk. In contrast to feelings, thoughts are our individual interpretations of what is happening internally (i.e., the meaning we attribute to our emotional/physical experience) or of events occurring in the world around us. Individuals with social anxiety tend to interpret social situations as threatening. That is, they make negative predictions about what will happen in social or performance situations (Clark, 2005; Clark & Wells, 1995; Heimberg, Brozovich, & Rapee, 2010; Hofmann, 2007; Rapee & Heimberg, 1997). For example, when faced with giving a presentation, socially anxious teenagers may interpret internal sensations (e.g., racing heart, sweating) as evidence that they are not prepared. External cues are interpreted similarly. Using the same example, if a socially anxious student notices classmates laughing during the presentation, he might assume that they are laughing at him. This negative attribution style, detailed in the next chapter, strengthens anxiety and avoidance.

Behaviors

The behavioral component of the anxious response, what we say or do, is typically the most observable to others. Escape from or avoidance of fear-inducing situations is at the core because it is a quick and easy way to reduce unpleasant physical and emotional feelings (Hofmann, 2007; Rapee & Heimberg, 1997). These behavioral patterns can be obvious, like leaving school if a presentation is scheduled, or subtle, such as avoiding eye contact with the teacher when he requests volunteers. Avoiding unpleasant events and emotions is a common and understandable human experience, and drastically reduces anxiety in the short term. However, repeated avoidance strengthens anxiety over time due to restricted opportunities to learn to effectively handle these situations.

HOW DO FEELINGS, THOUGHTS, AND BEHAVIORS WORK TOGETHER TO MAINTAIN ANXIETY?

The CBT triangle presented in Figure 4.1 illustrates the three main components of anxiety: physical/emotional feelings, thoughts, and behaviors. The triangle emphasizes how each one influences the others in all directions to create an ongoing cycle that fuels anxiety. Understanding the CBT triangle is an essential foundation for accepting the rationale behind the various intervention strategies that will be presented in later chapters. Thus, you will see this triangle reproduced multiple times throughout this book, and we recommend reminding your students of this model often. Because the anxiety components are intercon-

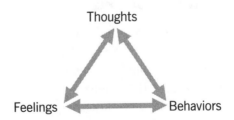

FIGURE 4.1. The CBT triangle.

nected, strategies aim to break this cycle by changing the negative thoughts and avoidant behaviors that fuel anxiety. Oftentimes, this will require students to push themselves out of their comfort zones to change their current patterns. As you might imagine, teenagers tend to be less resistant when they understand why they are being asked to engage in such difficult exercises.

> **Thoughts, behaviors, and feelings all interact to reinforce anxiety.**

Below are some examples of how this cycle maintains anxiety. We recommend sharing these examples or providing examples of your own with students to illustrate how the CBT triangle functions.

Negative Thoughts → Anxious Emotions/ Physical Symptoms → Avoidance

Start by teaching students about how interpreting situations with a negative lens increases anxious feelings and physical arousal, creating an environment in which avoiding the situation may seem like the best option (Clark, 2005). For example, a student who plans to start a conversation with Jen from history class at lunch but then thinks, "I won't know what to say and will sound boring" will likely feel nervous and decide not to speak to Jen at lunch, but rather continue to wait for Jen to initiate instead.

Anxious Emotions/Physical Feelings → Negative Thoughts → Avoidance

Additionally, sometimes students experience uncomfortable physical sensations in social situations prior to the awareness of negative thoughts. These internal cues may cause them to interpret their anxiety as severe or unmanageable (Anderson & Hope, 2009) or to interpret their surroundings as threatening, increasing the likelihood that they will leave the situation. For example, a teenager who feels anxious in a group may experience a racing heart and notice that her voice shakes a little. These sensations make her hypervigilant to both her own body and the facial expressions of others in the group as she tries to monitor whether anyone notices her anxiety. She thinks, "I'm so awkward and uninteresting," and remains silent instead of participating.

Past Avoidance → Negative Thoughts → Anxious Emotions/ Physical Symptoms → Future Avoidance

Pervasive avoidance of social situations reinforces negative thoughts about those events because of a lack of experiences to contradict the negative predictions (Hofmann, 2007). For example, if a student rarely volunteers to answer questions in class, thoughts such as "I will sound stupid" are strengthened because this prediction is never challenged. Such negative expectations exacerbate nervous feelings and physical symptoms, and make it unlikely that the student will risk speaking up.

HOW TO TALK ABOUT SOCIAL ANXIETY WITH STUDENTS

When beginning to help a student with social anxiety, we suggest starting by normalizing anxiety with a brief overview of the fight-or-flight response. Then follow with an explanation of the components of social anxiety and how they interact. We recommend asking students what feelings, thoughts, and behaviors they have in anxiety-provoking situations (Fisher et al., 2004). Selecting a universally difficult situation, like public speaking, as an example may make students feel more comfortable identifying feelings and thoughts. If a student is reluctant, we recommend providing a list of common symptoms (Handout 4.1: Common Anxious Responses) and asking the student whether any sound familiar. Once personal symptoms of each component have been identified, it is important to explain how they maintain the student's anxiety.

CONDUCTING PSYCHOEDUCATION IN A GROUP SETTING

While you might assume that socially anxious students would be hesitant to talk about themselves in front of a group of peers, providing psychoeducation in a group format can be helpful. It provides an opportunity for students to learn that others experience similar symptoms, which normalizes anxiety and increases students' awareness that many teenagers struggle with social anxiety. The group leader can use examples given by more expressive group members and ask more hesitant peers whether they sound familiar. This strategy fosters engagement and buy-in without requiring much verbal participation from severely anxious students at the initial stages, which can prevent overwhelming the most reluctant students. Additionally, peers are typically more effective than adults at prodding participation from quiet classmates.

COMMON CHALLENGES TO PROVIDING PSYCHOEDUCATION

Providing psychoeducation about anxiety is a simple but important intervention that helps students to better understand their own anxiety cycle, thereby setting the stage for justification of recommended interventions. However, some students struggle to identify or differentiate symptoms, and others are reluctant to disclose them.

Students Have Trouble Differentiating Feelings and Thoughts

Students often confuse feelings and thoughts or use the terms interchangeably (e.g., "I was thinking I felt nervous"). Utilizing Handout 4.1, clarify that feelings are mood states, while thoughts are our interpretations of what is happening around us (e.g., "I was thinking I would do something embarrassing at the party"). It is important to help students differentiate thoughts and feelings because evaluating negative predictions will be a main target for intervention. Students usually improve with practice, so it is worthwhile to spend time providing additional examples if necessary. If a student continues to struggle, at least make sure he understands that anxious feelings and thoughts will tempt him to avoid anxiety-provoking situations, but that avoidance will strengthen his anxiety.

Students Are Hesitant to Disclose Anxious Symptoms

It can be helpful to describe some common responses, like butterflies in the stomach or concerns about making mistakes in front of others, and ask students whether this has ever happened to them. It usually helps to use less threatening examples that all teenagers (not just socially anxious ones) can relate to in order to facilitate discussion. We recommend starting with examples such as giving a presentation in front of the class, trying out for a sport or school play, or meeting someone new.

Students may only acknowledge anxiety in one situation, even when you are aware they are anxious in many circumstances. It only takes one! Once you apply the model to the situation a student is willing to discuss, she may be better able to identify other situations in which similar patterns occur. In our experience, once students experience some success, their confidence in you and in these strategies will increase, and they will be more open to discussing other situations in which they may be experiencing anxiety.

LAUREN'S STORY

Ms. Hillman arranged a meeting with Lauren after speaking with her mother. Because Lauren expressed anxiety about missing class, Ms. Hillman suggested they meet during Lauren's gym class. She began the meeting by reviewing information obtained from Lauren's mother. This gave Lauren the opportunity to respond to this information and offer additional details if she wished to do so. Lauren presented as very quiet and rarely volunteered information spontaneously, but answered Ms. Hillman's direct questions. Ms. Hillman understood the importance of obtaining Lauren's buy-in, so she encouraged Lauren to imagine what her life might look like without anxiety. Acknowledging the ways that social anxiety holds her back and describing how her life would be better without anxiety prepared Lauren for a discussion about working with Ms. Hillman. Ms. Hillman thanked Lauren for her willingness to discuss situations she finds difficult and asked Lauren whether she would like to hear about strategies that could help her feel more comfortable in school. Lauren appeared anxious but hopeful and agreed that she wanted to learn more.

Ms. Hillman then moved on to educating Lauren about the three main components of anxiety: feelings, thoughts, and behaviors. She provided Lauren with Handout 4.1: Common Anxious Responses. Lauren identified her most common physical symptoms (i.e., racing heart, butterflies in stomach, sweating) and quickly related to the description of negative thinking: "I definitely do that all the time!" Together, Ms. Hillman and Lauren mapped out some of her common experiences on a big CBT triangle drawn on Ms. Hillman's office whiteboard. Lauren also wrote down her examples in a notebook.

Negative Thoughts → Anxious Emotions/Physical Symptoms → Avoidance
- "I'll give a wrong answer and everyone will think I'm stupid." → Racing heart, sweating → Avoid volunteering

Anxious Emotions/Physical Feelings → Negative Thoughts → Avoidance
- Butterflies in stomach, difficulty breathing → "I really hope the chorus teacher doesn't call on me for the solo." → Ask to go to the bathroom and leave class

Avoidance → Negative Thoughts → Anxious Emotions/Physical Symptoms → Avoidance
- Never going out with close friends in a larger group with unfamiliar peers → "I won't have anyone to talk to because my friends will be busy with other people. I'll just look awkward." → Racing heart → Decline invitation from best friend to go to the mall with a group

Ms. Hillman then asked Lauren to write down at least one more example of the triangle during an anxiety-provoking situation before their next meeting and suggested recording it in her agenda or on her phone.

Once Ms. Hillman felt that Lauren understood how the CBT triangle applied to her own experience with anxiety, she decided to introduce the skills and strategies in this book. Ms. Hillman explained how changing thoughts and behaviors is an effective way to stop anxiety in its tracks. She provided a brief overview of realistic thinking, social skills, and exposures before inviting Lauren to meet with her on an ongoing basis to try them together. She assured Lauren they would work together and take things one step at a time. Ms. Hillman also mentioned that she had used these strategies with other students, who had found them to be very helpful. Lauren hesitated, "It makes sense after everything we talked about, but I'm still not sure." Ms. Hillman challenged her to think about what they had reviewed and about the potential benefits that Lauren had previously stated were important to her, such as joining singing groups, making new friends, speaking up in class, and auditioning for the school play. After some prompting, Lauren expressed concern that other students might notice her frequent trips to the counseling office and assume something was wrong with her. Ms. Hillman and Lauren brainstormed ways to be discreet about their meetings (e.g., alternating days and times so Lauren rarely missed the same class), as well as explanations that Lauren could give if questioned. Ms. Hillman also made a note to herself to review these concerns at a later meeting when discussing anxious thinking.

Because Ms. Hillman provided Lauren with a clear description of the anxiety cycle, Lauren was able to understand how she and Ms. Hillman might start intervening. Providing psychoeducation about anxiety also helped Lauren to buy into the treatment strategies that Ms. Hillman described. It is not uncommon to find that even very reluctant students appear more willing to apply and practice these skills after being provided with psychoeducation about anxiety. The anxiety cycle often provides the best understanding of what this treatment approach involves and how it can be effective.

CHAPTER SUMMARY

- Anxiety is a universal biological process that protects humans by enhancing our ability to detect and steer clear of danger.

- Based on the CBT model, the anxious response is comprised of three components: (1) emotions and physical symptoms, (2) thoughts, (3) behaviors and avoidance.

- These components influence each other to create an ongoing cycle that fuels anxiety.

- Understanding the CBT triangle is an important foundation for accepting the rationale behind interventions that aim to modify the anxious cycle.

- Conducting psychoeducation in a group setting can normalize anxiety and help facilitate participation and engagement from reluctant students.

Common Anxious Responses

Feelings: Emotions	**Thoughts**
• Nervous • Scared • Anxious • Embarrassed • Self-conscious • Reserved • Ashamed	• Interpreting social and performance situations as threatening • "I know it is going to go badly." • "I have to be perfect or everyone will laugh at me." • "If I make a mistake it will be the end of the world." • "No one will want to talk to me."
Feelings: Physical Symptoms	**Behaviors**
• Racing heart or heart palpitations • Heavy breathing or shortness of breath • Blushing • Sweating • Butterflies in the stomach • Stomach pain • Frequent urination • Headaches • Dizziness • Shakiness • Muscle tension • Dry mouth	• Avoidance! • Stay home • Don't raise hand or participate in class • Don't attend the event • Go to the party but don't talk to anyone • Attend event but only stay with close friend • Don't initiate conversations • Don't ask for help • Don't join clubs, sports, or teams

CHAPTER 5

Socially Anxious Thinking 101

Understanding how socially anxious students think is critical for effectively implementing intervention strategies. Adolescents with social anxiety tend to have negative thought patterns that increase anxious feelings and physiological symptoms. Negative thinking also convinces teenagers that avoiding interactions and performance situations is their safest option when in fact it leads to more pervasive impairment. Socially anxious thinking contains specific types of cognitive errors, also referred to as cognitive distortions or thinking traps, whereby adolescents predict overly negative outcomes. Students must first be able to recognize negative thoughts and cognitive distortions as they occur in order to challenge them later through realistic thinking (Chapter 6) and exposure exercises (Chapter 12). This chapter describes some of the cognitive distortions common to social anxiety and explains how they contribute to avoidance. Chapter 6 will explain how school practitioners can teach students to challenge these thinking traps with realistic thinking strategies.

HOW DOES COGNITION DEVELOP IN ADOLESCENCE?

Adolescence is a period of enormous cognitive development, including the ongoing development of social cognition (Vetter, Leipold, Kliegel, Phillips, & Altgassen, 2013). During this developmental stage, teenagers gain the capacity to think abstractly about events outside of the present moment, allowing them to consider hypothetical situations. Developments in abstract thinking and perspective taking enable adolescents to understand that other people might have a different point of view or way of interpreting situations (Blakemore & Choudhury, 2006). Simultaneously, teenagers also experience an increase in egocentrism, or an inward focus on the self. This serves a healthy function in assisting with the primary tasks of adolescence, such as asserting independence or autonomy and establishing a social identity; however, it can also contribute to negative thinking about being judged. Specifically, egocentrism creates a phenomenon called the "imaginary audience," in which adolescents assume that they are being observed at all times (Ryan & Kuczkowski, 1994).

Adolescents' perception that they are the center of others' attention can lead to heightened self-evaluative fears and perceived dangers of negative social outcomes (Ryan & Kuczkowski, 1994). These developmental changes make adolescence a prime period for the onset of social anxiety.

> **Adolescents assume they are being observed at all times—a phenomenon known as the "imaginary audience."**

WHAT ARE THEY THINKING?: A GUIDE TO SOCIALLY ANXIOUS THINKING TRAPS

Among those adolescents predisposed to anxiety, perceptions that they are the center of others' attention coupled with their new ability to consider others' perspectives contributes to a cognitive style characterized by worry that they will perform poorly and be evaluated negatively in social or performance situations (Clark, 2005; Clark & Wells, 1995; Heimberg et al., 2010; Hofmann, 2007; Rapee & Heimberg, 1997). This negative and rigid approach includes overly perfectionistic expectations for how they should perform, inflexible rules about social interactions, assumptions of negative judgment by others, and worry that failed interactions will have drastic negative consequences (Clark & Wells, 1995; Foa, Franklin, Perry, & Herbert, 1996; Hofmann, 2007; Mellings, & Alden, 2000). While numerous thinking traps have been identified (Weems et al., 2001; Weems, Costa, Watts, Taylor, & Cannon, 2007), we detail some of the most common thought errors or cognitive distortions we have seen in socially anxious adolescents. These common thinking errors are detailed below and summarized in Appendix 5.1: Common Socially Anxious Thinking Traps.

Perfectionistic Expectations

Socially anxious students have overly perfectionistic expectations about how they should perform. These unrealistic expectations are impossible to meet, and students often become extremely critical of themselves when they (inevitably) fail to achieve perfection (Hofmann, 2007). They believe that they should never say anything that could be construed as rude or mean, and may also expect to be interesting, funny, and to look their best in every social interaction. In performance situations, they believe that they must avoid all mistakes and appear calm and relaxed in order to conceal their anxiety. Teenagers often erroneously believe that they are better off avoiding the situation altogether than facing the possibility that they may make an error, since they know that the chances of perfection are slim.

Preparing to give a presentation in class is a common situation that often elicits perfectionistic expectations. For example, Kai is a socially anxious student who becomes incredibly overwhelmed by giving presentations. He often thinks, "In order for this presentation to be a success, I can't make any mistakes." He erroneously believes that he must get every single fact correct, speak articulately, deliver the presentation smoothly without pausing or stuttering, and avoid getting flushed so no one will notice how nervous he is. He thinks that if he makes any mistake or if his presentation is not perfect, he will make a complete fool of himself. Because of these thoughts, Kai gets incredibly embarrassed and anxious every time he needs to give a presentation.

Rigid Social Rules

Socially anxious teenagers have rigid ideas about what is "allowed" during social interactions (Hofmann, 2007). These ideas often interfere with socializing in a number of ways. One common belief is that one must attain a certain level of familiarity with a peer before engaging in conversations, texting, and extending invitations. This thought perpetuates avoidance because it is consistent with socially anxious students' tendency to wait for peers to initiate conversation or invitations. They may also believe in strict codes about cliques and groups, specifically that they "cannot" extend invites to peers in different friend groups. Finally, students may have rules related to what topics are acceptable for conversation. For example, we have often heard adolescents say that they avoid talking about themselves because it sounds conceited. Sometimes it can be difficult to tell whether these rules are firmly held beliefs or excuses to avoid interaction out of fear of rejection or of being vulnerable.

Rules about when and who to contact are especially prevalent for socially anxious youth. A socially anxious teenager named Mary thinks that she can't text an acquaintance named Raven from class with a homework question. Even though Mary and Raven sit next to each other and often do classwork together, Mary thinks that they have not previously spoken or texted "enough times" for it to be "okay" to text Raven. She also believes that it is not okay to text someone for help until you have spent time together outside of school. Even though Mary has not been able to figure out the homework and there have been several signs that Raven would respond favorably to Mary's questions, Mary refuses to text for help.

Excessive Personal Responsibility

As is generally the case in life, social situations will sometimes go badly, albeit less often than socially anxious students expect. When this occurs, it is natural to attempt to make causal attributions or assign blame to explain the outcome. Socially anxious individuals tend to make internal attributions (Mellings & Alden, 2000), assuming personal responsibility for the negative outcome. For example, when the soccer team loses, a socially anxious player might believe that the loss was due to the one shot she missed and neglect other external factors, such as that their best player was injured, their goalie missed a save, or they played a better team. Another common situation in which excessive personal responsibility occurs is when a student invites friends to a movie that ends up being disappointing. Rather than accepting the idea that some movies do not live up to expectations, and that this is a common experience that does not upset most people, socially anxious adolescents will blame themselves for inviting others to a bad movie. They may even believe that others blame them for having a bad time or think they have bad taste for choosing the movie.

Excessive personal responsibility often occurs in ambiguous situations. For example, Hunter waves to a friend as he passes in the school hallway, but his friend does not wave back. Rather than considering alternative external possibilities, such as the friend didn't see him, was also nervous about the interaction, was having a bad day, or was preoccupied by an upcoming exam or a fight with a family member, Hunter assumes the friend's behavior is Hunter's own fault. Anytime this happens, the thoughts that run through Hunter's mind include "I must have done something to upset him," "He's probably mad at me," "Maybe he's embarrassed to say hello to me in front of his other friends," and "He probably just doesn't want to be friends with me anymore because I'm such a loser." Hunter ends up leaving the interaction feeling rejected and hurt. Additionally, Hunter is likely to feel more anxious around that friend now, and he is much less likely to try reaching out to that friend in the future.

Overestimation

Regardless of expectations, it is realistic to entertain the possibility that social interactions or performances may not have good outcomes. However, adolescents with social anxiety grossly overestimate the probability that negative events will occur in social situations (Foa et al., 1996; Lucock & Salkovskis, 1988). For instance, they assume that there is a 99% chance that they will make some type of embarrassing social mistake or that something else bad will happen, such as a friend saying no to an invitation to hang out. Although these feared outcomes or social mistakes (e.g., forgetting someone's name, giving the wrong answer in class) may occur from time to time, the chances are actually much lower than socially anxious adolescents believe.

A situation that often elicits overestimation errors is when a student would like to start a conversation with another student. For instance, Samuel thinks that his teammate Chris is cool and interesting. Even though Samuel would really like to talk to Chris after basketball practice, he "knows" that he will sound boring and Chris will be annoyed at him or ignore him. When asked to provide a percentage for how sure he is that this will occur, Samuel says 90% even though Chris has always been friendly with him. Obviously, there is a small chance that Chris might not enjoy talking to Samuel, but 90% is a gross overestimate.

Catastrophizing

In addition to overestimating the probability of disappointing or negative social outcomes, adolescents with social anxiety also catastrophize the implications of their perceived mistakes or poor performance, fearing these negative outcomes will have a terrible and long-lasting catastrophic impact (Foa et al., 1996). They attribute too much importance to brief interactions or small mistakes and fail to consider the "big picture": that others are rarely paying close attention and have much shorter memories for their mistakes than they do. If they have one awkward conversation, they believe that the peer will tell "everyone," everyone will think they are awkward, no one will want to talk to them, and their social reputation will be ruined forever. For example, whenever Darius gives a wrong answer in front of the class, he thinks that all his peers will think he is stupid and won't want to work on projects with him in the future. He also fears that his teacher will think he was unprepared for class and that he is a bad student. These thoughts persist even though his teacher praises him for volunteering, and giving a wrong answer in class is a common occurrence that happens to most individuals. As a result of overestimating and catastrophizing, socially anxious

> **Socially anxious teenagers assume the worst will happen.**

students "know" that something will go wrong, and are "sure" that when it does, the fallout and negative outcomes will be disastrous and intolerable.

WHY IS NEGATIVE THINKING PROBLEMATIC?

Many of these thinking traps share similar underlying distorted processes, in which negative assumptions are made without consideration of alternative explanations. Cognitive errors cause socially anxious students to overinflate risk associated with social or performance situations, thereby increasing motivation to avoid them. The choice to avoid is strengthened because students are relieved by not having to face the expected negative consequence. Unfortunately, avoidance deprives adolescents of positive experiences that will disprove their distortions. Over time, students' thinking patterns can become so ingrained that they do not even realize that they are having negative thoughts in anxiety-provoking situations. Without the recognition that thoughts are occurring, socially anxious adolescents are at risk for accepting these automatic thoughts as fact rather than assumptions or interpretations.

Increasing awareness of unhealthy thinking patterns is critical for supporting interventions aimed at changing and questioning these negative interpretations. Counselors must understand the thoughts that socially anxious students are having in order to help students recognize and label those thoughts before addressing them with realistic thinking and behavioral exercises. Additionally, being able to talk openly with students about these thinking traps allows students to feel understood. Particularly when they are discussed in groups, students may feel relieved that they are not the only teenagers who have those thoughts.

LAUREN'S STORY

As Lauren was fairly agreeable about committing to work on social anxiety with Ms. Hillman, and able to sufficiently identify her anxious thoughts in their first meeting, Ms. Hillman proactively provided Lauren with information about thinking traps (see Appendix 5.1). Ms. Hillman used Lauren's personal examples (e.g., assuming people would notice her visits to the counseling office, exaggerating the likelihood of giving a wrong answer in class, assuming that any singing mistake would mean the whole solo was a disaster) to illustrate each thinking trap while reviewing the CBT triangle. Lauren stated that she hadn't realized her thinking was overly negative and always just took her thoughts at face value and assumed that they were true. Ms. Hillman explained how when thoughts are so automatic, we often confuse them with facts rather than recognizing them as our own subjective (and inaccurate!) predictions.

Ms. Hillman informed Lauren that she would explain how to examine these thoughts more realistically at their next meeting but in the interim asked her to keep track of a few of her unhelpful or negative predictions when she feels nervous about a situation (i.e., what is she expecting to happen?). As Lauren wrote down examples of her thoughts, feelings, and behaviors throughout the week, she also wrote down which thinking errors she was making. The thinking traps that Lauren noticed she made most often were rigid social rules, overestimation, and catastrophizing. Below are some of Lauren's examples.

- *Rigid social rule:* "When my best friend hangs out with her soccer teammates, I can't join because I'm not on the team. Even when she invites me, it's just to be nice and she doesn't really want me to go."
- *Overestimation:* "If I go to the party, I'll just end up saying something stupid and embarrassing myself. It always happens."
- *Catastrophizing:* "I can't do a solo because I'll collapse under the pressure and ruin my chances to ever get another solo or singing part in the play."

Ms. Hillman followed up on the last example because it required some clarification. "Collapsing under the pressure" isn't very specific. When she probed Lauren about what she meant, Lauren said, "I guess I'm worried that I will forget the words and run off the stage, or throw up right there because I am so nervous." Ms. Hillman praised Lauren for pushing herself to be specific because identifying specific negative thoughts makes challenging them more effective.

With socially anxious thinking, something that may start with a grain of truth (i.e., "If I answer a question in class, I might get it wrong") gets blown out of proportion (i.e., " . . . and everyone will think I'm stupid and I'll never live it down!"), taken to the extreme, or twisted in some way. Just as Lauren frequently made certain types of thinking errors, we find that many students tend to make the same type of thinking errors over and over and over! You may notice a pattern early on, and it can be especially helpful to instruct students to watch for their "go-to" thinking traps. Even if students struggle with identifying the specific traps, just recognizing that the thoughts are distorted can be enough to prompt them to adjust their thinking.

CHAPTER SUMMARY

- Socially anxious students have a cognitive style characterized by overly negative and rigid thoughts about social situations, leading them to believe that they will perform poorly or be evaluated negatively.
- Common specific socially anxious cognitive errors include:
  - Perfectionistic expectations of their performance
  - Adherence to rigid social rules
  - Excessive personal responsibility for negative outcomes
  - Overestimation of negative outcomes
  - Catastrophizing negative outcomes
- Cognitive errors cause socially anxious students to overinflate the risk associated with social or performance situations, thereby increasing avoidance and exacerbating anxiety.

Common Socially Anxious Thinking Traps

Thinking Trap	Explanation	Examples of Common Thoughts
Perfectionistic expectations	Unrealistically high expectations about how one must perform in social, academic, athletic, or other situations	• "If I make a mistake, I'll make a fool out of myself." • "I have to do everything right or others will think I'm stupid."
Rigid social rules	Unspoken rules about social interaction that support avoiding the interactions	• "I can't say hi to her when she is with her other friends." • "I can't text him until we've talked more in school." • "I can't ask to join their lunch table in the middle of the school year."
Excessive personal responsibility	Assuming personal blame if something doesn't go right and ignoring any external possibilities	• "I must have done something to upset him." • "She's probably mad at me." • "He probably doesn't want to be my friend anymore because I'm a loser." • "I shouldn't have missed that goal. I made our whole team lose." • "If she doesn't have fun, it's my fault because I'm boring."
Overestimation	Overestimating the probability of negative outcomes; assuming negative outcomes are the rule rather than the exception	• "I'm sure that my mind will go blank and I won't know what to say." • "I'll probably trip in front of everyone." • "If I invite her to hang out, I just know that she'll say no."
Catastrophizing	Small mistakes are blown out of proportion and feel like the end of the world; the potential consequences of something going wrong are exaggerated	• "I'll never live this down." • "Everyone will think I'm dumb." • "No one will want to be my friend anymore." • "I'll be the laughingstock of the whole school." • "Everyone will know that I messed up."

CHAPTER 6

Realistic Thinking
Give It a Second Thought!

Socially anxious students tend to adopt a negative thinking pattern including specific types of thought errors or thinking traps that maintain anxious feelings, physiological symptoms, and avoidant behavior. Chapter 5 built the foundation by introducing the thinking traps that are common for socially anxious adolescents. Now we build on that foundation by teaching school practitioners how to explain thinking traps to socially anxious adolescents and how to guide these students toward "giving it a second thought." By identifying their negative thoughts as they occur, students can learn to actively challenge them through realistic thinking or behavioral experiments. Realistic thinking, or giving negative expectations a second thought by reevaluating their veracity, has been shown to be an effective strategy for reducing anxiety. Engaging in realistic thinking by replacing negative thoughts with more reasonable ones also increases the likelihood that students will approach anxiety-provoking situations rather than avoid them (Rapee, 1998; Taylor et al., 1997). Giving it a second thought utilizes questioning to challenge negative thoughts based on facts rather than emotions (i.e., anxiety). This chapter details the steps for teaching and practicing realistic thinking with socially anxious students.

WHAT IS REALISTIC THINKING?

Realistic thinking teaches teenagers to critically evaluate their thoughts based on evidence, rather than being guided by their anxiety (Rapee, 1998; Rapee et al., 2008). This strategy goes beyond simply telling students not to worry, or that negative thoughts are not true, because unfortunately, this is not effective. Rather, realistic thinking utilizes strategic questioning to encourage students to challenge the accuracy of their own assumptions—in other words, to give it a second thought. The central idea of this strategy is acknowledging that

45

feared outcomes will occur from time to time, but that this is the exception rather than the rule. It will go better than expected most of the time!

Replacing negative thoughts with more reasonable ones is theorized to be effective because it increases the chance that students will approach anxiety-provoking situations rather than avoid them (Rapee, 1998; Rapee et al., 2008; Taylor et al., 1997).

More realistic thoughts lead to decreased anxiety and avoidance.

For example, a 15-year-old student named Jayla is trying to invite her friend Priya to spend time together outside of school. When extending an invitation to a peer, Jayla thinks, "I talk to Priya all the time in class and we always have plenty to talk about, so it's not that different if we talk outside of school." This thought makes it more probable that Jayla will extend an invitation, compared to if she thinks, "If I invite Priya to hang out after school, she will probably say no and it will be really awkward." Realistic thinking and entering into anxiety-provoking situations provide experiences that allow students to learn that small social mistakes are manageable and negative social outcomes are both rare and tolerable. This new learning contributes to students feeling more comfortable in social situations and leads to more flexible thinking.

HOW IS REALISTIC THINKING DIFFERENT FROM POSITIVE THINKING?

Realistic thinking is not necessarily positive thinking (Rapee, 1998; Rapee et al., 2008). That is, like negative thinking, overly positive thinking is not realistic. Everyone knows that things will not always turn out as we hope. Most of the time, outcomes are neutral—not particularly good but also not catastrophic. For Jayla in the example above, excessive positive thinking, such as "This is going to be our best conversation yet and we are going to become best friends," also predicts an unlikely outcome. Furthermore, if the excessively positive outcome does not happen, Jayla will likely feel disappointed. Anxious negative thinking and positive thinking are two opposite poles of the same continuum, in which both ends represent unrealistic thoughts. Our goal is to encourage students to give their initial anxious thoughts a second thought and guide them toward the middle ground.

LAYING THE FOUNDATION FOR GIVING IT A SECOND THOUGHT

"Give it a second thought" is a relatively simple concept but can be challenging to apply. Adolescents are often stuck in rigid thinking patterns and negative predictions. Effective implementation requires flexible, on-the-spot thinking by school professionals to respond quickly to students' counterarguments to more realistic thoughts.

The first step is to discuss the connection of thoughts with feelings and behaviors. This relationship can be illustrated by explaining that different people often have different thoughts in the same situation, and that these differing thoughts result in opposite feelings and behaviors. Specifically, counselors should emphasize that negative predictions will lead to negative feelings and avoidance, while more realistic thoughts will foster confidence and approach behaviors (Fisher et al., 2004; Ryan & Masia Warner, 2012). This idea can be demonstrated through vignettes or visual aids but may be most powerful when personal student examples are used. For instance, two students on the football team are participating in the same pep rally, but one student is thinking, "I can't wait for everyone to see I'm part of the team and cheer for me," while the other is thinking, "I hope I don't do anything embarrassing while everyone is staring at me." Asking students to consider how each person will feel and act at the pep rally will demonstrate the critical point that thoughts affect how one feels and acts in any situation. Examples like this should help facilitate further discussion about students' anxious feelings, thoughts, and behaviors that will help them understand their connection. Handout 6.1: Same Situation, Different Thoughts! provides students with several examples of two teenagers in the same situation with different thoughts. It can be helpful to review each situation and ask students to reflect on how each teenager is likely feeling, given the thoughts that each is having.

Another critical concept to convey to students is that thoughts are merely our individual interpretations or hypotheses of what is happening internally (in our bodies, minds) and externally in the environment.

Anxious individuals tend to accept thoughts as fact rather than as individual assumptions that can be subjected to examination. Thoughts are subjective, individual opinions—they are not facts! Encouraging students to be open to the idea that thoughts are

> **Explaining that thoughts are not facts helps students learn to critically evaluate them.**

hypotheses and can be tested and evaluated is the basis for realistic thinking. For example, if Darnell is giving a presentation in class and notices a small group of students laughing, he might assume that his classmates are laughing at him for something he said or how he looks. What are some other possibilities? The classmates could be laughing at a private joke that had nothing to do with the presenter or at the teacher, who is falling asleep at her desk— the possibilities are endless. Below are step-by-step instructions for how to help students accomplish this more flexible approach to thinking.

Step 1: Identify Specific, Negative Expectations

Once students understand the idea that thoughts should not be accepted as fact but rather questioned for accuracy, the next step is for them to identify their own personal anxious predictions. Helping students identify *specific* thoughts is important for later success because the more explicit the negative expectation, the better it can be challenged. Sometimes students have an easier time relating to thoughts that are stated for them, rather than identifying their own thoughts.

We have provided a list of anxious thoughts that we have commonly heard from teenagers in Handout 6.2: Common Socially Anxious Thoughts and Worries. It may be helpful to first use this list to facilitate discussion by asking students if these thoughts are familiar. Then use Handout 6.3: Identifying Thoughts to have students brainstorm a list of their own negative thoughts that arise in different situations. Counselors may also wish to prime thoughts by providing certain scenarios so that students can anchor their common negative thoughts in familiar experiences. For instance, asking a student what goes through his mind when a teacher calls on him unexpectedly in class can more easily prime a socially anxious student to recognize that he often thinks, "Oh no! If I get it wrong, I'll look stupid and will be so embarrassed."

> **The more specific, the better! Specific thoughts are easier to challenge than vague ones.**

Step 2: Identify Thinking Traps

Negative thinking tends to fall into a few common categories, described in the previous chapter. We recommend presenting the thinking traps to students. Counselors can use the descriptions from Handout 6.4: Common Socially Anxious Thinking Traps and present the student stories from Chapter 5 to illustrate the thinking traps in action. Being able to label what kind of error their thought represents often helps teenagers buy into the fact that their negative socially anxious thoughts are actually thinking traps rather than accurate depictions or facts about what will happen. While it is not necessary for teenagers to memorize the exact names of these distortions, you can help students identify erroneous thinking by using the handouts. Sometimes several types of errors may be occurring simultaneously.

A summary of thinking traps presented in Chapter 5 is as follows:

- *Perfectionistic expectations:* Students have unrealistically high expectations about how they must perform in social, academic, athletic, or other situations.
- *Rigid social rules:* Unspoken rules about social interactions that support avoiding them.
- *Excessive personal responsibility:* Socially anxious teenagers assume personal blame and ignore other, external possibilities.
- *Overestimation:* Students overestimate the probability of negative outcomes. They are the rule rather than the exception.
- *Catastrophizing:* Small mistakes are blown out of proportion and feel like the end of the world.

Step 3: Give It a Second Thought! Are Your Initial Thoughts Realistic?

The most critical step is to teach students to generate questions that challenge the likelihood that their initial thoughts (thinking traps) are accurate. Handout 6.5: Giving It a Second Thought and Handout 6.6: Challenging Thoughts present helpful challenging questions for each type of thinking trap and facilitate student practice with realistic thinking. The goal is to treat thoughts as guesses rather than facts and to test them by identifying evidence that supports or discounts the predictions. Students may relate to the analogy that challenging thoughts is similar to participating in a debate or a cross-examination in a courtroom trial. Some general challenging questions, such as "What has happened before in this situation?" or "What would you say to a friend in this situation?" can be useful for many types of thoughts.

Let's take an example of a student named Nia whose friend did not answer her text. Nia has an initial thought reflecting excessive personal responsibility, such as "My friend didn't answer my text last night because she must be mad at me." You might challenge this thought by asking Nia whether there can be other reasons that are unrelated to her. Nia may simply respond by saying "I guess," but she is not convinced. Asking for some specific alternative explanations (e.g., her phone died, she was busy studying, she had a fight with her parents and her phone was taken away), and more information about the friend that might support these reasons (e.g., Does she usually answer when she is studying? Does she have frequent fights with her parents?), gives credence to alternative possibilities and decreases confidence in initial negative thoughts.

After challenging questions have been posed, it is important to ask students how true they think their initial thoughts were after evaluating the evidence. It can also be helpful to assess whether they feel less nervous about the situation and are less likely to avoid it in the future.

Step 4: Apply These Skills to Various Situations

Initially, school professionals may have to generate most challenging questions. However, as students begin to get more familiar with this technique, they should be encouraged to take more responsibility for challenging their own negative predictions. Application of this process to various situations is necessary to promote flexible thinking. It is common for students to doubt realistic thoughts at first, but with repeated practice, more flexibility in thinking and more confidence in alternative possibilities often develops. Students should understand that realistic thinking is a skill that requires practice in order for it to become more natural and effective.

Assigning students homework to practice this skill between meetings allows students to engage in it more readily in "real time." When assigning realistic thinking for homework, ensure that students understand how to use the worksheet by either providing Handout 6.7: Example— Completed Challenging Thoughts or by first filling in one worksheet together.

WHAT DO THESE STEPS LOOK LIKE ALL TOGETHER?

Below is a sample transcript of realistic thinking techniques in action. Ms. Hillman guides Lauren through each step using the example of attending a party, a commonly feared situation.

Step 1: Identify Specific, Negative Expectations

Ms. HILLMAN: So you mentioned you were nervous about this party coming up that you were invited to. What number from 0 to 10 would you use to rate how nervous you are about the party?

LAUREN: Maybe a 7.

Ms. Hillman: Okay, let's write that down [Handout 6.6]. What are some specific thoughts or predictions you are having about what might happen at the party?

Lauren: I don't know, I guess I'm worried that I will look awkward.

Ms. Hillman: Hmm, what would you be doing that would make you look awkward?

Lauren: Like if I don't have anyone to talk to, and I am just standing by myself.

Ms. Hillman: I can understand that. Nice job identifying your specific concerns. Are there other things you are expecting will go wrong at the party?

Lauren: Well, I'm worried that even if I can find people to talk to I'll run out of things to say. I guess I'm worried that people at the party will think I'm boring.

Ms. Hillman: That's a lot to worry about. No wonder you are not sure whether you want to go to the party. Let's see if those things are likely to happen.

Step 2: Identify Thinking Traps

Ms. Hillman: So we have three main guesses about the party: (1) you won't have anyone to talk to and will look awkward, (2) you will run out of things to say in conversation, and (3) others will think you're boring. Do you think any of these thoughts might be unrealistic? Are you falling into any thinking traps?

Lauren: I don't know, I have a hard time making conversation when I'm nervous.

Ms. Hillman: That's fair, I think a lot of people feel that way. But let's see if we can examine these thoughts to make you feel a little less nervous. Let's take one at a time. What about the worry that you won't have anyone to talk to? What do you think about that one?

Lauren: Well, it's my best friend's party and I know most of her friends, so I guess maybe I'm overestimating the chances that I won't have anyone to talk to.

Ms. Hillman: Yeah, I think you're right. What about the other thoughts—that you will run out of things to say and that people will think you're boring?

Lauren: That could definitely happen, but maybe I'm exaggerating a little and being too hard on myself [catastrophizing, perfectionistic expectations].

Step 3: Give It a Second Thought!
Is Your Initial Thought Realistic?

Ms. Hillman: I'm glad you can recognize that. How can you challenge the thoughts that you won't have anyone to talk to and will look awkward? You can use this list if you need help [Handout 6.4].

Lauren: Well, I could ask myself what usually happens. I sometimes have trouble at parties, but like I said before, I know most of the people going to this party and have talked to them before, so I guess it won't be too hard to start conversations with them. But sometimes it is hard to approach them when they are in a group.

Ms. HILLMAN: Okay, so you know pretty much everyone. What are the chances that at any moment everyone you know will be busy talking in groups, including your best friend?

LAUREN: I guess pretty small. I could always keep busy by getting a drink or checking my phone so I don't look awkward.

Ms. HILLMAN: Do you think everyone looks comfortable and busy all the time at a party except for you?

LAUREN: I guess I never thought about that because I'm only paying attention to myself.

Ms. HILLMAN: Interesting, do you think other people might be too busy paying attention to themselves to notice you in the minute or two you aren't talking to someone or to think about how you look awkward?

LAUREN: Probably . . . I never thought about it that way.

Ms. HILLMAN: Good, that's the point of all this! Now, how can you challenge the rest of the thoughts about running out of things to say and people thinking you're boring?

LAUREN: Well, I can ask myself how conversations usually go. If I know the person pretty well and am not that nervous, I can usually keep up an okay conversation.

Ms. HILLMAN: Okay, that's a good start. Can you think of any challenges about your expectations for yourself about conversations?

LAUREN: I could ask myself if I'm being too hard on myself?

Ms. HILLMAN: Do you think you are?

LAUREN: Maybe—I guess an okay conversation is better than standing awkwardly by myself.

Ms. HILLMAN: Definitely. If you experience an okay conversation with someone else, does it stick out in your mind as bad or do you think about that person as really boring?

LAUREN: No, I usually just think it was an okay conversation. I guess not every conversation can be really funny or deep.

Ms. HILLMAN: Exactly! Do you think maybe you're putting too much pressure on yourself?

LAUREN: Yeah, I do that a lot . . .

Ms. HILLMAN: So how are you feeling about the party now? What rating would you give it now?

LAUREN: I'm still nervous, but I think I can find people to talk to and keep myself looking busy and like I fit in. I'm feeling a little bit better about it. I rate it a 4.

Step 4: Apply These Skills to Various Situations

Ms. HILLMAN: That's great, you did a really nice job with this! You are really starting to understand how this works. It's important that you keep practicing. I'd like you to go through these steps on your own this week when you are feeling nervous about a situation. Use the example we did today and this worksheet [Handout 6.6] to complete the steps.

USING GROUPS TO TEACH REALISTIC THINKING

Implementing realistic thinking in a group format can be advantageous for several reasons. First, some students have difficulty identifying negative predictions or are reluctant to share them. In a group, students often express thoughts that others can relate to, prompting more students to participate and encouraging recognition and labeling of negative expectations. In this situation, directing questions to students who are more willing to share or better able to identify their thoughts can help get the conversation started. In a particularly quiet or reserved group, providing options and asking members whether each one sounds familiar to them can also be helpful.

In prior studies of this program (Masia Warner et al., 2016; Masia Warner et al., 2007), we have found that groups can be particularly effective in generating challenging questions. We have often seen students become actively engaged in challenging their peers' negative thoughts and raising alternative explanations. Facilitate participation by asking group members how they would challenge a thought volunteered by another student. Because teenagers have an easier time being realistic in situations involving others, helping group members challenge thoughts strengthens and reinforces their ability to challenge their own thoughts. Lastly, challenging questions and alternative explanations offered by peers tend to be received more credibly than suggestions from adults. Therefore, it is particularly advantageous to invite group members to generate responses to challenging questions, offer alternative explanations, and provide their perspectives on social rules.

PRACTICE, PRACTICE, PRACTICE!

To improve students' ability to challenge their thoughts, counselors should assign practice exercises for students to complete independently. Initially, providing students with a completed worksheet or Handout 6.7: Example— Completed Challenging Thoughts will remind them how the process works. It is often helpful to make several copies of Handout 6.6: Challenging Thoughts to give to students for weekly practice. Counselors might assign completion of three Challenging Thoughts worksheets about three different scenarios throughout the week and encourage students to monitor their anxiety and emotions before and after revising their thoughts to be more realistic. Over time as students become more fluid with these steps, counselors can forego using worksheets and ask students to verbally report in individual or group sessions how the challenging thoughts exercises went for them. In later weeks of the program, counselors will likely begin to notice that students' automatic thoughts about previous anxiety-provoking situations are becoming more realistic and students are entering into feared situations more regularly and with less distress. Alternatively, when students do still experience distress in anxiety-provoking situations, counselors may notice that with practice in challenging thoughts, socially anxious students will more quickly revise their thoughts and enter the feared situation anyway instead of avoiding it.

Realistic thinking and challenging negative thoughts are techniques that can be used throughout the entire course of the school program. Even when students are actively practicing social skills or exposures, they are likely to still experience negative thoughts for a time. Remember that changing the way we think is hard! Therefore, counselors should retain these techniques and weave them into behavioral exercises to address students' negative thinking in real time. When a student needs more practice with realistic thinking, we recommend asking the student to complete two to three Challenging Thoughts worksheets each week until revising their thoughts becomes more automatic. We refer to this chapter numerous times throughout the book to alert counselors to situations when reintroducing and implementing these techniques may be especially beneficial.

COMMON CHALLENGES TO TRAINING REALISTIC THINKING

Students Are Not Able to Identify Negative Thoughts or Predictions

Realistic thinking will not work for everyone. For some, especially those who can easily verbalize their thoughts, realistic thinking may be valuable. Other students who have less awareness of their anxious thoughts or who experience anxiety primarily with physical symptoms may benefit less from this skill. However, laying the foundation that thoughts should not be accepted as facts is helpful for other techniques we will discuss in later chapters.

Students Do Not Provide Examples of Negative Thoughts

Students may not share thoughts either due to anxiety that they might be negatively evaluated or to a lack of awareness of their thoughts. Sometimes it is difficult to tell the difference. A good starting point is to provide a list of commonly experienced anxious thoughts and ask students to identify which ones sound familiar (Handout 6.2). This strategy can help students feel more comfortable because they realize that their thoughts are not unusual. We have had students frequently appear surprised and relieved that we know the thoughts they are having and have heard them before. It is best to start by identifying thoughts in less threatening situations, such as giving a verbal presentation, trying out for a competitive team, or auditioning for a school play. If a student continues to struggle identifying thoughts, you may need to spend some extra time increasing awareness. Asking students to keep a journal or find a place to write down (or electronically track in phones) what they are thinking right before or after a challenging situation may be beneficial.

Thoughts Are Framed in a Way That Is Difficult to Challenge

There are a few common reasons why particular thoughts may seem difficult to challenge. The first is that a student tends to provide vague, nonspecific thoughts—for example, "Starting a conversation with a new peer is going to be a disaster." The problem with vague thoughts is that they do not provide adequate information about what negative outcome the student expects. Encouraging students to be as specific as possible can help to clarify their concerns: "I understand that you are concerned about starting this conversation, but what are you worried might happen? What would make it a disaster? What do you expect to happen?"

A similar problem arises when students frame thoughts as questions, such as "How is this going to go?" Though they may disguise their thoughts as questions, teens usually have specific predictions about the outcome. Therefore, these "question thoughts" should also be pursued further to identify the feared outcome—for example, "How are you thinking it might go? Sounds like there is a way it could go that you are worried about."

Finally, students sometimes substitute feelings for thoughts: "I'm thinking that I'm really embarrassed about starting this conversation." The student is merely identifying the emotional feeling (embarrassment), but not the prediction that is causing the emotion. Again, this should be queried for further clarification, for example, "You've done a nice job identifying how you are feeling about starting a conversation, but what are you thinking about how the conversation might go that is causing you to feel embarrassed?"

Students Do Not Believe Alternatives to Their Negative Predictions

It takes students time to be convinced by alternative possibilities. This is to be expected, as many students have been thinking negatively for years, and they believe their negative predictions are 100% true. In a way, the negative thinking has "protected" them from anxiety because it justified avoiding anxiety-provoking situations. However, students' thinking will become more flexible with repeated practice as well as with strategies we will discuss later to directly change behavior. We often observe a shift in students' thinking when they are able to challenge their thoughts more independently. When students still doubt more realistic possibilities, we recommend creating a behavioral experiment to test whether the negative thoughts are exaggerated. For example, if a student is convinced that it is against social rules to smile at strangers or acquaintances in the hallway, and that no one will smile back, ask her to try smiling at 10 people and keep track of how many people smile back. Chances are the student will have grossly underestimated the number of smiles she will receive.

LAUREN'S STORY

At the start of their next meeting, Ms. Hillman asked Lauren what she had noticed over the past week regarding the connection between her thoughts, feelings, and actions. Lauren sheepishly said that she did not write it down but had thought about it often. It was apparent to Ms. Hillman that this was true because Lauren began recounting several relevant examples. In addition to the example about attending a party, described in the dialogue above, Lauren had also noticed that her math teacher made a mistake grading her test. She checked with several friends and her mother to be 100% sure it was a mistake. Despite her certainty, she was nervous about approaching the teacher and had been avoiding it. At first when Ms. Hillman asked her to identify her thoughts, Lauren stated, "I was thinking, how is she going to react?" Ms. Hillman reminded Lauren that when stating anxious thoughts as questions, it's usually the predicted answer to the question that is actually causing anxiety. Ms. Hillman asked, "Lauren, how would you answer that question? How did you think your teacher would react?" Lauren then identified several anxious thoughts, such as "She is going to tell me that I'm wrong," "She is going to think I'm being disrespectful," "She is going to get angry," and "I'm going to make her feel like she's a bad teacher." Ms. Hillman reiterated the importance of questioning your initial negative thoughts, in other words, the importance of giving it a second thought. Using Handout 6.5 and Handout 6.6, Ms. Hillman illustrated how each of these thoughts could be evaluated for evidence to determine how realistic it is.

- "What is the probability that you are wrong?"
- "If you are right, what is the probability that the teacher will say you are wrong?"
- "How does she usually respond when someone points out a mistake?"
- "Do good teachers make mistakes sometimes?"
- "What evidence do you have that she will get upset?"
- "Even if she tells you that you are wrong, would that be so bad?"

At first, Ms. Hillman had to offer most of these questions, but after the first example, Lauren caught on. "I knew I was probably exaggerating, at least that is what everyone tells me, but I never really thought it through like this." Ms. Hillman suggested that they do a few more examples using Handout 6.6. Together, they worked through another example about singing a solo. Ms. Hillman asked Lauren to take some blank copies and practice a few times before their next meeting, and Lauren decided to also type the challenging questions into her phone so she would always have them accessible.

Ms. Hillman continued to weave realistic thinking strategies into later meetings. As is often the case with realistic thinking strategies, Lauren required occasional coaching to refrain from presenting thoughts as questions or as feelings, and she continued to be inconsistent in filling out worksheets for realistic thinking. Even though she sometimes did not complete any worksheets, Ms. Hillman noticed over time that Lauren generated alternatives to anxious thoughts more quickly. Lauren sometimes even corrected her thoughts and verbally generated alternatives immediately, without going through any challenging questions. When Ms. Hillman noticed this, she praised Lauren for practicing realistic thinking and highlighted for Lauren how her realistic thoughts were becoming more automatic.

Just as Lauren was inconsistent about completing worksheets, counselors may notice that their students seem to "never do the homework." As frustrating as this may be, remember that even when students do not complete worksheets, they often spend time thinking about the skills and strategies presented to them. We encourage counselors to notice and praise small changes that students make in their thinking over time. The more counselors include realistic thinking within their conversations with students and the more students are praised or reinforced for their practice, the more likely students are to actively engage in challenging their thoughts.

CHAPTER SUMMARY

- Realistic thinking teaches adolescents to critically evaluate their thoughts utilizing strategic questioning to challenge the accuracy of their assumptions based on evidence.

- After laying the foundation, realistic thinking steps include (1) identifying specific negative predictions, (2) recognizing thinking traps, (3) evaluating the probability of the feared outcome or generating possible alternatives, and (4) practicing by applying these skills to various situations.

- Teaching realistic thinking in groups can facilitate discussion about negative thinking. In addition, receiving suggestions and feedback from peers can enhance credibility of the strategies.

- Common challenges include students' difficulty identifying specific negative predictions and skepticism about alternative explanations.

Same Situation, Different Thoughts!

Relaxed Reggie and Anxious Annie have been in a lot of the same situations but have very different thoughts while they are there. How do you think each one of them is feeling in each of the following situations after they think these things?

Situation	Relaxed Reggie	Anxious Annie
Playing softball in gym class	"I love gym-class softball! It's so much fun, and it doesn't matter if you win or not."	"I'll probably strike out in front of everyone and my team will be mad at me."
Losing a mock debate in history class	"Wow, he made some really great points. I'll have to remember to ask him where he found those sources."	"I must have looked like an idiot in front of the whole class."
Attending a friend's birthday party and not knowing anyone	"I'll get to meet her other friends. She's really nice, so I bet her friends are nice too."	"I won't have anyone to talk to, and I'll just look awkward standing alone the whole time."
Performing in a school talent show	"I can't wait to show everyone what I've been working on in my drum lessons."	"If I mess up, I'll be the laughingstock of the whole school! I'll never live it down."
Having a friend cancel weekend plans to hang out	"He probably needs to finish that big science project due on Monday. I know he's really trying to get an A on it."	"He really just didn't want to hang out with me because he thinks I'm boring or too unpopular."

Common Socially Anxious Thoughts and Worries

Below is a list of common socially anxious thoughts and worries. Read the list and mentally (or physically) check off which thoughts you often experience. Does this sound like you?

. . . In the Classroom

- "If I volunteer in class, I'll probably give the wrong answer and look stupid."
- "If I ask the teacher a question, he will think I'm stupid or that I haven't been doing the work."
- "If I make a mistake during my presentation, I'll make a fool out of myself."
- "I have to do everything right or others will think I'm stupid."
- "If I give my opinion during the class discussion, everyone will think that what I say is weird or dumb."

. . . With Friends or Acquaintances

- "I have no friends" or "No one will want to be my friend anymore."
- "If I try to talk to her, I will say something stupid, weird, or boring."
- "I can't talk to him because I will just run out of things to say."
- "If I go to the party/out with a large group, I won't have anyone to talk to."
- "If I invite someone to hang out, she will say no."
- "He only agreed to hang out with me because he feels sorry for me."
- "If I invite her to hang out, she won't have fun or won't want to hang out ever again."
- "If I invite him over, he will think I'm a loser and have no other friends."
- "I can't say hi to her when she is with her other friends."
- "I can't text him until we've talked more in school."
- "I can't ask to join their lunch table in the middle of the school year."
- "She will probably think I'm annoying and bothering her."
- "He probably doesn't want to be my friend anymore because I'm a loser."
- "If she doesn't have fun, it's my fault because I'm boring."
- "I'll probably trip in front of everyone and never live it down."
- "I'll be the laughingstock of the whole school."
- "Everyone will know that I messed up."

Identifying Thoughts

What are your nervous thoughts?

What are you expecting to happen?

Common Socially Anxious Thinking Traps

Thinking Trap	Explanation	Examples of Common Thoughts
Perfectionistic expectations	Unrealistically high expectations about how one must perform in social, academic, athletic, or other situations	• "If I make a mistake, I'll make a fool out of myself." • "I have to do everything right or others will think I'm stupid."
Rigid social rules	Unspoken rules about social interaction that support avoiding the interactions	• "I can't say hi to her when she is with her other friends." • "I can't text him until we've talked more in school." • "I can't ask to join their lunch table in the middle of the school year."
Excessive personal responsibility	Assuming personal blame if something doesn't go right and ignoring any external possibilities	• "I must have done something to upset him." • "She's probably mad at me." • "He probably doesn't want to be my friend anymore because I'm a loser." • "I shouldn't have missed that goal. I made our whole team lose." • "If she doesn't have fun, it's my fault because I'm boring."
Overestimation	Overestimating the probability of negative outcomes; assuming negative outcomes are the rule rather than the exception	• "I'm sure that my mind will go blank and I won't know what to say." • "I'll probably trip in front of everyone." • "If I invite her to hang out, I just know that she'll say no."
Catastrophizing	Small mistakes are blown out of proportion and feel like the end of the world; the potential consequences of something going wrong are exaggerated	• "I'll never live this down." • "Everyone will think I'm dumb." • "No one will want to be my friend anymore." • "I'll be the laughing-stock of the whole school." • "Everyone will know that I messed up."

Giving It a Second Thought

Like a lawyer, ask yourself and answer these questions to see what is true based on the evidence, not just feeling nervous or worried.

Thinking Trap	Challenging Questions
Perfectionistic expectations	• "Are you being too hard on yourself?" • "Could you live with a less perfect outcome?" o Examples: having a good game instead of a great game, getting a supporting role instead of the lead in play, having an okay conversation rather than a perfect one • "Wouldn't a less than perfect outcome be better than not trying at all?"
Rigid social rules	• "If that 'rule' is true, how do other teens do it (make new friends, make plans to hang out, find a lunch table)?" • "Can you think of a time you or someone else did it and it turned out okay?" • "If it seemed less difficult or scary, do you think it might be an option?"
Excessive personal responsibility	• "Even if it doesn't go well, could there be another reason that doesn't have to do with you?" • "Do you always want to talk to everyone, even if you are having a bad day or feeling nervous?"

Overestimation	• "What is the probability that your prediction will happen?"
	  o Rate 0–100%
	
	• "Do you think you might be overestimating?"
	
	• "What evidence do you have to support this high estimate?"
	
	• "What usually happens in this situation?"
	  o (Only helpful if the student usually performs pretty well in the situation)

Catastrophizing	• "Even if the worst outcome comes true, so what?" • "Could you live with that?" • "Even if the worst outcome comes true, will you care about this a week from now? A month from now? A year from now?" • "In the grand scheme of things, how will it really affect your life?"

Challenging Thoughts

Situation: _____

What are you worried might happen? Identify thinking traps: _____

_____

_____

_____

Feelings (Rate 0–10*): _____

Challenging questions: Check questions below that apply to these thinking traps.

☐ What is the evidence that this will happen? What is the evidence that it won't happen?

☐ What is the probability that this is going to happen (0–100%)? Am I exaggerating? Am I jumping to conclusions?

☐ What else might happen in this situation besides what I'm worried about?

☐ Are there other possible explanations? Are there other ways to think about this?

☐ What usually happens in this situation?

☐ What do I think when I see this happen to someone else?

☐ Are other people really paying as much attention to me as I think they are?

☐ Am I making things worse than they really are?

☐ Am I being fair to myself? Can I really expect to never make a mistake?

☐ Can I expect everyone to like me? Does it mean that no likes me?

☐ What advice would I give a friend who was worried about this?

☐ What's the worst thing that can possibly happen? Could I live with that?

☐ Will I remember this a week, month, or year from now? Will it really matter?

Answers to challenging questions: _____

_____

_____

_____

_____

_____

_____

Feelings after challenging (Rate 0–10*): _____

*0 = not having the feeling at all
*10 = the most you've ever had the feeling

Example—Completed Challenging Thoughts

Situation: Trying out for fall play

What are you worried might happen (thinking traps): I'm just a freshman, everyone is better than me, I'm going to forget my lines, if I make a bad impression now I'll never get a part any other year

Feelings (Rate 0–10*): Nervous = 8, Embarrassed = 5, Confident = 1

Challenging Questions: Check questions below that apply to these thinking traps.

- ☑ What is the evidence that this will happen? What is the evidence that it won't happen?
- ☑ What is the probability that this is going to happen (0–100%)? Am I exaggerating? Am I jumping to conclusions?
- ☑ What else might happen in this situation besides what I'm worried about?
- ☐ Are there other possible explanations? Are there other ways to think about this?
- ☑ What usually happens in this situation?
- ☑ What do I think when I see this happen to someone else?
- ☐ Are other people really paying as much attention to me as I think they are?
- ☑ Am I making things worse than they really are?
- ☐ Am I being fair to myself? Can I really expect to never make a mistake?
- ☐ Can I expect everyone to like me? Does it mean that no likes me?
- ☑ What advice would I give a friend who was worried about this?
- ☑ What's the worst thing that can possibly happen? Could I live with that?
- ☑ Will I remember this a week, month, or year from now? Will it really matter?

Answers to challenging questions: I might have tougher odds as a freshman, but some freshmen get parts. Maybe I can ask my brother if some people get a part in later plays after getting cut as a freshman. I've been in drama for years so I have a decent chance – maybe 50%. I'll never make it if I don't try. I would tell a friend it's worth a try. The worst that can happen is I can ruin my chances but I can always get involved in other plays outside of school.

Feelings after challenging (Rate 0–10*): Nervous = 5, Embarrassed = 3, Confident = 5

*0 = not having the feeling at all
*10 = the most you've ever had the feeling

CHAPTER 7

Go Ahead, Start the Conversation

Adolescents with social anxiety typically avoid numerous social and performance situations. This pervasive avoidance of socialization often starts early in childhood, hindering the development of social competence and resulting in social skills deficits (Beidel et al., 1998, 1999; Kearney, 2005). Socially anxious students who exhibit these deficits may also experience less successful social interactions, which in turn increases their anxiety and the likelihood that they will continue to avoid social situations in the future. Thus, enhancing social skills helps students feel more prepared to interact socially and bolsters their confidence to enter into new social situations. The next four chapters focus on training socially anxious students in critical social skills, including initiating and maintaining conversations, extending invitations to peers, attending to conversations with others while managing anxiety interference, and practicing assertiveness. This chapter provides a rationale for teaching social skills in school groups. It also provides guidance on teaching students to initiate conversations and display appropriate and welcoming nonverbal behavior.

WHY IS SOCIAL SKILLS TRAINING IMPORTANT?

The development of key social behaviors is often impeded by a history of inadequate socialization experiences for anxious youth. Socially anxious adolescents are more likely to perceive themselves as less socially competent, and they often anticipate performing poorly in social situations (Alfano, Beidel, & Turner, 2006; Beidel, 1991). Consistent with their own evaluations, socially anxious adolescents show interpersonal skills deficits. They are rated by others as less socially skilled and are less likely to receive positive peer responses (Spence et al., 1999). Specifically, they express greater anxiety in conversations, interact and initiate less, are more withdrawn, use less assertive responses, and speak with fewer words and longer speech latencies than their nonanxious peers (Alfano et al., 2006; Beidel et al., 1999, 2007; Spence et al., 1999). High anxiety in social situations may interfere with attending to and processing the social situation because students are hypervigilant to potential threats and focus on their own performance rather than attending to their conversational partner (Alfano et al., 2006).

These underdeveloped social skills are likely a contributing factor in the development and maintenance of social anxiety. Spence and colleagues (1999) suggest a model in which social skills deficits increase negative expectations about social situations, thereby encouraging anxiety and avoidance. For example, Jordan is a teenager with rusty skills for starting conversations. He often predicts that he will not know what to say and is hesitant to approach peers. He almost never initiates interactions, and his subsequent withdrawal from social situations has reduced his opportunities to practice and improve conversational skills, thereby maintaining his anxiety (Rapee & Heimberg, 1997). His lack of practice has resulted in actual awkward performance when he has tried to initiate conversations. Poor social interactions confirm his negative predictions and strengthen his avoidance. This is a vicious cycle that intensifies social anxiety by maintaining exaggerated negative thinking, deficient social skills, and avoidance.

Also placing socially anxious teenagers at a disadvantage are their nonverbal and verbal social behaviors, such as limited eye contact, speaking at a low volume, mumbling, fidgeting, and appearing tense. These behaviors, caused by social discomfort, often give the impression that socially anxious students are unfriendly or unwilling to engage in social interactions. Peers may then avoid approaching them, which may strengthen beliefs of socially anxious students that they are uninteresting or unapproachable, or that initiating conversation with unfamiliar peers is unwelcomed (Ryan & Masia Warner, 2012).

For all of the aforementioned reasons, it is becoming increasingly accepted that social skills training for socially anxious adolescents may be critical for achieving maximal treatment benefits (Alfano et al., 2006; Herbert et al., 2005; Kendall et al., 2012; Mesa, Beidel,

> **Social skills training may be critical for maximal treatment benefits.**

& Bunnell, 2014). Delivering explicit coaching in conversational skills and facilitating student practice through role plays provides students with a foundation for success in exposures and in everyday social situations.

TRAINING SOCIAL SKILLS IN SCHOOL GROUPS

We find that it is valuable to implement social skills training with a group of students in school. The group format and inclusion of peers allow opportunities for students to practice skills and receive feedback. Several students can be involved in brainstorming potential opportunities for conversations with others and ways to initiate interactions. Additionally, it is generally more realistic for students to start conversations with peers about topics they would normally discuss, rather than practice with counselors or other adults.

Social skills training conducted one on one with a therapist in a traditional clinic office can feel artificial and constrained. Practicing conversations with an adult (i.e., the therapist), who may not be fully aware of how teenagers speak to each other or what conversation topics are most relevant, may have limited benefits. Oftentimes skills practiced in this manner do not generalize as well to real-life interactions. Adolescents may also discount positive and skilled interactions with adults. For example, they may discount successful conversations with thoughts like "I only did well because I was talking to an adult" or "That was only easy because adults are nicer than peers." "My therapist made it easy for me," "My therapist carried the conversation," or "My therapist has to be nice to me" are other common thoughts that can interfere with generalizing skills to interactions with peers. Without an opportunity to practice with peers, students may dismiss what they learned when practicing with adults because they do not believe it applies to people their age.

Groups also provide opportunities for continuous practice because counselors can pair students for role plays, assign various discussion topics, and have them switch partners repeatedly. When implementing role plays in groups, counselors may have students identify a few things they enjoy and then have them start and maintain conversations on those topics. In addition, sometimes students will want to invite other group members to get together outside of meetings. A school group can be a safe place for socially anxious students to start extending invitations to others and developing outside friendships. We recommend having some general awareness of how group members feel about each other so you can guide them accordingly.

Additionally, unlike training in a clinic office, implementing social skills training at school provides a more realistic context and affords natural opportunities for students to practice these skills outside of the therapy room. In addition to group role plays, social skills practice can be implemented by enlisting the assistance of prosocial school peers in a controlled setting (i.e., the counselor's office) or in various natural places throughout the school. Students can leave the room during sessions to go practice social skills with peers in the hallway or library and then report back to the counselor or group about what happened. Practicing conversations with peers also enhances the likelihood that conversations will feel more natural. Peer interactions increase the probability that conversations will center around realistic topics such as well-known eccentric teachers, cafeteria food, current television shows, or frustrating locker assignments.

Below we describe how to train social skills in a group context (Fisher et al., 2004; Ryan & Masia Warner, 2012), but therapists should feel free to adapt these lessons for use in individual sessions when they have determined that individual treatment is preferred for a particular student. The same strategies for teaching, brainstorming, and modeling skills can be used, and therapists can role-play with students one on one before eventually having the student practice with other peers in the school.

LAYING THE FOUNDATION FOR SOCIAL SKILLS PRACTICE

To begin the conversation about social skills training with students, it may be helpful to remind them of what they have learned regarding how thoughts, feelings, and behavioral avoidance increase anxiety. The counselor can ask students how they feel when they interact with less familiar peers, what their experiences in conversations are like, or how they might describe their typical interactions with unfamiliar peers. It's likely that the students will offer up descriptions like "It's awkward!," "It feels weird!," or "I look like a fool." At this point the counselor can remind students that exaggerated negative self-evaluations are common with social anxiety but should also empathize with students' feelings that social situations are indeed awkward for them. Counselors can then use this as an opportunity for presenting the rationale for social skills practice.

We recommend explaining that interacting with others to initiate and maintain conversations or extend invitations requires us to use our social skills. Social skills, like all skills, can be practiced. The more we practice, the more comfortable we are and the less awkward we feel doing those things. Because students want to get more comfortable around people and want to stop avoiding interactions with others, they need to practice engaging in social situations and using social skills.

The counselor can focus on students' subjective experiences of not feeling comfortable as the rationale for engaging in social skills practice, rather than emphasizing potential actual social skills deficits. Discussing explicitly how socially anxious students often present with social skills deficits when introducing social skills training would likely only serve to make students even more self-conscious in social situations.

> **Social skills, like all skills, can be practiced!**

INITIATING CONVERSATIONS

Counselors should present that the first social skill the group will focus on is initiating conversations with others. Counselors can empathize with the idea that starting conversations is a significant struggle for students with social anxiety. Students often have a difficult time approaching others and initiating interactions, which severely limits opportunities to create new relationships. Ask the students for feedback on how they feel when initiating conversations, particularly with unfamiliar peers. (Remember, they likely feel differently with their best friends!). We have often heard from students that they do not know how to start conversations or what to say in conversations. In addition, they have trouble identifying appropriate times to begin talking and often report feeling uncomfortable or awkward being the first to "break the silence." Teaching students to initiate conversations includes (1) discussing how to identify opportune times for interactions, (2) reviewing what to say to initiate conversations, (3) demonstrating how to look friendly and approachable to others, and (4) role-playing initiating conversations.

Step 1: When Is a Good Time to Start a Conversation?

Start this topic with teenagers by asking them, "When do you think would be a good time to start a conversation with someone else?" When running group programs, the counselor can have the group generate a list together and can write the results on a whiteboard if one is available. Often teenagers have a lot of difficulty generating ideas. It helps to prompt students to think about different places they might be during the day that are conducive to conversations. Scenarios to offer might include (1) when you are introduced to someone, (2) when you run into neighbors or peers in different settings (e.g., at the mall, the swimming pool, a local restaurant), (3) before or after you attend a structured event (e.g., before dance class, after baseball practice, after a school assembly), and (4) when you are in close proximity to someone else (e.g., sitting next to someone in class or on the bus, in an elevator, or in line in a store).

Next, discuss with students how to decide whether to start a conversation in one of these situations. We have found it helpful to have teenagers think about the following questions:

1. Does the person look busy? For example, are they reading, writing, or preoccupied with their thoughts?
2. Does the person look friendly? Are they smiling or making eye contact?
3. Does the person provide an opening (e.g., say something first)?

Modeling examples of these nonverbal behaviors and asking students whether they should approach you can also be helpful in highlighting these points.

We must inform you that your students with social anxiety will likely be overly cautious. That is, they often interpret social cues negatively, and they erroneously assume the person is not interested in talking. Therefore, it is important to emphasize that most people are friendly and open to conversations unless they are busy with something else. Skeptical students may take some convincing and might require confirmation from outgoing peers or a behavioral experiment. Counselors can have students poll their friends or family to find out how people feel when others initiate conversations with them. We have also found it valuable to assign a "smile experiment." This involves asking students to smile at as many people as possible and to notice and record how many smile back. Ask them to report how many times out of 10 the person they smiled at responded in a positive way.

Step 2: What Do I Say to Start a Conversation?

Now that you have convinced your students that there are several times when conversations are possible, it is important to help them break the ice. Initiating conversations focuses on simple things to say to begin a social exchange and on nonverbal behaviors that help facilitate positive communication. We find it helpful to be as lighthearted as possible and to have students brainstorm options for how to initiate interactions. Remember, socially anxious students believe that they must say something perfect, witty, or brilliant to start a conversation. Therefore, you may want to tell them that they will not believe how easy it is. Starting conversations is as simple as commenting on something they have in common with the other person or on something going on around them. Examples include: "We live on the same block," "My dad is in the Navy too," "I see you at the pool sometimes," "Have you tried out for soccer before?," "This is a really nice place," "The bus is crowded today," or "What did you think of the homework?" Make sure to stress that the statement does not have to be the "perfect statement." Any comment will usually break the ice and get the other person talking too. Emphasize that most people are friendly and respond positively to friendliness from others.

Step 3: Looking Friendly and Approachable

Remember that socially anxious students often appear shy or tense, which may turn others off or make it unlikely that others will approach. Furthermore, socially anxious students are usually unaware of how they appear to others. It can be helpful to model inappropriate or unhelpful nonverbal behavior in a lighthearted style (e.g., looking down, frowning, looking annoyed, slouching, crossing arms, speaking low). Ask the students, "What is wrong with the way I look? Do you think anyone would want to talk to me if I looked like this? How could I look more friendly and approachable?" Have the students generate reasons why certain nonverbal behaviors are unhelpful, and brainstorm what other nonverbal behaviors might be helpful for looking sociable and inviting. It can also be helpful to discuss how others sometimes perceive shy people as "stuck up" because of nonverbal behaviors such as not smiling or looking tense. Students are often shocked to hear that others would ever interpret these behaviors as uninterested or condescending. Ask students how they think they appear to others (e.g., friendly vs. unfriendly) and why.

In your review of nonverbal behaviors, make sure to present and model the helpful nonverbal behaviors from Table 7.1 below. You will also provide feedback on these important nonverbal behaviors when students practice initiating conversations in role plays. It can be beneficial to remind students to practice these behaviors as they converse with you and with other group members, if implementing a group program. Furthermore, Handout 7.1: Helpful and Unhelpful Nonverbal Behaviors can be given to students as a summary after the discussion to remind them about which nonverbal behaviors you want them to practice and why. We recommend having students practice different nonverbal styles such as looking nervous or looking relaxed. For groups, counselors might instruct students to take turns picking three helpful or three unhelpful nonverbal behaviors from Handout 7.1 and modeling them for the group. Other group members can then call out which behaviors the student is trying to portray.

TABLE 7.1. Helpful Nonverbal Behaviors

1. Facing the person with an open posture (i.e., not crossing arms)
2. Making eye contact
3. Smiling
4. Not fidgeting or shuffling feet
5. Speaking in an audible, confident voice
6. Speaking clearly and slowly
7. Looking relaxed and confident

Step 4: Role-Playing Initiating Conversations

Role plays are a great intermediate step between introducing a skill and assigning practice in uncontrolled settings. After students have discussed and practiced when to start a conversation, what to say, and friendly body postures to use, it is time to start role-playing in the group. If working with a student individually, these role plays should be started with just the counselor and student. Appendix 7.1: Role-Play Scenarios for Practice—Initiating Conversations can be helpful for school personnel just beginning to structure role plays for students. Counselors can either assign role-play situations from the potential scenes listed in Appendix 7.1 or can brainstorm with students to identify situations they would like to use for practicing this skill (i.e., attending a school meeting, sitting on a bench, or attending a sports event). Arranging role plays is often easier in a group. Pairs of students can be enlisted in different role-play scenarios to practice initiating conversations while other students observe. Try to incorporate those elements that are problematic for each student (e.g., starting a conversation with someone who is older or who is a popular classmate at school). Once the situation is selected, choose one student to start the conversation. Frequently switch who is assigned to initiate the conversation and rotate which students are participating in the role play. At this stage, each role play can be very short (e.g., less than 1 minute), since maintaining and lengthening conversations will be the topic of the next social skills session. This also allows enough time to have students rotate partners and practice multiple times.

A good goal for a group training session is to have each group member practice initiating conversations at least twice. Keep in mind that performing in front of others will likey be difficult for students. Emphasize that the goal is to become more comfortable just getting a conversation started and that this quick exchange is the focus. To decrease pressure and reinforce that conversation starters do not need to be "perfect," group members can be told that their conversation starters should be as dull as possible. To lighten things up, other students can provide feedback on whether their conversation starters were dull enough. Remind students that avoiding practicing this skill will only make their anxiety worse, and that the best way to decrease anxiety and improve their skill is to practice and receive honest feedback from peers about how students look and sound. Make sure to practice repeatedly until each group member feels and looks more comfortable with this skill before moving on to maintaining conversations.

Feedback is a crucial aspect of learning through role playing. In group treatment, invite other members of the group to give feedback by saying, "What went well? What can he do to appear friendlier?" Encourage group members to comment on whether the student spoke loudly enough or made eye contact. They can also provide examples of other statements that would have worked in the same situation to initiate the interaction. One thing we like to do is to have each student share a different statement that could have been used to start the conversation. This exercise promotes flexibility and creates additional practice for all group members. When working with students individually or in a group, if there are areas of particular difficulty (e.g., they do not make eye contact, they speak too softly), provide directive but encouraging feedback and have the student repeat the exact same role play with emphasis on improving the target behavior (e.g., looking more confident, smiling more, saying something else instead).

It is important to be positive by commenting on specific things the student did that were successful (e.g., "I like how you looked really friendly" or "Commenting on the class you have together was such a good conversation starter"). It is equally important to point out anything the student could improve upon, but counselors should frame this feedback in terms of the behavior they want students to do more of, rather than what the counselor thinks was not effective. For instance, if a student did not make eye contact with his role-play partner, the counselor can say "I want you to try looking in her eyes more next time," rather than the less effective "Don't look at the floor so much next time." After providing feedback, model and practice the appropriate eye contact, tone of voice, or other behavior, and have students repeat the same statements using improved facial expressions or nonverbal behaviors. On the other hand, you may comment that the student's nonverbal behavior was friendly, but the comment she made to initiate the conversation was overly complicated. In this case we recommend brainstorming alternative comments and then repeating the role play with the same effective nonverbal behavior and one of the new statements.

Once students seem to understand the skills and are comfortable practicing with the counselor or group members, we suggest trying conversations with other school personnel (e.g., the librarian, other counselors). If possible, we recommend having school peers (e.g., prosocial peer leaders) help with role-play practice. After a school has implemented these strategies for multiple years, counselors may invite back program "graduates" from the prior year to help role-play the skills in individual or group sessions. During individual or group sessions, counselors can also use naturally occurring opportunities around the school by assigning students to go initiate a short conversation with one or two other students or school personnel in the building. For example, counselors can have students leave the room briefly to go practice starting conversations with peers in the library or cafeteria, with hall monitors, or with students running a bake sale. Students can then report back to the counselor or group and debrief the experience afterward, reflecting on the skills that were discussed and practiced.

PRACTICE, PRACTICE, PRACTICE!

It is very important that practice take place outside of your role plays with the students in order to facilitate generalization of skills. The goal is for starting conversations to become a routine part of the students' lives—something they do every day. As previously mentioned, after the first session on initiating conversations, we recommend assigning students the "smile experiment," where they smile at as many people as possible and record how many out of 10 people respond positively. Additionally, encourage students to practice some of the helpful nonverbal behaviors throughout the week. You could have students practice by themselves at home in a mirror or with family members. Students could even practice looking relaxed and approachable when sitting alone at the school bus stop or when standing in line in the cafeteria.

Following some effective role plays with group members or school personnel, we recommend challenging students to initiate a specific number of conversations per day as homework. Initially, counselors may assign only a few conversations per day, and then gradually increase the number until students are regularly initiating too many to count! Remember to emphasize that most people are friendly and respond positively to friendliness from others. Identify easy situations or conversation partners that students can begin with, as well as harder situations to be addressed after students have mastered the easier situations. It can be helpful to have students check in with you a couple of times during the week (i.e., before school or during a nonacademic period) to ensure they are practicing, and to help your most nervous or reluctant students by discreetly practicing with them around the school building.

Counselors can also initially ask students to keep running logs of the conversations they initiated with notes about where the conversations took place (e.g., gym class, bus stop) or who the conversation was with (e.g., friend, unfamiliar peer, teacher). These logs can be helpful in determining how to expand on students' practice. For instance, a counselor may notice that students only initiate conversations with certain peers or in one class. The counselor can then challenge them to start a conversation with a less familiar peer or with a classmate during lunch. However, because some students might faithfully practice the skill but regularly forget to write down their interactions, counselors should remember that the important part is that students are *practicing* the skills and starting conversations, not that they are writing down what they did! For some students, logs may not be helpful and so should be used at the counselor's discretion.

COMMON CHALLENGES TO INITIATING CONVERSATIONS

Students Are Reluctant to Practice Initiating Conversations

If you are having trouble getting students to practice conversations, we recommend that you actively engage in the practice with them. We do not mean that you hold their hands and stand next to them (awkward!). Rather, set up a time to go around the building with them and assign various tasks or identify opportunities to start conversations. You might start with school nurses, secretaries, or other counselors if talking with peers is more challenging for a student. In addition, you may want to explore whether students are making negative predictions about starting conversations with others and use realistic thinking strategies from Chapters 5 and 6 to help them to overcome their reluctance.

Students Are Rigid in Using Social Skills

Another common difficulty we have found is rigid use of skills, such as when students repeatedly say the same thing to start a conversation. They may become overly reliant on one statement, such as "the homework was confusing." It is essential that flexibility be specifically trained. Teach flexibility by having students practice initiating conversations multiple times in the same scenarios while requiring them to use different opening statements.

You and other group members can also take turns offering alternative suggestions for conversation starters in the situations.

Students Continue to Look Unfriendly

Students may get good at starting conversations but continue to look unfriendly, for example by frowning or avoiding eye contact. To address this, it is important to teach students to become aware of their unintended nonverbal messages to others and reinforce more friendly and confident behaviors (i.e., smiling, eye contact, speech volume, intonation, and relaxed and engaged body posture). You may ask them to observe their posture and relaxed behavior when they are interacting with someone close to them, such as their sibling or even their parents. When you draw their attention to situations when they do look friendly, students can become aware of how the helpful nonverbal behaviors feel in their body when they are using them naturally. If students are open to doing so, it can also be helpful to videotape them while they are interacting with you and to view the video together, paying attention to their nonverbal behaviors when they are less comfortable.

Students Use Too Many Negative Statements

A final observation we have made is that socially anxious students tend to start conversations using negative statements (e.g., "This teacher is boring," "This bus is crowded," "It is hot in here"). While it is reasonable to make occasional negative comments, overreliance on negativity can come across as whiny or rude. Therefore, it is important to help students practice starting conversations with positive statements by repeating role plays with alternatives. Additionally, as students recount their experiences starting conversations outside of the group, be attentive to what statements students chose. Intervene early if students are falling into a negative comment pattern by having the student generate alternatives to their negative statements. Then have them practice using those alternatives either in the group, with the counselor individually, or with other peers or school professionals throughout the day.

LAUREN'S STORY

Ms. Hillman reinforced Lauren's dedication to working on realistic thinking and reminded her that the next set of techniques would focus on improving her conversation skills. At first, Lauren was thrilled, exclaiming, "Good, I really need that!" However, as soon as Ms. Hillman told Lauren that the best way to hone conversation skills is in a group with peers, Lauren clammed up. Ms. Hillman provided Lauren with information about the group and addressed initial concerns that Lauren expressed. Ms. Hillman then asked Lauren if this was another good opportunity for giving it a second thought, and guided Lauren through the steps to challenge her negative expectations about being in a group. After practicing some more realistic thinking, Lauren reluctantly agreed to join the group.

Ms. Hillman formed a group of four 9th- and 10th-grade students with whom she and another counselor had been working individually. She sent passes to each of the students during a period in which most had a nonacademic class. Each of the students attended, albeit reluctantly. Ms. Hillman briefly reiterated the purpose for meeting as a group and addressed confidentiality concerns. She asked students to introduce themselves by saying their name, grade, and one thing they liked to do. Lauren followed instructions but offered minimal information.

Ms. Hillman then introduced the skill of initiating conversations. She explained that many people find initiating conversations to be difficult but said that with practice, everyone can improve. She taught the group how to identify opportunities for conversation, decide what to say, and look friendly and approachable. First, Ms. Hillman asked the group to brainstorm aloud a few initial lines for starting a conversation. Ms. Hillman made sure to give a lot of praise but also provided feedback to each student and asked group members to do so as well. When Lauren seemed to gravitate toward comments related to academics, such as "the homework was really hard," one of the other students suggested she try statements unrelated to school. Lauren agreed it was a good idea and experimented with a few comments related to other events that were going on or to something she and the other person might have in common like music and movie preferences.

Next, Ms. Hillman explained nonverbal communication and provided group members with Handout 7.1: Helpful and Unhelpful Nonverbal Behaviors. To help students loosen up before role plays, Ms. Hillman demonstrated several of the nonverbal behaviors in an exaggerated manner and instructed students to shout out the behaviors being modeled. Lauren eventually laughed out loud at Ms. Hillman's demonstration of slouching and shuffling one's feet. Ms. Hillman then chose helpful behaviors for looking friendly and approachable and asked each student to demonstrate these behaviors. Lauren was guarded at first, displaying her usual limited eye contact. However, she benefited from feedback about her facial expression. Ms. Hillman urged Lauren to repeat conversation starters with special attention to maintaining eye contact. Lauren gradually improved her nonverbal communication and seemed proud when the other group members noted that she appeared much friendlier by the end of group. Finally, Ms. Hillman split the students into pairs and asked them to practice role-playing various conversation starters with their partners. Lauren made the most of the opportunity and continued to improve her eye contact. Ms. Hillman concluded the group by asking each student to commit to using these ideas to start conversations at least three times before their next meeting.

As is often the case when beginning groups, Ms. Hillman's students were nervous about participating with other peers. By varying the activities, encouraging active participation, and offering lots of praise for hard work, Ms. Hillman was able to create a supportive environment where group members allowed themselves to take risks. Counselors who implement skills groups are likely to find that these groups are not only effective at helping students practice skills and reduce anxiety, they are also fun for both students and counselors! Skills groups are a great way to facilitate rapid improvement. They also help students build feelings of self-efficacy and competence that prepare them for tackling more difficult skills or challenging exposures later on.

CHAPTER SUMMARY

- Underdeveloped social skills likely contribute to the maintenance of social anxiety.

- Teaching social skills at school is ideal because it affords natural opportunities for practice with peers not available in other settings, including use of a group format.

- Conducting training in a group format may be optimal because it facilitates practice with peers and allows for feedback from peers in a safe environment.

- Training in initiating conversations includes the following:
  - Identifying appropriate opportunities for initiating conversation
  - Providing guidelines about what to say to initiate conversation
  - Teaching students how to look approachable or friendly
  - Practicing using role-play situations with positive and constructive feedback
  - Assigning homework for practice with peers

- Be aware of challenges to initiating conversations such as students' reluctance to practice, rigid use of social skills, unfriendly nonverbal behavior, and excessive use of negative statements.

Role-Play Scenarios for Practice—Initiating Conversations

SCHOOL SITUATIONS

1. Sitting in class waiting for the teacher
2. Standing by your locker before or after school
3. In line in the cafeteria
4. Sitting in the cafeteria or school library
5. Sitting in the auditorium for an assembly
6. Standing near someone in gym class
7. Sitting next to someone on the bus to school or the bus for a field trip
8. In the locker room after practice or backstage after rehearsal
9. At sports or play practice waiting for the next structured task
10. Standing near someone at a school science fair or art show

OUTSIDE-OF-SCHOOL SITUATIONS

1. At a party of a mutual friend
2. Seeing an acquaintance in a store or restaurant
3. Standing in line in a store or at the mall
4. In a dance, gymnastics, or karate (or other) class outside of school
5. At sleep-away camp meeting new bunkmates
6. Seeing an acquaintance at the town pool
7. Seeing a peer at a park or baseball/soccer field after school
8. Sitting near a classmate in the public library doing homework after school

Helpful and Unhelpful Nonverbal Behaviors

Below are examples of nonverbal behaviors that are helpful and unhelpful when we are trying to look friendly, approachable, and engaged in conversations with others.

👎	👍
Unhelpful	**Helpful**
☒ Turning body away	☑ Facing the person with an open posture
☒ Crossing arms	☑ Making eye contact
☒ Looking down or away	☑ Smiling
☒ Frowning	☑ Not fidgeting or shuffling feet
☒ Fidgeting or shuffling feet	☑ Speaking in an audible, confident voice
☒ Slouching or keeping head down	☑ Standing or sitting up straight
☒ Mumbling or speaking in a low voice	☑ Speaking clearly and slowly
☒ Looking annoyed or angry	☑ Looking relaxed and confident

CHAPTER 8

Maintaining Conversations and Extending Invitations

In the last chapter, we discussed how to provide students with skills for starting conversations. Once students are initiating conversations more regularly, it is time for the next step: maintaining conversations and extending invitations. We have found that even when socially anxious teenagers become comfortable "breaking the ice," they continue to struggle with expanding conversations. They might feel like they have failed at a conversation if any awkward pauses occur or if they "run out" of things to say. They frequently also have a difficult time knowing when or how to shift topics during conversations. Moreover, even after several pleasant conversations with a peer, socially anxious adolescents remain reluctant to invite someone to get together outside of school. These limitations make it difficult for students to establish new relationships or deepen existing friendships. Therefore, this chapter focuses on skills for maintaining conversations and extending invitations to peers with the goal of developing friendships with others.

LAYING THE FOUNDATION FOR PRACTICING CONVERSATIONAL SKILLS

Begin by telling students that starting conversations is only the first step in becoming more comfortable during social interactions. Socially anxious adolescents typically experience significant anxiety during longer exchanges. Students have told us that they avoid starting conversations because they worry that they "won't know what to say after." Their main concerns are (1) pauses or moments of silence, (2) "running out of things to say," and (3) others' perceptions that the conversation is boring or awkward. It may be helpful to open up the discussion by asking what concerns they have regarding maintaining conversations. Offer up one or two potential concerns if students seem "stuck." Remind them about how negative predictions feed avoidance and strengthen social anxiety, and briefly see if they can come up with more realistic thoughts (Chapter 5 and 6). Then explain that they will be practicing how to maintain conversations and extend invitations to peers.

ENHANCING CONVERSATIONAL SKILLS

Because socially anxious students are concerned about running out of things to say, they often fire a lot of questions at others without commenting or responding. This can be off-putting to peers and can make others feel like they are being interrogated. We have also seen students awkwardly change topics prematurely, too frequently, and too abruptly. In addition, the anxiety students experience during conversations can distract them from genuinely listening to what the other person is saying. Therefore, they may appear uninterested or may miss information that is essential to natural follow-up comments or questions. (Helping students attend to and use relevant conversational cues will be discussed in Chapter 9.) Unfortunately, all of these behaviors may result in conversations that are indeed awkward, with long pauses or clunky transitions (Alfano et al., 2006; Beidel et al., 1999, 2007; Spence et al., 1999). These uncomfortable experiences reinforce students' negative thoughts about conversations and exacerbate their fears about inviting peers to get together, thereby fueling a vicious cycle of negative experiences and avoidance of social opportunities. To remediate this pattern, we teach socially anxious students essential skills to sustain natural conversations. Specifically, we focus on replacing closed-ended questions with open-ended ones, staying with topics for longer periods of time, and changing topics more smoothly. We then teach students how to extend invitations to friends and acquaintances and have them practice this skill through role plays (Fisher et al., 2004; Ryan & Masia Warner, 2012).

Step 1: Asking Open-Ended Questions

To improve students' conversational skills, we recommend teaching them how to use open-ended questions. Begin by explaining to students that no one likes to feel as if they are taking an oral exam or being interrogated. Questions delivered in a rapid-fire fashion tend to make others feel uncomfortable. In addition, this type of interaction does not allow for the reciprocal exchange of information that facilitates the identification of mutual interests, which build friendships. It can be helpful to demonstrate this type of interaction by inviting a student to be a volunteer. Ask her a string of yes or no questions. To make it fun and light-hearted, be silly and exaggerate the interrogative nature of the yes/no questions, and do not allow the volunteer time to expand on her answer. Afterward, get feedback from the group on how the "conversation" went and brainstorm with the students why it did not go well. The students will likely point out that you asked only yes or no questions and that your partner did not have a chance to elaborate or contribute to the conversation in a meaningful way.

At this point, transition to highlighting the differences between closed-ended questions like the ones you asked (e.g., "Do you like sports?"), to which the other person is most likely to respond with one-word answers ("yes" or "no"), and open-ended questions that promote more dialogue (e.g., "What kinds of sports do you like to play?"). It can be fun to provide students with about 10 questions and have them identify whether they are open or closed. Handout 8.1: Is It Open or Closed? provides some examples for this activity, along with its companion answer key in Appendix 8.1: Answer Key—Is It Open or Closed? Counselors may elect to use the worksheet with students but should also feel free to make this as inter-active and flexible as possible by generating closed and open-ended questions that may be more relevant or interesting for their students. Some counselors prefer using worksheets, others like writing on whiteboards, and still others like to lead this activity as a completely oral exercise with students shouting out the answers. Counselors are encouraged to find the style that best works for them and their students.

We next recommend having students practice changing closed questions to open ones by either revising sentences in Handout 8.1 or by using Handout 8.2: Creating Open-Ended Questions. Sample answers are provided in Appendix 8.2: Answer Key—Creating Open-Ended Questions. Counselors may also generate original sentences for the group to revise. Explain to students that generating open-ended questions and remembering to use them naturally during conversations is a skill that requires consistent practice. Occasionally, students may attempt to *never* use a closed-ended question and may seem stuck in role plays or conversations because of it. To prevent this from happening, it may be helpful to clarify for students that closed-ended questions are not always bad and are often appropriate and helpful in the conversation to move things along in a natural way. The goal is not to *never* use closed-ended questions, but rather to use *more* open-ended ones so that we do not inter-rogate our conversation partner. If this becomes a problem for some students, have them practice mixing up open- and closed-ended questions by assigning them a specific number of both types of questions to ask in a role play or practice conversation. For instance, you may have them ask a closed-ended question (e.g., "Did you start the social studies project yet?") and follow it up with an open-ended question, depending on whether the answer was "yes" (e.g., "What did you do for your project?") or "no" (e.g., "What historical event[s] are you thinking of choosing for your project?").

Step 2: Staying with a Topic

It is important that students understand that asking a few open-ended questions is not enough to keep a conversation flowing smoothly. We encourage them to take an interest in the topic and in what the other person is saying. Interest can be conveyed by asking a follow-up question based on information another person has given. Providing students with a scenario to demonstrate what this looks like and asking them to weigh in throughout the story can be helpful. For instance, if Constance asks Jean on the first day of school, "Did you go on vacation this summer?" and Jean says it would be appropriate for Constance to follow up. Have the students generate possible follow-up questions (e.g., "Where did you go?"; "What did you do?"; "What was your favorite part?") that Constance could ask Jean.

If using the example above, present to students the possible scenario that Jean has just finished telling Constance all about her vacation. *Now what?* This is another place where students sometimes feel stuck. They might feel that after the other person was done talking, the conversation just "died" or there were awkward pauses when they couldn't think of any additional questions to ask. Explain to them that another easy way to maintain a conversation is to offer your own thoughts about the person's response or answer your own question once the other person finishes. Ask the students to generate examples of how Constance might do this when Jean finishes talking about her vacation. If the students have difficulty coming up with things to say, you might prompt them by noting that a response could include commenting on which activity during Jean's vacation seemed most exciting (e.g., "I think I would have liked the water park best. Wave pools are my favorite!"). Alternatively, it would be appropriate for Constance to follow up by explaining some of the things that she did over the summer (e.g., "I went to soccer camp this summer instead of going on a family vacation"). These strategies help keep the conversation on the same topic rather than quickly jumping to something else. They also allow the conversation to have some depth. Emphasize for students that all of these strategies aim to increase their comfort staying on the same or similar topics for longer periods of time. Next, students will need to understand when and how to appropriately transition topics.

Step 3: Switching Topics

We recommend pointing out to students that you can only talk about summer vacation for so long; eventually it will be necessary to change the subject, and it is important to allow the conversation to have some depth and to go in directions that may be unexpected. We emphasize "letting go" of trying to excessively control and structure the conversation just to avoid any moments of silence. For instance, some socially anxious students feel panicked when others shift conversations toward new topics because the students didn't "prepare" what they would say on that topic. Instead of rolling with the new, unexpected conversation, some might then try to end the conversation or abruptly shift toward something they do feel prepared to talk about. We try to teach students that the key is to move smoothly from one topic to the next, and some moments are better for transitions than others. For example, Jean probably wouldn't want to start talking about her new dog when Constance has just started telling her about soccer camp. Instead, after Constance finished talking about soccer camp, Jean might naturally shift the conversation away from summer vacation and toward the fall soccer season in school, a distinct but related topic given the type of camp that Constance attended.

Teach students that appropriate times to switch topics are when (1) there is a long pause (i.e., when no one is talking), (2) there is nothing left to say about a subject (i.e., there have already been a lot of follow-up questions and comments), or (3) someone thinks of a related topic (e.g., Jean mentions fall soccer after Constance talks about soccer camp). Some counselors might write this list on a whiteboard and then have students brainstorm examples of when these would be applicable, either from real-life interactions that have already happened or hypothetical examples. Remember that students who struggle with social anxiety may require assistance evaluating typical behavior in these situations because they are often overly concerned about pauses. It helps to educate them that brief silences are a natural part of conversations and do not always signal that it is time to change topics.

It may also be helpful to explore what types of negative assumptions they are making about pauses and to encourage more realistic thoughts (see Chapters 5 and 6).

Step 4: Extending Invitations

Having longer conversations more easily can be very rewarding, and you will notice that your students' confidence will increase with success. We must caution, however, that students can get stuck at the conversation stage rather than moving on to develop friendships outside of school or at organized activities. Students get stuck because of intense fears of being rejected should they invite others to get together. For students to establish more meaningful friendships, the next important step is to assist them in extending social invitations. To begin talking about extending invitations, counselors should verbalize their understanding that socially anxious students often worry about rejection, specifically someone saying no to an invitation.

Socially anxious students are extremely worried about rejection.

Counselors might have students generate a list of automatic thoughts that occur when they imagine inviting a friend to get together. It is important to review what distortions (Chapter 5) the student might have about peers refusing invitations (e.g., "No one likes me" or "I am a loser"), and to revisit thinking strategies from Chapter 6. Explain to students that practicing the next skill of extending invitations can help them increase comfort in reaching out to others, establishing meaningful friendships, and challenging automatic thoughts. Noting the rationale and many benefits of practicing social skills can help students buy in and engage with these strategies.

Students often feel reluctant to start inviting peers, particularly if they have numerous negative expectations about what might happen. Therefore, we teach them to start inviting others in a less direct way that tends to feel less risky. Specifically, counselors could suggest statements like, "Maybe we can get together sometime." Phrasing a request this way gives students a chance to evaluate the other person's reaction before actually making a specific invitation. Then, if the other person seems positive or interested (e.g., "That would be great, I would like that"), students can follow up by saying something more specific like "How about seeing a movie this Saturday?" Following up with a specific suggestion is important because it increases the chance that the social engagement will actually occur and creates a natural opportunity to exchange contact information (e.g., "Let me get your number so I can text you about this later").

We encourage counselors to explain that if a peer responds positively to the idea of hanging out but rejects the specific idea, it doesn't mean an invitation failed or that the student "blew it." Encourage students to brainstorm what they might say if they offered a suggestion that their friend turned down. For instance, counselors might present the following scenario:

"You asked your classmate Andre if he would want to hang out and he seemed interested. Andre said yes, but when you invited him to play basketball, his response was 'I don't really like basketball.' What are some options for what you could say next?"

Encourage students to generate several options to promote flexibility in responding. Students might offer other suggestions for activities, ask Andre what his favorite hobbies are, or directly ask Andre what he would like to do instead.

Counselors should also warn students that peers may not always seem wildly enthusiastic even if they agree to get together. Because socially anxious students tend to expect negative reactions in social situations, it can be beneficial to remind them about automatic thoughts that might come up if their peers do not seem overly excited about their invitation (e.g., "They are just agreeing out of pity," "They don't really want to hang out with me"). Encourage your students to then challenge those thoughts (Chapter 6). Some ways to challenge those thoughts could include, "She wouldn't have agreed to hang out with me if she really didn't want to." A counselor might also have students generate other possibilities for why their peers did not respond more enthusiastically (e.g., "She was nervous about our math test in the next class"). Alternatively, the counselor might mention the nonverbal behaviors discussed previously and ask students, "Are you always extremely animated and outwardly enthusiastic when someone else asks you to do something?" (Chances are, the answer is no!)

At times when another's response to an initial invitation is more neutral (e.g., "Maybe"), encourage students to let it go for that moment, and instead try again later if a future conversation seems to be going well. Another situation that is possible but not common is, of course, if a peer's response is negative (e.g., "No, why would I want to do that?"). Counselors should present this possibility and openly address it in the individual or group session because this is a very common fear in socially anxious students. Many students will feel less worried about this possible situation if they have strategies to handle it. If a peer responds very negatively, encourage students to end the conversation and walk away. We like to make sure that teenagers know that outwardly negative or mean responses are atypical, especially from peers they have been talking with regularly and have experienced as positive and friendly. Students can be informed that typically, the worst-case scenario would be that others may be noncommittal.

Figure 8.1 on the next page is a flowchart summarizing the potential outcomes of extending invitations to peers. As with many strategies contained in this book, counselors may present this information in different ways. Some might wish to photocopy the flowchart as a handout, while others may draw the flowchart on a whiteboard. Still others prefer to present this information in a list or just as a conversation. We encourage counselors to be flexible in their delivery of this material and adapt their presentation to the students in the program or group.

Step 5: Role Plays to Practice Conversational Skills

As illustrated in Chapter 7, role plays are an effective strategy for facilitating students' practice and mastery of skills. By now, students have practiced role plays for initiating conversations. To enhance conversational skills, role plays should increasingly focus on maintaining

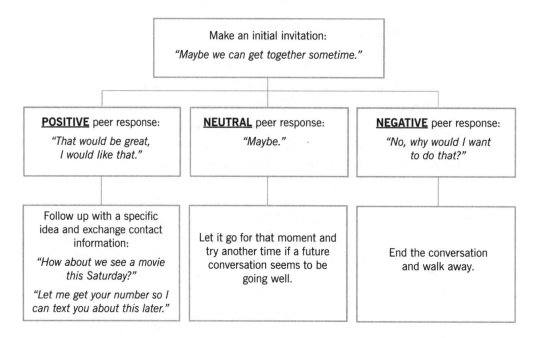

FIGURE 8.1. Flowchart for extending invitations to peers.

conversations by using open-ended questions, transitioning conversational topics at appropriate times, and extending invitations to peers.

We recommend setting specific goals for the student during each role play (e.g., ask at least two open-ended questions, stay on a topic for 3 minutes). See Appendix 8.3: Role-Play Scenarios—Maintaining Conversations and Extending Invitations for potential ideas related to role plays for these skills. Similar to what was discussed in Chapter 7, it is essential that students receive both positive reinforcement and constructive feedback about their skills use and nonverbal behavior. Have students repeat skills when additional practice is necessary. Potential strategies for setting up conversational role plays are discussed below.

> **Enhance conversational skills with role plays for maintaining conversations and extending invitations.**

We suggest that one role play include initiating and maintaining a conversation after meeting someone new. It can be helpful to present the goal of the conversation as getting to know the other person by listening and taking an interest in what she says. You may want to conduct other role plays where students are expected to ask at least two open-ended questions on one subject, and then appropriately shift to another topic and ask two more open-ended questions. Variations such as having students remain on topic until you signal that it is time to switch (to ensure that they do not switch prematurely) can also be helpful (see Appendix 8.3). Allowing students to struggle a little to maintain the topic during role plays is preferable to allowing them to abruptly change subjects.

Role plays can be done in individual sessions between the student and counselor or in group sessions by having group members role-play with each other. In group sessions, counselors can present the various options for role plays (see Appendix 8.3), or group members can brainstorm other goals for role plays. As with the role plays for initiating conversations, two students can role-play in front of the group and then the group can weigh in or give feedback. This may be beneficial for discovering what specific skills may be difficult for individual group members. Alternatively, students may be paired up, and each pair can role-play at the same time. For instance, a counselor might assign the students to talk about one topic for 3 minutes before switching to another topic. After pairing the students up, the counselor can say "Go" and have multiple pairs of students talking at the same time. After 3 minutes, the counselor might call out "Switch topics!" and all the pairs will need to find a smooth way to transition to a new topic. This strategy allows all of the students to get more individual practice; however, the counselor will need to be sure to move around the room and observe each pair so that he can give feedback afterward. Counselors should also be careful to rotate group members so that students are not always with the same partner. After a few role plays, the group can come back together and discuss their experiences collectively: What challenges did they face? Which skills did they feel like they mastered? Which skills do they need more practice with? What role play should the group try next?

Another goal for student role plays should include ending conversations by inviting peers to get together. For example, you may ask students who are talking about movies to end the conversation by suggesting that they attend a movie together (e.g., "It sounds like we like a lot of the same types of movies. Maybe we can go to a movie sometime"). It is helpful to ask students to practice a general invitation first. Then, depending on the tone of the response, have students follow up with specific plans. Like role plays for maintaining conversations, role plays for extending invitations can be done in individual sessions or groups. Counselors should be sure to use the same strategies discussed above for effectively conducting group role plays (e.g., observing different pairs, rotating partners, debriefing role plays afterward). In individual sessions, the counselor can act out different reactions to an invitation (i.e., positive, negative, neutral) and have the student practice responding appropriately. In group sessions, counselors can assign which partner is going to invite and which partner is going to react. Then either the counselor or group members can decide which type of reaction (i.e., positive, negative, neutral) is going to be played. Additionally, role plays for extending invitations should include practicing with a partner who turns down the invitation for a specific reason, so that students can follow up with new suggestions for alternative activities, days, or times.

PRACTICE, PRACTICE, PRACTICE!

It is essential that students practice these skills in "the real world" between meetings. At least twice per day, they should practice making their conversations a little longer by using open-ended questions and transitioning to new subjects when appropriate (e.g., less often). Brainstorm with students about possible places to practice conversation skills (e.g., unstructured time before class, before or after religious services, at after-school programs, at school club meetings, and during organized athletic events, dances, or music programs), as well as who might be a less risky conversation partner to start with (e.g., classmates, teammates, a friend of a friend). As your students practice more, have them increasingly initiate and maintain conversations with more unfamiliar peers and acquaintances, such as classmates they don't regularly talk to but sit near.

After some practice maintaining conversations, assign students the specific goal of inviting a friend to get together at least once per week. At first, students can invite friends they are comfortable with or have known for a long time. However, it is important to work toward having them invite new or less familiar peers. It is recommended that you assist students in identifying who they plan to invite and generating ideas for what they might do together prior to the end of your meeting. This helps remove the additional barrier of deciding who to ask and increases accountability. For instance, your student has spoken with someone a couple of times in class and they seem to get along well. This peer would be a potential person to invite to get together. In sessions, it is often helpful for students to brainstorm various activities that might be enjoyable to do with peers. In a group, students are usually able to come up with even more ideas, and group members can then select potential activities from the list when they invite a friend to get together.

COMMON CHALLENGES IN PRACTICING CONVERSATIONS

Students Repeatedly Change a Conversation Topic Too Quickly

Even with practice, we find that some teenagers still get very nervous about running out of things to say and will change the subject too rapidly. We recommend practicing conversations with the student with the stipulation that she cannot change the topic until you raise your finger. You can vary the time depending on how challenging you wish to make it for the student. If the student is still struggling, revisit negative predictions about pauses in conversation and practice some realistic thinking techniques covered in Chapter 6. You might also assign homework to observe conversations and pay attention to how they flow and what types of pauses are typical. Students can even be instructed to time pauses in others' conversations

Students Express Concern That It Is Too Soon to Invite Someone to Get Together

Socially anxious teenagers tend to overestimate the amount of time they should spend getting to know someone before inviting them someplace. We have found that some students even have specific rules about the number of times they should have spoken prior to getting together, or they insist on waiting for the other person to invite them somewhere first. This can obviously interfere with making friends. If a student has been enjoying talking with a peer who is responding positively, chances are that peer will also feel positively about doing something together. Most people feel good when someone invites them to do something. Use realistic thinking to help students recognize how they would feel if someone they had talked to a few times expressed interest in hanging out with them. They might feel nervous, but they will most likely say that they appreciate being asked. The important part is to get the student to actually take the risk and invite others to get together.

Even with Encouragement, Your Student Will Not Invite a Peer to Get Together

Students with social anxiety are very nervous about rejection, and getting them to invite a peer can be particularly difficult. You may have to start with someone very safe (a good friend) and gradually progress to less familiar peers. It may be necessary to ask students to bring potential contacts (i.e., phone numbers) to your office and encourage them to send a text while you are with them to get the dialogue started. Additionally, when running a group program, you might find that students in the groups start to become friends. For some very anxious students, it may be helpful to have two group members who are friendly with one another plan to do something together. Then encourage them to invite another outside peer to join the two of them, or assign each student to individually invite one other classmate to create a small group get-together.

Students Believe It Is Their Responsibility to Ensure the Get-Together Is Fun

Students may not only have concerns about extending an invitation, they may also worry that the person will say yes, meaning the student will actually have to go! This anxiety may be partially attributed to beliefs that if they do the inviting, they are responsible for the other person having a good time. These concerns can be especially magnified if the get together occurs at the student's house or if they choose a place to go or an activity to do. Of course, these beliefs about sole responsibility are not realistic. Remind students that if someone agrees to make plans with you, he is interested in having fun with you, just as much as you want to have fun with him. Most likely, both individuals have common interests, and the fun will come naturally. Use realistic thinking to help students evaluate why they believe it is their responsibility to make sure the other person has fun, and help them identify what their thoughts would be if they were invited by someone but then did not enjoy the activity (e.g., would students really blame the person who invited them if a movie was worse than expected?). As you can see, adolescents with social anxiety will often create their own roadblocks that you will help remove so they can progress in establishing new skills.

LAUREN'S STORY

The group met during a different period the following week to practice a new skill. Ms. Hillman asked the group whether they had completed their assignment of initiating conversations. Lauren and another student reported that they had, and they were surprised by the positive responses they received. Lauren admitted that she practiced with a fairly comfortable acquaintance at first, but when that went well, she pushed herself to try with someone who was less familiar. Ms. Hillman praised Lauren and the other student for completing the homework and reminded the group about the importance of practice. She then encouraged the group to collectively challenge negative predictions about starting conversations to help the group members who found the assignment too difficult.

Ms. Hillman then presented new material about maintaining conversations and extending invitations. She explained the difference between open-ended and closed-ended questions and led the group through a few exercises aimed at rephrasing closed questions into open ones. Ms. Hillman also discussed with students how to determine appropriate times to change topics in a conversation. Ms. Hillman split the group into two pairs again and asked them to role-play one at a time, with the observing pair providing feedback. Lauren grasped the usefulness of open-ended questions but tended to switch topics too quickly because of her discomfort with pauses in conversations. Although Lauren had improved in her ability to start conversations, she was very restricted in her responses once the conversation got going. Her eye contact was improved compared to the previous session, but it was still fleeting when she became nervous about what to say next. Group members helped Lauren brainstorm ways to elaborate on her responses to extend the conversation longer. Ms. Hillman also helped Lauren challenge her negative expectation that she would ramble and be uninteresting to her conversation partner. Group members provided the helpful feedback that even when Lauren gave longer responses, they were relevant and didn't sound like rambling. They also told her that she was a more interesting conversation partner when she said more, not less!

Finally, Ms. Hillman tackled the anxiety-provoking topic of inviting others to get together. The group discussed socially acceptable ways to extend invitations and identified some guidelines on how to determine when it is appropriate to invite a peer to get together. Lauren's cognitions about rigid social rules quickly became apparent: "It would be weird for me to ask that person to hang out because we have never seen each other outside of school before." Two of the other students were able to challenge some of these thoughts, which seemed particularly helpful to Lauren: "But you said you talk every day after math class. Would you think it was weird if she asked you to hang out?" Ms. Hillman then asked the students to role-play extending invitations with a partner. She had the group practice multiple times, encouraged them to vary their style, and suggested activities to promote flexibility.

Ms. Hillman provided a homework assignment to initiate and maintain conversations with two new peers, and to extend at least one invitation. She also encouraged Lauren to practice elaborating on her responses to conversational partners. Before excusing group members to their next class, Ms. Hillman had each student identify a few possible peers they might invite to get together.

Some of Ms. Hillman's strengths as a group facilitator are particularly notable. She regularly incorporated prior skills that students learned, such as realistic thinking and friendly nonverbal behaviors. Additionally, by pushing students to identify their thoughts and by encouraging other group members to challenge those thoughts, she ensured that each student's example was a learning opportunity for all. Ms. Hillman also encouraged students to get specific! She challenged students to generate more specific thoughts, required audience group members to provide specific feedback, and ensured that homework exercises were specific about the number of times each skill should be practiced and who the skill would be practiced with. We encourage counselors to draw on some of the strengths demonstrated by Ms. Hillman that were discussed in this chapter, in order to integrate skills practice into group treatment and maximize the benefit that students receive from these social skills groups.

CHAPTER SUMMARY

- Socially anxious students have difficulty maintaining conversations because they worry about moments of silence and running out of things to say, or they worry that others will be bored.

- Negative predictions, anxiety, and insufficient social skills can result in awkward conversations characterized by rapid-fire questioning and changing topics prematurely or too frequently.

- Teach students to have more natural conversations by:
  - Replacing closed-ended questions with open-ended ones
  - Staying with topics for longer periods of time
  - Transitioning between topics more smoothly by identifying related topics

- Socially anxious students have trouble inviting others to get together because they are overly concerned with rejection (i.e., someone saying no).

- Teach students to extend invitations by:
  - Inviting others in a way that feels less risky (i.e., "Maybe we can get together sometime")
  - Determining the tone of the response and following up positive responses with a more specific plan ("Maybe we can go to a movie this weekend?")

- Practice is essential! Role plays should focus on specific goals, such as maintaining conversations using open-ended questions, transitioning conversation topics at appropriate times, and practicing extending invitations to peers.

APPENDIX 8.1

Answer Key—Is It Open or Closed?

1. What did you do last weekend?—**OPEN**

2. Did you see the new *Star Wars* movie?—**CLOSED**

3. Are you going to the football game this weekend?—**CLOSED**

4. Which classes are you taking this year?—**OPEN**

5. Do you have a favorite teacher?—**CLOSED**

6. What did you think of the science test last week?—**OPEN**

7. Did you do the math homework?—**CLOSED**

8. Are you going to try out for the school play?—**CLOSED**

9. What are your plans for summer vacation?—**OPEN**

10. How did you get interested in art?—**OPEN**

APPENDIX 8.2

Answer Key—Creating Open-Ended Questions

Keep the conversation going: Here are potential alternatives for the closed-ended questions.

1. Have you ever (been to this restaurant/done this activity)?

   a. What kinds of restaurants do you usually go to? Do you have a favorite?

   b. When was the last time you did this activity? (e.g., went rock-climbing, bowling)

2. Do you like (food/musician/movie/hobby/sport)?

   a. What do you think of (food/musician/movie/hobby/sport)?

   b. What types of (food/musician/movie/hobby/sport) do you like?

3. Are you going to (school event/party)?

   a. What are you doing this weekend?

   b. What do you think about the upcoming (school event/party)?

4. Do you play (sport/video game)?

   a. Which sports do you play?

   b. What types of video games do you like?

5. Are you trying out for/auditioning for (sport/play/concert)?

   a. How are you feeling about trying out for (sport/play/concert)?

   b. What are your thoughts about trying out for (sport/play/concert)?

6. Are you a (sports/sports team) fan?

   a. Which sports do you like to watch?

   b. Which sports teams do you follow?

7. Did you see (TV show/movie/news event)?

   a. What did you think about (TV show/movie/news event)?

   b. What types of (TV shows/movies/news events) do you watch?

8. Are you taking (class/elective) this year?

   a. What (classes/electives) are you taking this year?

   b. What is your favorite (class/elective)? Why?

9. Did you do the (homework/class project)?

   a. What did you think of the (homework/class project)?

10. Did you go (on vacation/to camp/away for the summer)?

    a. Where did you go (on vacation/to camp/this summer)?

    b. What was your favorite part about your (vacation/camp/summer)?

Role-Play Scenarios—Maintaining Conversations and Extending Invitations

SCHOOL SITUATIONS

1. Sitting in class waiting for the teacher

2. Standing by your locker before or after school

3. In line in the cafeteria

4. Sitting in the cafeteria or school library

5. Sitting in the auditorium for an assembly

6. Standing near someone in gym class

7. Sitting next to someone on the bus to school or the bus for a field trip

8. In the locker room after practice or backstage after rehearsal

9. At sports or play practice waiting for the next structured task

10. Standing near someone at a school science fair or art show

OUTSIDE-OF-SCHOOL SITUATIONS

1. At a party of a mutual friend

2. Seeing an acquaintance in a store or restaurant

3. Standing in line in a store or at the mall

4. In a dance, gymnastics, or karate (or other) class outside of school

5. At sleep-away camp meeting new bunkmates

6. Seeing an acquaintance at the town pool

7. Seeing a peer at a park or baseball/soccer field after school

8. Sitting near a classmate in the public library doing homework after school

POTENTIAL ROLE-PLAY GOALS

1. Ask only open-ended questions

2. Ask two or more open-ended questions before switching topics

3. Keep talking with other person for 3 minutes before switching topics

4. Keep talking for 5 minutes

5. Practice with a partner who is very talkative or not talkative at all

6. Talk about a movie or activity and then extend a general invite related to it

7. Extend an invite that includes a specific day or plan

8. Practice with a partner who acts positive, neutral, or negative following your invite

9. Practice with a partner who turns down your invite for a specific reason

Is It Open or Closed?

Identify whether the following questions are OPEN-ENDED or CLOSED-ENDED questions. Remember that open-ended questions allow for longer responses, but closed-ended questions can usually be answered with one word.

1. What did you do last weekend?

2. Did you see the new *Star Wars* movie?

3. Are you going to the football game this weekend?

4. Which classes are you taking this year?

5. Do you have a favorite teacher?

6. What did you think of the science test last week?

7. Did you do the math homework?

8. Are you going to try out for the school play?

9. What are your plans for summer vacation?

10. How did you get interested in art?

Creating Open-Ended Questions

Keep the conversation going: Turn these closed-ended questions into open-ended questions.

1. Have you ever (been to this restaurant/done this activity)?

2. Do you like (food/musician/movie/hobby/sport)?

3. Are you going to (school event/party)?

4. Do you play (sport/video game)?

5. Are you trying out for/auditioning for (sport/play/concert)?

6. Are you a (sports/sports team) fan?

7. Did you see (TV show/movie/news event)?

8. Are you taking (class/elective) this year?

9. Did you do the (homework/class project)?

10. Did you go (on vacation/to camp/away for the summer)?

CHAPTER 9

The Secret
to Meaningful Conversations
Listening to What Others Say

Socially anxious teenagers often struggle with anxiety interference, which occurs when anxious thoughts and feelings (e.g., negative self-evaluation, clammy hands) or excessive self-monitoring (Clark & Wells, 1995), impede one's ability to concentrate and pay attention in social and performance situations. This interference, which can occur during social interactions, classroom instruction, and other school-related situations, often impairs social and academic performance. This chapter discusses techniques to conquer anxiety interference by teaching students to attend and listen to interactions going on around them (e.g., conversations, teacher's lessons) rather than to the "anxiety noise" in their brains. Tailoring training to meet the specific needs of socially anxious adolescents will increase the value of these strategies for students.

LAYING THE FOUNDATION: WHAT IS ANXIETY INTERFERENCE?

Classroom Interference

Imagine the following scenario: Mariana is in math class. She becomes aware that she does not understand the concept being taught and would like to ask a question about the material. Instead of raising her hand immediately to ask the teacher to repeat or explain something she does not understand, Mariana becomes preoccupied with finding the perfect way to phrase her question and concerns about what others will think of her question. Thoughts start racing through her head: "Will I sound stupid?," "I am the only one who does not understand," "Will the teacher get mad at me for interrupting the class?" All of this probably feels like a wildly confusing mess in her mind, a jumble of thoughts and images. This is because her attention is focused on multiple things at once: (1) trying to comprehend what the teacher is saying, (2) trying to form the perfect or smartest-sounding question in her mind, (3) evaluating her behavior and how she appears to others, and (4) worrying about what her classmates and the teacher will think of her if she asks a question. Having one mind do all these things at once is impossible for anyone! In fact, the number of demands on her attention will lead to negative outcomes. Due to becoming overwhelmed and pre-occupied by anxiety, Mariana never asks her question and does not get the information clarified. In addition, because her focus was disrupted by evaluative concerns, her ability to comprehend and remember the class material is now compromised even further. This may go on for several minutes or even the rest of the class period.

We recommend that counselors begin by using this scenario or a similar one with students when explaining the concept of anxiety interference (Fisher et al., 2004). You can make this example interactive by asking teenagers what they think Mariana might be think-ing when she does not understand the classroom material. You can also ask them what they think will happen in this scenario given that she was distracted by so many thoughts. You may also want to probe for personal instances when this has happened to your students in their classes. We have found that most students can really relate to this example, and that discussing it often encourages them to share personal anecdotes. Research supports the accounts we have heard from students, with studies demonstrating academic impairment for anxious students, including increased memory disturbances and impaired academic performance (Woodward & Fergusson, 2001), such as increased likelihood of failing a grade (Stein & Kean, 2000), higher rates of school dropout (Stein & Kean, 2000; Van Ameringen et al., 2003), and decreased likelihood of pursuing advanced education (Kessler, 2003; Kessler et al., 1995).

Conversational Interference

After students understand what anxiety interference looks like in the classroom, transi-tion to talking about anxiety interference in unstructured social situations, such as during conversations. Counselors might introduce the idea that the same types of difficulties may occur when meeting new people and having conversations. Socially anxious teenagers are nervous when speaking to others. They can become preoccupied with (1) worry about how others are evaluating them, (2) planning what to say next, and (3) working hard to ensure that others are not bored. Experiencing these distractions makes it impossible to genuinely listen to the content of the conversation. In turn, these competing demands make it dif-ficult for your socially anxious students to engage in conversations with a natural flow that is actually enjoyable, rather than feeling like work. Helping students experience success and feel more confident during conversations will reinforce their efforts to engage in social interactions with others. Therefore, it will be important to work with students to train their attention to actively listen and remember what others are saying during conversations.

We recommend explaining to students how anxiety interferes with their conversations. Engage students in this discussion by asking them to recall times their anxiety has gotten the best of them when talking to peers or adults, thus making conversations awkward or difficult. Similar to classroom interference, we have found that many students who struggle with social anxiety can easily relate to this experience during conversations.

We also suggest reviewing the reasons why it is important to listen to, as well as remember, what others say about themselves during conversations. It may be helpful to ask students to remember a good conversation they had and inquire about what factors made it a positive experience. We emphasize the following points: (1) people who actively listen to what others say and take an interest in others are perceived as more genuine and often make better friends, (2) people enjoy speaking with others who remember what they have told them, and (3) peers will often reveal information about themselves during conversations that students can use to maintain conversations or initiate future interactions. Emphasize that the key to more naturally flowing conversations is to attend only to what the person is saying rather than worrying about how you appear or what you will say next.

> **Social anxiety interferes with paying attention and participating in social exchanges.**

HOW DO I TRAIN STUDENTS TO LISTEN AND REMEMBER?

In an effort to enhance students' focus, we have used two attentional exercises when working with students (e.g., Masia Warner et al., 2016). Like the skills we discussed in the last chapter for maintaining conversations, whenever feasible, we recommend conducting these exercises in a group of students. However, if only individual meetings are possible, it may be useful to enlist the help of another school staff member.

Step 1: Memory Game

After students understand what anxiety interference is and how it negatively impacts their interactions, introduce the Memory Game. This game consists of a stack of cards that contain brief stories about fictional characters. We have included eight completed cards, as well as four blank "create your own" cards in Handout 9.1: Memory Game—Fictional Characters for Practice for counselors to photocopy and use with students. Alternatively, school practitioners may use index cards or create other fictional characters to ensure that characters are representative of their school's student body.

Introduce the game by telling students that they will be acting out the parts of various teenagers who are meeting at a party for the first time. Each person involved in the game (students, counselors, and other staff members) chooses one card and reads it aloud. The goal is for students to remember the names and background information for each of the other characters with 100% accuracy. However, counselors should not tell students the goal of the game until all players have read their cards. Once all group members have introduced their characters, ask each player to recall one piece of information about each of the other characters. Alternatively, players can take turns asking each other questions to assess group members' memories about their characters (e.g., "What was my name?," "How many sisters do I have?," "How old am I?," "What do I like to do?"). We recommend repeating this game (i.e., introductions, questions about each character) until students are able to respond to the questions about the other characters with 100% accuracy. However, keep in mind that this exercise should probably not take more than 10 minutes. If you are implementing this with an individual student, we recommend that you pick two cards at a time and do this repeatedly until the student is more quickly recalling information about your characters or until you finish all the characters in the deck.

Step 2: Personal Memory Game—Make It a Conversation!

This next activity is fun for students, particularly if conducted with a group of about four school peers. Again, if a group is not feasible, we recommend at least trying to enlist one other school staff member to join you. For this exercise, each player should create a personal introduction that is similar in format to those of the previously assigned fictional characters in the Memory Game, including names and four bits of personal information (e.g., My name is Linda Creevey. I live with my dad, my grandmother, and my little brother. I have a dog named Willow. I like horror movies, and I once went skiing). School counselors should model the format by saying their name and giving four pieces of information. Once all players have created their personal introductions, they should share them.

The purpose of this game is to challenge students to practice initiating and maintaining conversations based on the information they just learned about others (e.g., name, hobbies, personal facts), rather than simply recalling the information. However, as with the Memory Game, do not tell students what they are going to do until everyone has finished providing their introductions. If you are conducting this exercise in a group, one pair of students will interact at a time while the rest observe. You should designate one student in the pair to be responsible for starting the conversation based on something the other student said in his introduction. We recommend continuing to practice until all students have had at least two chances to participate in role plays: one in which they were responsible for starting and maintaining the conversation and the other in which they were the conversational partners. We also recommend switching partners between role plays so that students have an opportunity to interact with more than one person. It is important to remind students to maintain conversations by listening to information provided by their partners and using it to respond.

To make the game more challenging, when the student initiating the conversation cannot remember any of her partner's personal facts, she is responsible for asking the other student to repeat his facts. This is an important part of the exercise because it is typical for students to forget what others have said and to feel embarrassed about it. Therefore, it provides them with practice in making minor social mistakes and assertively asking others about themselves in a safe environment. After the student has had ample opportunity to initiate and maintain the conversation, if the pair seems stuck (which does happen, especially if you allow the conversation to go on for longer periods of time), you might invite other group members to provide suggestions of things the student can say to maintain the conversation. Finally, make sure to pay attention to nonverbal behaviors during conversations, and to provide feedback or invite group members to comment on this.

We have found this exercise to be very valuable for a few reasons. Teenagers find that it allows them to practice having more natural and pleasant conversations, and thus these skills generalize well to real situations. In addition, students often show significant improvement over time in their focus and recall of important information. Finally, this experience provides clear evidence for how listening and remembering what others tell you about themselves can make having conversations easier and enjoyable, and can facilitate developing friendships.

Step 3: Nonverbal Listening—What Does It Look Like?

Active listening is important, but we have to *show* others that we are listening! Therefore, this can be an important time to once again review appropriate nonverbal behavior. In Chapter 7, we reviewed nonverbal behaviors that are helpful for initiating conversations and appearing friendly or approachable. Now, we turn our attention to nonverbal behaviors that communicate to others that we are engaged and interested in conversations. We recommend starting this discussion by inviting students to offer suggestions on how to look interested when others are speaking. Counselors may also prefer to have students demonstrate these nonverbal behaviors. We summarize key behaviors indicative of active listening in Table 9.1 at the bottom of the page.

The main aspect we like to emphasize is to make eye contact with the person who is talking. Due to anxiety, adolescents frequently look down or away from conversational partners' faces (Chen, Ehlers, Clark, & Mansell, 2002), which may give the impression that they are not engaged while others are speaking. We tell them that, in our culture, we can briefly glance away while we are talking but should not break eye contact for long while the other person is speaking. Looking away while another is talking is a sign of disinterest or signals that you are ready for the conversation to end. Of course, this does not mean we should stare blankly at others the entire time they are speaking. Rather, we suggest staying in a comfortable position, nodding your head occasionally or verbalizing listening (e.g., "yeah," "uh huh," "hmmm"), and actively thinking about and responding to what is being said.

TABLE 9.1. Signs of Active Listening

1. Facing the person with an open posture (i.e., not crossing arms)
2. Maintaining eye contact
3. Smiling
4. Occasionally nodding head
5. Verbalizations (e.g., "yeah," "uh huh," "hmm")
6. Remembering and responding to what the other person says

We recommend having students practice these behaviors and providing feedback and coaching as needed. Counselors can also get creative in having students practice looking interested. Additional practice could include extra rounds of the personal memory game or having a brief conversation about anything interesting and engaging. One fun practice activity could also include having your student pretend to be interested and practice active listening behaviors while you tell him a very boring story. In groups, this activity can be done in pairs. One student can be assigned to tell a boring story while the other one practices acting engaged and interested. Pairs should switch roles and partners so that each student gets a turn to tell the boring story and practice active listening behaviors with multiple partners.

PRACTICE, PRACTICE, PRACTICE!

Just like the other skills we have introduced, we cannot expect lasting change following a few illustrative exercises. Building on the out-of-session conversational practice that students are already doing, counselors should assign students active listening exercises. Students could be asked to initiate conversations with at least two unfamiliar peers and report back to the counselor or group one nice new thing they learned about their conversation partner when talking to her. Any information that students report back should be factual and generally public knowledge or openly shared with others, such as "I talked with Sakina and learned that she plays basketball on the school varsity team" or "I talked with Tim and learned that he is an editor on the school newspaper." It is also important to encourage students to be mindful of staying focused on the interactions they are involved in during their everyday life—both in the classroom and with peers.

> **Encourage students to be mindful of staying focused during everyday interactions.**

Continue to remind students to practice active listening prior to having them engage in exposure exercises that involve conversation. Over time, these skills will become more natural and will pay off by producing more pleasant and positive conversations.

COMMON CHALLENGES TO LISTENING AND REMEMBERING

Students Are Still Having Trouble Listening and Remembering in the Classroom

It may be necessary to coach students to challenge negative thoughts related to struggles with understanding class material and/or asking questions in class (refer to Chapter 6). If a group setting is feasible, you may also use the opportunity to get feedback from peers to help normalize the experience of having to ask a question in class. In addition, helping students feel more comfortable with asking questions using exposure exercises covered later in Chapters 11 and 12 will reduce anxiety that can interfere with attending during classroom instruction. Students might benefit from practice with phrasing questions and role-playing with you prior to attempting this in class. Additionally, if anxiety interference in the classroom is actively impairing the student academically and he refuses to ask questions in class, it may be necessary to encourage him to approach the teacher before or after school to ask questions or request clarification. Over time, you and the student can work up to asking questions in front of others.

Students Are Generally Having Trouble Remembering What Others Say

Some students require more practice than others, so be patient! Continue practicing skills with the student and assigning them practice exercises. Challenging anxious thoughts about one's role in a conversation or expectations in the classroom may also be helpful (Chapter 6). If you are not noticing progress, consider the possibility that there may be other reasons the student has difficulty paying attention (e.g., other types of worries, ADHD). We recommend consulting with teachers and other school professionals to better understand whether the student is having trouble paying attention across many different situations, even ones that do not elicit anxiety. It may also be helpful to discuss this directly with the student as well. When difficulty attending and remembering appears to be pervasive, consider referring the student for further evaluation.

LAUREN'S STORY

Ms. Hillman began the next group meeting by asking Lauren and the other students whether they had attempted to initiate and maintain conversations since their last meeting. Ms. Hillman was pleasantly surprised when they all reported positive results. However, it was another story when Ms. Hillman asked whether they had extended invitations! Lauren admitted it felt too difficult to ask her classmate to hang out. However, Lauren was excited to tell Ms. Hillman that she had accepted an invitation to go out with her best friend, Ashlyn, and Ashlyn's soccer teammates, who were less familiar to Lauren. Lauren reported that she was very nervous beforehand and almost canceled, but forced herself to go and felt better once she was there. Lauren told Ms. Hillman that she focused on using open-ended questions, making good eye contact, and elaborating on her responses. Encouraged by this positive experience, Lauren told the group that she was going to invite a classmate to walk into town after school this week.

After reviewing progress since the past meeting, Ms. Hillman introduced the idea of anxiety interference. Lauren related to this idea both in the classroom and during conversations. She always knew that she spent a lot of time figuring out what to say or exactly how to phrase it, but she hadn't realized this was causing her to miss out on what was going on. She seemed surprised about how anxiety about saying the "perfect" thing actually increased the chance of saying something off topic. Ms. Hillman introduced memory games and role plays. After repeated practice, Lauren commented, "It's a lot easier to have a conversation when you actually focus on what the other person is saying!" Ms. Hillman challenged the group to continue pushing themselves to initiate and maintain conversations with less familiar peers, making sure to stay in the moment and allow the conversation to flow as naturally as possible.

CHAPTER SUMMARY

- Socially anxious teenagers struggle with anxiety interference during social interactions and academic situations. Anxiety interference occurs when anxious thoughts (e.g., fear of negative evaluation, planning what to say next) and feelings (e.g., heart racing) impede one's ability to concentrate and pay attention.

- Improving one's active listening is important because people enjoy speaking with others who remember what they have said. It also results in useful information for maintaining conversations and initiating future interactions.

- To enhance students' focus, we recommend utilizing two attentional exercises, in a group setting when possible.

  o Memory Game: Students recall facts about fictional characters without knowing they will be asked to remember this information.

  o Personal Memory Game: Students use facts about a partner to initiate and maintain conversation.

- Throughout practice exercises, give feedback and invite peers to provide feedback, offering other ideas on how to use information learned through the interaction to maintain conversation.

- Offer a review of nonverbal behaviors and coach students on communicating their interest and engagement during conversations.

Memory Game—Fictional Characters for Practice

Use these examples flexibly. You may need to adapt these characters in order to make them more representative of your student population. You can also create your own characters in the blank spaces.

Kevin McDonald: I am in the 11th grade. I play soccer. I play the guitar. I want to be a pilot in the Air Force.	*Bryan Johnson:* I am in the 12th grade and I have four older brothers. I play basketball and I love to draw. I love animals and have three pets.
Hector Juarez: I am 16 years old. I like to go mountain biking. My parents are doctors. We mostly speak Spanish at home.	*Melissa Richardson:* I am in the 10th grade. I like to sing and perform in shows. I also like to write my own songs. I live with my grandmother and two sisters.
Sara Dillon: I am 16 years old. I love learning new languages. I hope to become an ambassador to a foreign country. I'm traveling to France this summer for vacation.	*Lashonda Edwards:* I am 15 years old and the youngest in my family. I won our school science contest. I want to become an environmental scientist.
Ji-Won Kim: I am in the ninth grade. I do gymnastics after school. I love to read, and I hope to become a teacher someday.	*Jamarious Walker:* I am 17 years old. I just earned my driver's license. I work after school at the local video game store. I enjoy drawing and painting.

CHAPTER 10

Your Needs Matter
Learn to Speak Up!

Learning to be assertive is a difficult skill for most adolescents, but particularly for those with social anxiety. Socially anxious students tend to communicate passively, quietly acquiescing to others' requests or preferences even when requests are incompatible with their own. Anxious students often prioritize others' needs at the expense of their own due to fears of displeasing others or being negatively evaluated. Learning how to communicate assertively is a critical part of overcoming social anxiety because it supports more genuine, mutually beneficial relationships. In this chapter, we review different styles of communication and discuss how to help students skillfully and assertively express their needs, refuse requests, and communicate with adults in authority positions.

LAYING THE FOUNDATION FOR ASSERTIVENESS TRAINING

Individuals with social anxiety often favor a passive communication style (Schlenker & Leary, 1985), in which they do not openly express thoughts, feelings, opinions, or preferences. This behavior is perceived as a way to avoid judgment, conflict, or disapproval from others.

For example, when a socially anxious teenager is asked where he would like to go on Friday night, he is likely to say something like "I don't care, wherever you want to go" even though he may have a preference. Rather than communicating directly, passive communicators expect others to read their minds or somehow guess their preferences. Unfortunately, when this does not happen, adolescents with social anxiety may feel overlooked or angry, leading to unhealthy interactions in their relationships that can make it difficult for them to maintain friendships. This ineffective communication style can fuel negative expectations about social interactions (e.g.,

> **Socially anxious students often have difficulty asserting themselves.**

"She doesn't really care about what I want," "Everyone walks all over me") and negative self-perceptions (e.g., "I have no control over my life," "What I want doesn't matter," "I can't keep any friends"). Furthermore, adolescents may avoid certain friends or family members because they fear being unable to refuse requests and they feel "forced" to do things that make them uncomfortable. Overall, passive communication exacerbates social anxiety by reinforcing negative cognitions and avoidance of social interactions.

We recommend introducing the concept of passive communication by explaining its meaning using examples and asking students whether this approach sounds familiar. You can elicit other examples, possibly even personal ones, from students. Ask students to identify the pros and cons of a passive approach and explain how it affects their relationships. It is okay to acknowledge the positive aspects of passive communication in the short term, such as avoiding conflict and pleasing others. However, be sure to communicate that the downside of being passive is that they rarely get what they want! It can also lead to the feeling that relationships are one-sided and produce feelings of resentment that will eventually ruin those friendships and other relationships.

Next, have students brainstorm more effective ways to communicate their needs, and praise them when they provide examples of assertive communication. Following this discussion, introduce the term "assertiveness" and ask students what it means while highlighting any assertive communication strategies they just generated. Explain to students that assertive communication is the direct and honest expression of thoughts, feelings, and needs, and is the most effective approach for communicating with others and getting our needs met while also respecting the needs and rights of others. Because socially anxious students often communicate in a passive way and believe that being direct is rude, many will confuse being assertive with being aggressive. It is helpful to distinguish between the two styles, noting that assertive communication *respects* the rights, feelings, and needs of others. Aggressive communication, on the other hand, prioritizes our own wants or needs while disregarding the rights, feelings, or needs of others. Additionally, clarify for students that being assertive does not mean that we must try to get our way all the time and that we should never compromise. On the contrary, mutual compromise or taking turns is a part of respecting the rights of others as well. Illustrate the differences between the three styles of communication (i.e., passive, assertive, and aggressive) by providing examples, asking students to identify the style, and, when applicable, asking students to generate their own into assertive statements. Counselors may also provide students with Handout 10.1: Understanding Communication Styles. This handout provides several examples of the three styles and facilitates students' practice in converting passive and aggressive statements into assertive ones. Once students understand the differences between these communication styles, it is time to practice being assertive!

ASSERTIVENESS TRAINING

Given socially anxious students' difficulties asserting themselves (Ginsburg, La Greca, & Silverman, 1998; Strauss, Lease, Kazdin, Dulcan, & Last, 1989), we focus on various assertiveness skills including: expressing preferences, making requests, refusing requests, and expressing their feelings (Fisher et al., 2004; Ryan & Masia Warner, 2012). We also train students to practice assertiveness with important adults in their life, such as asking a teacher for help or requesting clarification about a grade. Role plays are a particularly effective method for teaching assertiveness skills (Fisher et al., 2004; Ryan & Masia Warner, 2012). As with the skills presented in previous chapters, it is also important to train students in nonverbal communication related to assertiveness and to reinforce these concepts through in-session role plays whenever feasible. Additionally, assertiveness training is best taught by conducting these exercises in groups of students because they provide various practice partners. If only individual meetings are possible, it may be helpful to enlist assistance from your school colleagues.

Step 1: Assertive Nonverbal Communication Skills

One reason socially anxious students may have trouble asserting themselves is that their nonverbal behaviors do not match what they are saying. For instance, if a socially anxious student looks down, hesitates, or shuffles his feet when trying to refuse a request or favor from a peer, the peer is likely to guess that when pushed a little bit more, the student will cave—and he usually does! Socially anxious students may confuse assertive behavior with aggressive behavior, and thus be hesitant to practice assertive postures or assertive nonverbal behaviors. Because of this, we recommend beginning assertiveness training by teaching students about what assertive nonverbal behavior looks like.

Counselors might begin by asking students to explain or demonstrate what passive, assertive, and aggressive nonverbal behavior might look like if someone was asking for a favor or refusing a request. Alternatively, the counselor might explain or demonstrate that passive communication could include looking down, speaking softly, or hesitating when talking. At the other extreme, aggressive communication would likely include raising one's voice, frowning, or leaning forward so as to encroach on another person's space. Finally, demonstrate that assertive nonverbal behaviors fall in between these and should communicate that the individual is making a firm statement while respecting the person she is speaking to. Specifically, assertive nonverbal communication includes maintaining eye contact, standing up straight and facing the other person, and using a firm but calm and pleasant tone of voice. We recommend that counselors demonstrate assertive nonverbal behaviors presented in Table 10.1.

TABLE 10.1. Assertive Nonverbal Communication

1. Maintain eye contact
2. Stand up straight and face the person
3. Use a firm and clear, but calm and pleasant tone of voice
4. Speak at a medium speaking volume (e.g., not whispering, but not shouting)
5. Speak at a consistent speed (e.g., not hesitating or pausing with "umm")

Just as with other social skills, we recommend having students practice these behaviors. Counselors may have students briefly role-play or demonstrate acting passively, assertively, or aggressively so students can see the difference between these communication styles and experience how each one feels in their body. If conducting assertiveness training in groups, students can take turns demonstrating how they would act when communicating in each of these styles. To keep the practice lighthearted, counselors can ask students to vote on who in the group seemed the most passive, assertive, or aggressive in their demonstrations. Additionally, during role plays or demonstrations of assertiveness skills described below, counselors should give specific feedback related to nonverbal behaviors so that students can refine their skills. Group members can provide feedback to one another as well.

Step 2: Expressing Preferences or Needs

Adolescents with social anxiety tend to appear indecisive or void of opinions because they rarely express their preferences (e.g., where to eat, what game to play, what movie they prefer to see) for fear of judgment from others (Cuming & Rapee, 2010). We have commonly heard students worry that others will judge their choice, or that if something goes wrong or is unsatisfactory, it will be their fault. When choosing a restaurant, for example, a socially anxious adolescent might worry that her friends will think her choice is too expensive (or inexpensive), or that if someone dislikes the food it will reflect poorly on her. It is important for students to learn that these beliefs are often unrealistic. Counselors should communicate that most peers (and adults!) will appreciate that the student has interests and opinions about things, even if it is not what they would choose. Sharing our preferences and interests with others helps to deepen friendships and results in more authentic interactions.

> **Sharing preferences and interests with others helps deepen friendships.**

We recommend using some realistic thinking strategies from Chapter 6 to address these thoughts, since we know they are commonly present and often interfere with student's ability to be assertive.

Teach students to use "I" statements to express their preferences and needs ("I would like to go bowling tonight instead of going to the movies," "I think this project would get done faster if we split it up"). It can be helpful to begin practice by having students make one direct and assertive statement about something they like and do not like. We recommend students participate in at least one short role play specifically related to expressing preferences or needs. For example, students could be instructed to pretend they are trying to plan what to do with a friend over the weekend. In doing so, they need to express a preference for at least one activity and assert something that they would like to do. See Appendix 10.1: Expressing Preferences or Needs for tips and examples of additional role plays to help students practice.

Step 3: Making Requests and Getting Involved

Teenagers with social anxiety are often reluctant to make requests or ask for help because they worry about imposing on others. They may have strongly held negative beliefs, such as belief that making requests will result in being viewed as difficult, needy, or incompetent. This makes them uncomfortable because they believe they are inconveniencing others and being negatively evaluated. Students who have difficulty advocating for themselves may limit their academic success, and failure to make requests can lead to missed opportunities to get involved in school activities, such as clubs or sports. For example, a socially anxious student named Timothy was absent at the beginning of the school year on the day that students all signed up for clubs. He was disappointed when he learned that he missed the opportunity to include his name on the e-mail list because he really wanted to get involved in the volunteer club at school. Instead of contacting the student leaders and requesting that his name be added to the list so that he could attend meetings and events, Timothy assumed it was too late and that the club leaders would think he would not be a good or reliable member since he couldn't even manage to sign up on time!

In teaching students to make requests and pursue their interests, we recommend using Timothy's story or a similar one and reinforcing the use of "I" statements to express preferences. For instance, Timothy could have contacted the student leader and expressed his interest in the club (e.g., "I am really interested in the volunteer club. You guys do such great work!"), and then followed up by making a request to be added to the e-mail list (e.g., "I'd really like to be involved. Please add my name to the e-mail list so I can know when and how to help out").

Similar to other assertiveness skills, we recommend that students role-play making requests. Students might role-play making a request of a peer (e.g., "I'd really appreciate if you could explain the last math homework problem to me") or even a salesperson (e.g., "I would like some help. Could you show me where the shoe section is?"). We especially recommend that students role-play asking to join a club, team, or musical ensemble. Many socially anxious students would like to be more involved in their school community but struggle with how to achieve their goal. Practicing how to ask for information about activities or request joining a club allows students to gain the confidence they need to pursue their interests. These role plays can be very helpful in supporting students' increased engagement in school, which ultimately has a ripple effect by increasing the number and quality of interactions and relationships with similar peers. Appendix 10.2: Making Requests and Getting Involved describes a number of potential tips, role plays, and out-of-session practice exercises that counselors can use with students.

Step 4: Refusing Requests

Individuals with social anxiety also have difficulty refusing requests because they worry about others becoming angry or disappointed, or having a negative opinion of them (e.g., thinking of them as a bad friend or as inconsiderate). Remind students that while it sometimes feels easier in the short term to begrudgingly agree to something, we often regret it later and end up feeling bad because we have neglected our own needs. Ask students for examples of requests that have been difficult to decline, what they ended up doing, and how they felt about it afterward.

Once students understand the value in learning to refuse requests, introduce the steps for doing so (see Appendix 10.3: Refusing Requests). Emphasize the importance of assertive nonverbal behavior: maintaining eye contact and using a firm but pleasant tone of voice. For the verbal reply, we recommend using the phrase, "I'm sorry, but . . . ," repeating the request, and providing a brief and direct reason for refusal. For example, "I am sorry but I can't give you a ride because I need to be home in time to get my sister off the school bus." We emphasize providing an honest reason instead of an excuse to increase comfort with being assertive and to avoid getting caught in a lie. However, we support minor "white lies," at least initially, if it helps students take the first steps in being more assertive. An example of a small "white lie" could be "I'm sorry, but I can't run that errand for you. I have too much homework tonight" when the student only has some or a moderate amount of homework. With practice, students will gain more confidence being direct.

Finally, we aim to prepare students for situations when others will persistently try to persuade them to agree to something even after they have refused. For example, when a neighbor asks you to babysit, and you say no. She proceeds to tell you how important the wedding is that she has to attend and that you are the only person she trusts with her kids! In this case, we instruct students to simply repeat what they've said ("I am sorry but I can't . . .") rather than start making excuses or give in. We discuss how the more explanation you provide, the more likely it is that someone might sense you feel guilty or are reconsidering and then try to persuade you to change your mind.

To practice refusing requests, we start with the scenario that another student has asked to copy homework. We suggest saying "I'm sorry but . . ." with a reason to refuse, and have students brainstorm various statements they could make. We have found this situation to be common and distressing for socially anxious students. If you are conducting this exercise in a group, you can have each student practice by giving a different reason for refusing the same request. Next, we suggest that students participate in at least two role plays (see Appendix 10.3: Refusing Requests for examples). In the first scenario, the person asking for the favor will be understanding and easily accept the refusal. Then, to make the situation more challenging and possibly more realistic, we recommend repeating the role play with the other person giving the student a difficult time about saying no. Encourage the student to confidently repeat her refusal. Following each role play, provide students with feedback about their nonverbal behavior. How was their eye contact? Were they able to keep their voice firm without becoming tense or aggressive? In addition, offer feedback about the reason students provided and whether it seemed plausible and adequately expressed their needs. Similar to other skills in this book, conducting role plays with a group of students is beneficial because it allows for repeated practice with varied partners and peer feedback, which helps to strengthen generalization.

Step 5: Expressing Feelings

Finally, we recommend helping students become more comfortable expressing feelings, both positive and negative. This tends to be the most difficult step in assertiveness training because it requires the student to be vulnerable. Expressing positive emotion, such as appreciation or closeness, is important for building relationships. However, socially anxious students tend to be hesitant to express positive feelings such as excitement because they work very hard to be "cool" and don't want to appear needy. Students might falsely believe that positive statements like "I had a really great time at your party. Thanks for inviting me" or "I am really excited to go bowling with you and your friends on Saturday" might suggest to others that they have no other friends or will become clingy, and that these statements might make other people not want to hang out with them. Students fail to realize that everyone likes positive feedback, especially when others have made themselves vulnerable by extending an invitation. We recommend using realistic thinking strategies (see Chapter 6) to take alternative perspectives and communicate to students that most people feel good and appreciate when others express positive feelings toward them. Counselors might ask students how they would feel if someone said those positive statements to them. Counselors might also have students reflect on whether they would want to spend more or less time with a peer who expressed appreciation or enjoyment. Emphasize again how positive feelings build relationships.

The ability to express negative feelings, such as disappointment, sadness, or anger, is also critical for deepening relationships, as well as for resolving conflict and protecting oneself. These are difficult interactions for all teenagers, especially for socially anxious ones, so direct instruction and repeated practice are necessary. We again recommend using "I" statements to effectively communicate hurt or frustrated feelings because this phrasing minimizes blame and possible defensiveness. For example, "I felt embarrassed when you made that joke about me at lunch" expresses one's point of view more effectively than "You were a jerk to me at lunch today." "I" statements are more likely to be well-received because they are less accusatory and difficult to argue because they simply state how someone else feels. We also instruct students to include a request about how they would like to be treated in future interactions, such as "I felt embarrassed when you made that joke about me at lunch. Please don't do that in front of other people in the future." Assertive nonverbal behavior is also paramount here. Students must project confidence by maintaining appropriate eye contact and a firm tone of voice at an adequate volume. Utilize role plays (See Appendix 10.4: Expressing Feelings for examples), as instructed for other skills, to practice "I" statements.

Step 6: Assertiveness with Adults

In addition to struggling with being assertive with friends or peers, socially anxious adolescents often struggle in assertively communicating with adults, such as teachers, coaches, or school administrators. They might believe that it is disrespectful to express themselves to an authority figure, and they especially fear negative consequences from accidentally angering or disrespecting a teacher or coach. They also fear asking for help because they worry that these adults might think poorly of them. For instance, students may avoid asking a teacher for help in understanding a class lesson or avoid asking a teacher for clarification about a grade. They may also avoid expressing preferences to their team coach for a certain playing position (e.g., "I really enjoyed playing shortstop, and feel more comfortable there than second base"). To further support teenagers in developing assertiveness, we believe it is important to encourage adolescents to express their needs and preferences to the adults in their lives.

We recommend that counselors explain to students that the adults in their lives, especially those at school, are invested in students' development, and want them to succeed and flourish! Emphasize for students that it is possible to be assertive while still respecting adults in authority. Remind students that when being assertive, we are always respectful—that's part of the definition! Help students to challenge negative thoughts about asking for help or expressing themselves with adults and encourage them to rely on their "I" statements. One example that counselors can use to help students challenge negative thoughts includes asking a teacher for a college recommendation letter. For instance, a socially anxious senior who asks a teacher for a college recommendation letter might think, "They don't really want to do it," "I'm sure they have better things to do," or "It's too much work for them." The student might assume that the teacher will be annoyed, even though the vast majority of teachers expect to be asked for letters, write college recommendation letters all the time, and are happy to help their students take the next step to further their education. Have students practice challenging their anxious thoughts and generate more realistic alternatives.

Becoming more comfortable with teachers and coaches is also important for increasing the number of supportive adults that a student has in his life. When students feel supported and cared for by the adults in their school, they are more likely to engage in the school community and to ask for help when needed. Role plays for communicating with adults should always include communicating with a teacher, such as asking a question about class content or requesting assistance of some sort. It is also helpful to have students complete at least one role play regarding expressing a preference or making a request to a coach, musical director, or club adviser. See Appendix 10.5: Assertiveness with Adults for additional role-play and practice ideas. Chapter 15 will elaborate specifically on classroom strategies for getting teachers involved in students' treatment to further address these goals.

Step 7: Dealing with Bullies

Assertively asking people not to engage in hurtful interactions may not be sufficient to stop persistent teasing or bullying. Socially anxious students tend to be easy targets for bullies because peers know that they will often become visibly upset and not stand up for themselves. They may be surrounded by fewer friends, thereby increasing their vulnerability. Research has also demonstrated associations between social anxiety and peer victimization, with socially anxious students being more likely to report a history of bullying (Storch, Brassard, & Masia-Warner, 2003; Storch & Masia-Warner, 2004). It is critical to directly address fears related to bullying to optimize treatment success because being a victim of bullying at school can worsen social anxiety and may lead to school avoidance.

Given the recent focus on bullying in the national dialogue, we recognize that many states have developed comprehensive anti-bullying legislation and policies that may inform school professionals' response to bullying. For example, New Jersey's Anti-Bullying Bill of Rights Act (Public Law 2010, chapter 122), which was signed into law in 2011, addresses harassment, intimidation, and bullying (HIB). The law requires each school district to appoint an anti-bullying coordinator, anti-bullying specialists, and safety teams at the school level to investigate and mediate all reports of bullying and provide school programming to prevent bullying. Therefore, we recommend addressing bullying with your students according to your school, district, and state policies.

In general, you may help students by brainstorming possible responses to hypothetical bullying situations or examples of past bullying experiences and weighing the pros and cons of each solution. Responses might include ignoring or avoiding the bully, planning to be with a friend during times when one might encounter the bully, and reporting the bully. Discussing bullying is particularly helpful after role-playing assertiveness with adults. Counselors can help students decide which safe adult to confide in when bullying occurs, what factors might necessitate reporting bullying to the appropriate school professional, and which school professionals will ultimately need to know in order to best intervene. As always, role-playing selected responses to bullies and role-playing asking an adult for help better prepares to students to enact these solutions compared to simply talking about it.

PRACTICE, PRACTICE, PRACTICE!

Following adequate role-play practice with you or other school personnel or peers, brainstorm some ways for your students to practice assertiveness in their everyday lives. The Chapter 10 Appendices provide ample ideas for practicing assertiveness, including expressing preferences (Appendix 10.1), making requests (Appendix 10.2), refusing requests (Appendix 10.3), expressing feelings (Appendix 10.4), and being assertive with adults (Appendix 10.5). Before resorting to these lists, however, we recommend that counselors ask the students about situations in which they may be communicating passively with friends, family members, and school personnel, or times they avoid speaking up for what they want. For example, a friend always asks for a ride home or a sibling frequently chooses where to go out for dinner. Maybe it is difficult for a student to order food with substitutions or send back a wrong order. Ensuring that assigned exercises are relevant to your students' lives helps to optimize their skills practice. Encourage each student to express a preference, make a request, or express his feelings at least one time per day until the next time you see him. If you feel the student is up for the challenge, instruct him to refuse all requests until the next time you see him, even requests he doesn't mind. You may need to clarify that exceptions to this rule include reasonable requests or assignments by parents and teachers (e.g., students don't get to opt out of homework for the rest of the year!). Students may use this as an excuse to turn down social invitations, so we explicitly state that declining social invitations because of anxiety is not part of their homework! You may also challenge them to practice assertiveness with adults such as asking a teacher for help or expressing a preference to a coach.

COMMON CHALLENGES IN TRAINING ASSERTIVENESS
Students Insist That Passive Communication Is Effective

Sometimes students will insist that what they are doing is working for them. Of course this is possible, but we have found that they usually mean that they are able to avoid conflicts. It helps to explore how this makes them feel and to talk about how they feel they are treated by others. Explain that while it is okay to be easygoing, and that some people have fewer preferences than others, it is important that they be able to express themselves on the few occasions when they do feel strongly about something. It may also be useful to challenge students about how they might be viewed for never having an opinion.

Students Continue to Have Trouble Communicating Assertively

Realistic expectations are important. Students have developed their communication style over many years, and it will often take repeated practice with many different people across a variety of situations before assertive communication begins to feel natural. Encourage the student to continue practicing with a variety of people. Start with friendly or more easygoing partners and then work up to more difficult ones. Provide lots of praise and reinforcement for their efforts, and emphasize how it felt when they were able to be assertive—even if they did not achieve the intended result.

Family Members or Friends Do Not Respond Well

There may be people who prefer getting their way all of the time and find it difficult to handle students' increase in assertiveness. They may try to discourage assertiveness because it means they will have to compromise more often. Examples might include an aunt who has the student babysit, friends who often ask for help with homework, or significant others who prefer to make the decisions. It is important to discuss the interpersonal experiences students are having and to understand the students' feelings and possible negative interpretations of these events (e.g., "This is not working," "No one likes me anymore," "Everyone is getting angry at me"). It might be necessary to explore more realistic thoughts or possibly whether the current relationships are healthy or reciprocal. Counselors may also elect to practice further role plays with the students to assess whether the student is coming across as aggressive or even passive, rather than assertive. Fine-tuning of the student's nonverbal skills may be necessary.

LAUREN'S STORY

At the final skills group meeting, Lauren excitedly reported that she extended an invitation to her classmate, who accepted it. Ms. Hillman and the group members praised Lauren for her efforts and asked for more details about what she said and how it went. Ms. Hillman was careful to ask Lauren whether this experience weakened her belief in her "rules" about hanging out with friends outside of school. Lauren acknowledged that maybe her rules were partially how she convinced herself that it was okay to continue avoiding. Ms. Hillman reminded Lauren and the group that one of the most helpful things they will learn is that facing fears gets easier with time and practice, and is the only way to overcome anxiety.

Ms. Hillman began the assertiveness group by providing an overview of the different styles of communication. Lauren, as well as the other group members, related to the idea that passive communication is easy in the short term but can lead to resentment and other negative feelings in the long run. Ms. Hillman reviewed assertiveness in expressing preferences or needs, making requests, getting involved in school, refusing requests from others, expressing positive and negative feelings, and engaging with adults. She then allowed group members to choose specific assertiveness situations they wanted to role play to ensure that practice exercises were as relevant as possible to each student. Using various partners, group members role-played some of the specific difficult situations they had recently encountered. Lauren particularly connected with examples of assertively making requests and expressing feelings and preferences to others. She role-played situations such as asking a teacher to review the grade on a test, voicing her preference about what movie to see with friends this coming weekend, and expressing gratitude to her best friend for her patience and persistent efforts to bring Lauren along to social events with her teammates.

While Lauren's eye contact had steadily improved during other conversations, Ms. Hillman noticed renewed difficulty in maintaining eye contact while role-playing assertiveness. Ms. Hillman provided feedback and Lauren expressed frustration: "I thought I was finally better at that! There are so many things to remember." Ms. Hillman reminded her that she had improved and highlighted all of the other skills she had mastered. "Remember, there is no such thing as a perfect interaction! This is just something that needs a little more practice, especially when you are saying something you are nervous about. I am confident that you will keep improving. You have been working so hard and have already improved in maintaining eye contact during conversations and in elaborating your responses." Ms. Hillman encouraged Lauren to repeat the role play a few more times with special attention to her eye contact. Lauren was eventually able to do this successfully, and her partner provided positive feedback.

As homework, Ms. Hillman assigned students to choose two of the situations they had practiced during the session to try out before their next meeting. Lauren chose thanking her best friend and talking to her teacher about her grade. Ms. Hillman informed the group that they would next meet with her individually to create fear ladders and to complete their first exposures. She suggested they meet at least a couple more times as a group to help each other with exposures. She also offered to revisit assertiveness role plays again in a few weeks because several students had demonstrated significant difficulty and asked for more practice. All group members agreed that assertiveness was among the most challenging of the skills they had practiced together.

CHAPTER SUMMARY

- To avoid potential disapproval, conflict, or negative evaluation, socially anxious teenagers tend to communicate passively. They often comply with others' demands and do not openly express their thoughts and feelings.

- Assertive communication is the direct and honest expression of thoughts, feelings, and needs in a way that respects the rights and feelings of others.

- Assertive nonverbal behavior includes appropriate eye contact and speaking in a firm yet pleasant tone of voice.

- Training students in assertiveness includes demonstrating, practicing, and role-playing . . .
  - Assertive nonverbal behaviors, including appropriate eye contact and speaking in a firm, yet pleasant tone of voice.
  - Using "I" statements to directly express preferences, make requests, refuse requests, and express feelings.
  - Practicing assertiveness with adults, such as teachers or coaches.
  - Helping students brainstorm possible responses to bullying, including whom they may confide in and when to report bullying to the appropriate school professional.

APPENDIX 10.1

Expressing Preferences or Needs

TIPS FOR EXPRESSING PREFERENCES OR NEEDS

- Use "I" statements:
  - My favorite thing to do is _(insert activity)_
  - I really enjoy _(insert activity)_
  - I don't enjoy _(insert activity)_
  - I would like to _(insert activity)_
  - I need _____
  - I need help with _____

SAMPLE ROLE PLAYS

- Making plans with a friend and being decisive about what you want to do
- Talking with a friend and disagreeing with his opinion
- Talking with a friend and expressing a need (e.g., to go do something, run an errand)

PRACTICE—SAMPLE HOMEWORK EXERCISES TO ASSIGN TO STUDENTS

- Tell your friends or peers something you like to do even if you are not sure it is "popular"
- Offer a suggestion for something that you want to do or a place you want to go
- When you and your friends are making plans, disagree with someone's suggestion or express dislike of an activity, and provide an alternative idea
- Before you begin an activity with a friend, say that you need to do something else first (e.g., finish homework, run an errand) and ask to change the time of the get-together
- Provide an opinion (in class or when hanging out) that is purposely different from your peers' opinions

Making Requests and Getting Involved

TIPS FOR MAKING REQUESTS AND GETTING INVOLVED

- Use "I" statements:
  - o I would appreciate if you _____
  - o I would like you to _____
  - o I would like to _____
  - o I need help with _____

ROLE-PLAY EXAMPLES

- You need help with homework and want to ask a classmate
- You need to finish a chore at home and want to ask your friend who came over for dinner to help you
- You need to borrow something (e.g., spare change, a book, a phone)
- You want to invite a friend to come with you to a specific social event
- You are at a concert with reserved seats, but there is a jacket on your seat so you have to ask the person to move it

PRACTICE MAKING REQUESTS— SAMPLE HOMEWORK EXERCISES TO ASSIGN TO STUDENTS

- Ask to try on jewelry that is inside the display case and then don't buy anything
- Ask a salesperson for a shoe in your size
- Ask a salesperson to check if they have any more of an item in the back (in your size)
- Return an item at a store
- At a restaurant, send back food or make a special request
- Ask a classmate for help with homework
- Ask for help with a chore or something at home
- Ask to borrow something (e.g., spare change, a book, a phone)
- Ask someone to come with you to a specific social event
- Ask a classmate for feedback on a paper or creative writing assignment
- When hanging out with a friend, ask to change the television channel or the music

PRACTICE GETTING INVOLVED— SAMPLE HOMEWORK EXERCISES TO ASSIGN TO STUDENTS

- Ask for information about a school club
- Ask student leaders about joining a school club
- Submit artwork or creative writing to a school art show or literary magazine
- Submit an article and ask the school newspaper to run it
- Join a school club (e.g., debate team, school newspaper, literary magazine, yearbook)

Refusing Requests

TIPS FOR REFUSING REQUESTS

- Start with an apology and repeat the request
  - "I'm sorry I can't babysit this weekend . . ."
- Provide a *brief, true* reason why you are refusing
  - "I'm sorry I can't babysit this weekend, but I have other plans."
- If the other person tries to change your mind, stay calm and repeat your refusal
  - "I'm sorry, I can't."

ROLE-PLAY EXAMPLES

- A relative or neighbor asks you to babysit but you can't or don't want to
- A classmate asks to copy your homework. She says she will fail if she doesn't pass this assignment
- Your best friend asks you to walk his dog while he is on vacation. You have a lot of tests that week and don't have time
- Your friend asks you to play the piano for her singing audition. It will take a lot of time to learn the song, and you are in the middle of preparing for your own audition
- Your teammate asks you to drive him home, but your parents don't allow you to drive with other teenagers in the car
- Someone asks you out on a date, but you aren't interested in him
- An acquaintance asks if she can come with you to a party you were invited to, but you aren't sure if she would be welcome

PRACTICE—SAMPLE HOMEWORK EXERCISES TO ASSIGN TO STUDENTS

- Practice refusing one request per day (e.g., to run an errand, to copy homework)

Expressing Feelings

TIPS FOR EXPRESSING FEELINGS

- Use "I" statements:
    - I feel _____
    - I felt _____ when you _____

ROLE-PLAY EXAMPLES

Expressing positive feelings

- You were invited to an event or party and you had a really great time
- Someone did a really nice favor for you
- You enjoyed spending time with someone

Expressing hurt or angry feelings

- Someone is whispering about you
- You learn that someone said something mean about you or spread a rumor
- You are not invited to something by a friend you usually include in plans
- You do a favor for someone and they criticize how you did it
- Your sibling messes up your stuff in your room or takes things without asking
- Someone cuts before you in line
- A group member doesn't do her fair share of the work on a class project

PRACTICE—SAMPLE HOMEWORK EXERCISES TO ASSIGN TO STUDENTS

Expressing positive feelings

- Express positive feelings to a friend or peer (e.g., that you had fun together, that you appreciate something he did)
- Express appreciation for being invited to or included in an event where you had fun
- Thank someone for a favor or something she has done for you
- Share a positive memory about a friend with that person

Expressing hurt or angry feelings

- Let someone know you are upset with him (e.g., if someone hurts your feelings or does something that makes you angry)

Assertiveness with Adults

TIPS FOR BEING ASSERTIVE WITH ADULTS

- Be polite (e.g., "Excuse me").
- Use "I" statements:
  - I need help with _____
  - I don't understand_____
  - I would like to _____
  - I would really appreciate if _____

ROLE-PLAY EXAMPLES

- You didn't understand the class lesson and ask the teacher for help
- You believe a teacher gave you an unfair grade and wish to talk to her about it
- You want to tell your coach that you dislike playing a certain position and plan to request a position that you prefer
- You want to ask your band director for a solo in the next concert
- You approach a club adviser to inquire about joining
- You have an idea for a project in your volunteer club and pitch it to the club adviser

PRACTICE—SAMPLE HOMEWORK EXERCISES TO ASSIGN TO STUDENTS

- Interrupt the teacher and ask a question in class
- Approach a teacher after class to say that you did not understand the material presented in class
- Ask a teacher with help on either classwork or homework
- Ask a teacher for clarification about a grade
- Ask a teacher to provide a reference for a job or recommendation letter for college
- Express a preference for where to sit in a class if the teacher assigns seats
- Ask a club adviser about joining a club or ask for certain responsibilities (e.g., being in charge of the next fundraiser)
- Talk to your coach and express a preference for playing a certain team position (e.g., shortstop instead of second base)
- Talk to your band or choir director and ask for a solo
- Ask a coach or music director for help on a certain skill (e.g., pitching, playing a difficult musical piece)
- Ask to interview a teacher, coach, or school administrator for an article or class paper
- Provide school administrators with suggestions for school improvement

Understanding Communication Styles

The chart below describes three different kinds of communication styles and gives examples of what these styles might look like in various situations. Review the sample situations and then practice creating an example of your own.

Passive	Assertive	Aggressive
"You can keep playing the video game, it's okay if I don't get a turn."	"I would really like a turn to play."	"You're being selfish. Give me that controller, it's my turn!"
"I don't care what we do tonight."	"I would really like to go see that movie."	"I'm going to see that movie. I don't care whether you come or not."
"It doesn't bother me if you copy my homework."	"I spent a lot of time on my homework, so I don't think it's fair for you to copy it."	"Stop being lazy and do your own homework."
"I guess we can invite your friend to come along."	"I would prefer if we hung out just the two of us tonight because sometimes your friend can be mean to me."	"I hate your friend—if she's going I'm not!"
"It's okay, I didn't really want to go to the party anyway."	"It really hurt my feelings when you didn't invite me to your party."	"You aren't a good friend. Now I'm not going to invite you anywhere ever again!"

CHAPTER 11

Facing Your Fears
Creating a Fear Ladder

Most students are familiar with the expression "face your fears." For socially anxious teenagers, however, this is easier said than done. The anxious cycle of negative thinking and uncomfortable physical sensations increases the likelihood that students will avoid social situations that induce anxiety (Hofmann, 2007; Rapee & Heimberg, 1997). For example, if a teenager experiences stomachaches and thinks, "I'm going to say something to embarrass myself" when in a group of peers, he will likely avoid participating in conversations. Such avoidance will strengthen the physical symptoms and negative predictions on subsequent occasions, leading to more frequent and persistent avoidance of other group events. Pervasive avoidance results in significant impairment as students miss out on opportunities to initiate and maintain social interactions, attend social events, and participate in academic, athletic, and other extracurricular activities. Therefore, we must teach students to move toward their fears rather than away from them. Chapter 11 teaches school personnel how to begin the process of helping students face their fears through exposures by collaboratively identifying students' fears and developing a fear ladder or hierarchy.

HOW DOES EXPOSURE WORK?

The most effective way to disrupt the anxiety cycle is to coach students to *gradually* engage in the situations they have been avoiding (Foa & Kozak, 1986; Foa & McNally, 1996). There are several possible reasons why exposure to avoided activities is effective. First, when we face our fears, we often learn firsthand that the experience is not as bad as we had predicted. In other words, we compile evidence that our negative predictions are usually not accurate. Learning through experience that feared outcomes are unlikely is more convincing than simply being told (Rescorla & Wagner, 1972; Salkovskis, Hackmann, Wells, Gelder, & Clark, 2007). In addition to disproving unrealistic expectations of social and performance situations, exposure helps us habituate or get used to the uncomfortable physical feelings associated with anxiety in these situations (Foa & Kozak, 1986; Foa & McNally, 1996; Lader & Mathews, 1968). As reviewed in Chapter 4, anxiety activates our fight-or-flight mechanism (sympathetic nervous system), which creates uncomfortable physical symptoms that accompany anxiety. However, our bodies also have a built-in "cool-down" system (parasympathetic nervous system) that returns our system to homeostasis, or how we usually operate (Stratakis & Chrousos, 1995). The longer we allow ourselves to remain in an anxiety-provoking situation, the calmer and more comfortable we become. With repeated

> **Exposure is the most effective way to interrupt the anxiety cycle.**

practice over time, the anxious response will be extinguished. Finally, facing and persevering through anxiety-provoking situations builds confidence that uncomfortable feelings can be tolerated and overcome. In summary, when we facilitate students' successful experiences facing their fears, confidence increases while anxiety and avoidance decrease over time.

HOW DO I PRESENT EXPOSURE TO STUDENTS?

The idea of entering into feared situations can sound very intimidating to students. We are asking students to intentionally place themselves in circumstances that they have been avoiding, possibly for years! Therefore, it is important to spend adequate time reviewing the anxiety–avoidance link and carefully explaining the rationale for exposure. We often start by telling them that there is bad news and good news. The bad news is that while avoidance seems to work in the moment because it quickly eliminates anxiety in the short-term, it also makes everything harder in the long run and prevents us from experiencing many good things in life. For example, a student may choose to remain silent when a teacher asks a question because it removes any chance of being judged negatively and reduces anxiety temporarily. However, this choice will lead to continued anxiety about participating in class, and over time, perhaps a lower participation grade. Avoidance also results in missed opportunities for students to feel engaged at school, receive positive feedback, and build confidence. Sometimes the reward is worth some risk! In addition, when we don't give things a try, we never learn that they are usually not as bad as we thought they would be or that we can handle them. For example, giving the wrong answer in class may be temporarily embarrassing but is not the end of the world.

The good news is that we can learn to overcome anxiety. Facing difficult situations one step at a time helps us feel more comfortable with every try. Therefore, our goal is to intentionally enter the situations we find uncomfortable so these situations become less scary and we feel less nervous over time. As an introduction to this idea, we suggest asking students for several examples of times when social or performance situations turned out to be easier than they expected.

A counselor might introduce exposures with the following script that we have used when working with students in the past:

> "The bad news is that when we avoid doing something because we are shy or embarrassed about it, we make it even harder for ourselves the next time and we miss out on important opportunities. How many times have you heard people say that if you fall off a bike, you should get back on as soon as possible? When we avoid things, what tends to happen is that we blow them out of proportion in our minds and they become harder to deal with. Avoidance prevents us from learning that if we face the situation, it will usually be okay in the end. Is there anything you thought would be much harder than it was when you actually did it? Have you ever stressed over something for days and then when you did it wondered why you had worried or stressed about it so much? The good news is that by gradually easing ourselves into these situations, we can learn to feel comfortable and safe instead of feeling nervous. The more we do something, the easier it becomes. Therefore, in order to overcome our anxiety, we must face our fears and intentionally do things that make us feel nervous and shy. That sounds cruel, doesn't it? Well, it is not meant to be cruel, but it is how we get used to being in these situations and how we overcome our nervousness and fear."

Additionally, Handout 11.1: Rationale for Exposure Exercises can be used to help counselors present the rationale of exposures to students.

GETTING STARTED: DEVELOPING A FEAR LADDER

Once students grasp the central concept of exposure, the next step is to develop a fear ladder or fear hierarchy. A fear ladder or fear hierarchy is a list of situations that the student avoids or fears to the extent that it ruins the experience. The ladder should gradually progress in difficulty as you climb up it, with the bottom steps being the most manageable and the top steps more challenging (Lang & Lazovik, 1963). A ladder that includes about 10 situations of varying difficulty is a good starting point.

Assisting students in developing a fear ladder requires familiarity with commonly feared situations among teenagers with social anxiety, as well as specific situations feared by the individual student. Fear hierarchies should be based primarily on a student's unique fears and avoided circumstances. Some of this information may have already been obtained through prior discussions with students. However, some additional assessment may be warranted to generate specific situations for the ladder. We recommend having the student complete the Liebowitz Social Anxiety Scale for Children and Adolescents (LSAS-CA; Masia Warner et al., 2003b). The LSAS-CA assesses adolescents' level of fear and avoidance in 24 situations and thus highlights which situations are problematic as well as the corresponding difficulty levels. The counselor and student should then create the ladder collaboratively.

Additionally, a counselor and student may choose to create a separate hierarchy that specifically addresses a particularly difficult area for a student, such as one that has been resistant to change. For instance, Melanie fears giving her opinion because she is afraid that others will think she is dumb. She and her counselor developed a mini-ladder to address this fear in particular. From least distressing to most anxiety provoking, her fear ladder included (1) expressing her preference or opinion to a close friend about an activity she wanted to do, (2) expressing her preference for an activity to an unfamiliar peer and (3) to a small group of friends, (4) giving an opinion that is consistent with her peers' opinions during a class discussion, and (5) giving an opinion that was different from most of her peers during a class discussion. Breaking down fears in this way can make them more manageable for students to tackle gradually.

WHAT MAKES AN EFFECTIVE FEAR LADDER?

There are two goals to keep in mind when creating a fear ladder: (1) steps should be well defined, clear, and specific and (2) steps should slowly increase in difficulty from lowest to highest. A blank fear ladder is provided for photocopying and use with students (see Handout 11.2: My Fear Ladder). Additionally, the end-of-chapter appendices provide counselors with several completed sample fear ladders (Appendix 11.1: Example—Performance Fears Hierarchy, Appendix 11.2: Example— Social Fears Hierarchy, Appendix 11.3: Example— Combination of Social and Performance Fears Hierarchy). Some examples of tasks that students might include on a fear ladder are answering questions in class, ordering food at a restaurant, making eye contact and smiling at classmates, telling a personal story to a group of friends, and starting conversations while waiting in line. If counselors and students are having difficulty coming up with potential feared situations to add to the ladder, the appendices in Chapter 12 provide comprehensive (although admittedly not exhaustive!) lists of potential exposure ideas. Counselors and students may refer to these lists to help identify which situations are the most anxiety provoking for the particular student. Once the most important situations have been identified, the next step is to ask students to assign difficulty ratings (0–10) to each situation. These ratings form the basis for arranging the exposure tasks in a hierarchical order. To ensure fear ladders work well for your students, we recommend the following considerations.

Include Items with a Range of Difficulty

It is important that the fear ladder include tasks representing a wide range of subjective difficulty. The student may require some encouragement to generate higher-difficulty items for the ladder because they may seem impossible to accomplish. Of equal importance, you may need to work together to identify easier tasks, such as situations the student may already be facing but still finds uncomfortable. These easier goals are a good starting point because they help students understand the exposure process, experience success, and gain confidence. In fact, the first exposure step should be constructed to ensure that the student is capable of handling it with only some difficulty and that it will be a successful and positive experience. Additionally, each individual step or task can be made easier or more difficult by varying aspects of the task slightly, such as who is involved, where it takes place, or how long the student needs to stay in the situation.

Include Classroom or Academic Activities

When constructing the fear ladder, it is essential to incorporate situations that can be practiced at school. Socially anxious students spend the largest proportion of their day and often experience the most distress at school. Therefore, the school environment provides them with countless opportunities to challenge their anxiety with different people (i.e., students, teachers, other school personnel) and in different situations (i.e., hallway, class, cafeteria, gym, extracurricular activities). We recommend that students always include fears that occur in the classroom (e.g., asking or answering a question during class, contacting the teacher for extra help, participating or giving an opinion in group work, giving a presentation). Students should include fears related to interacting with their peers as well as interacting with adults. Other important circumstances throughout the school day might include saying hello to peers in the hallway, joining a group activity during gym class, talking with others during downtime in school (i.e., before or after class), or eating lunch with a group of acquaintances. In the next chapter, we will discuss how to capitalize on the natural school environment when implementing exposure such as by incorporating teachers, administrators, and peers into the process and using various school locations (e.g., cafeteria, library). The availability of such clinically relevant situations is why school is the optimal setting to treat adolescent social anxiety.

Include School Engagement or Additional School-Based Exercises

Because socially anxious students often do not feel connected to their school community, counselors should also guide students to add school engagement and extracurricular activities to their fear ladder. This may require that counselors have additional discussions with students about their hobbies, talents, or interests. Including extracurricular activities provides students with opportunities to get involved in activities they are interested in but may have been too scared to try. It also affords opportunities to engage with peers, communicate with additional school personnel, and feel more connected with their school at large. School engagement might include submitting a painting to the school art show, a creative writing piece to the literary magazine, or an article to the school newspaper, or even signing up for the school science fair. To further facilitate school engagement, we recommend that students join a school club as a regular member (e.g., volunteer club, debate team, literary or art magazine, school newspaper, photography club, yearbook), audition for a play or musical ensemble (e.g., choir, band), or try out for a team sport. Students might also run for school office or for a leadership position in a club in which they are already involved. Joining at least one extracurricular activity, or getting more involved in the activities students are already a part of, facilitates increased exposure to social and feared situations and helps students initiate and deepen friendships with peers who have similar interests.

Always Include Inviting Peers to Get Together

Because adolescents with social anxiety are reluctant to engage in exposures with a higher potential for rejection or failure, it is challenging for them to extend social invitations. While inviting peers to get together may result in harsh rejection, it is more likely that the peer will politely decline or accept the invitation. Sometimes students avoid extending invitations because they are worried that they will not know what to say or how to act appropriately when hanging out if the peer says yes! If this occurs, help the student engage in realistic thinking (Chapter 6) and spend time practicing how to initiate (Chapter 7) and maintain (Chapter 8) conversations. Extending invitations is a central step in establishing meaningful, long-term relationships. These relationships are also especially important for decreasing social withdrawal and increasing social engagement and support for socially anxious students. Therefore, inviting peers to get together should be practiced repeatedly throughout the course of intervention until students are doing so more routinely.

Include Items That Expose Students to the Core Fear of Embarrassment or Rejection

Students avoid social situations largely as a means of preventing embarrassment, social mistakes, and rejection. As part of the exposure process, it is crucial that students learn that social mistakes are a normal part of life and rarely result in catastrophic consequences. In addition, students should be encouraged to take social risks in order to learn to cope with embarrassment and rejection. Although some minor embarrassment is naturally experienced during exposure practices, the majority of experiential exercises go quite well without negative outcomes and may even result in positive consequences. For example, if a student auditions for a part in the school play, he may forget his lines, trip onstage, or embarrass himself horribly. However, it is more likely that he would simply not make the cast just like many other students, or he might do well and get a part! Therefore, it is necessary to include some ladder steps that directly target fears of humiliation and negative evaluation—the core of social anxiety disorder! Adding a few extremely difficult exercises that challenge students to purposely embarrass themselves may facilitate enduring treatment success. Examples of this type of exposure include trying out for a sports team, intentionally dropping belongings or tripping in the hallway, yelling across the hallway to say hello, interrupting others, calling someone the wrong name on purpose, spraying water under your arms before a presentation, or providing the wrong answer on purpose.

FEAR LADDERS IN A GROUP SETTING

It can be helpful to explain the rationale for facing one's fears in a group setting, where some students will strongly support the concepts involved and promote confidence in others. In addition, students can work as a group to identify some target hierarchy goals they have in common and can give feedback to each other about potential situations to include. Students are incredibly creative, and brainstorming as a group can provide counselors and students with countless ideas for exposures! However, even when conducting treatment in a group, we do recommend short individual meetings to refine tasks, rate difficulty, and finalize the fear ladder so that each ladder is tailored to the unique needs of individual students. Once fear ladders are prepared, it is time to start implementing exposures, which we discuss in detail in the next chapter.

LAUREN'S STORY

Ms. Hillman met with Lauren individually about a week after the assertiveness group to create her fear ladder. Ms. Hillman began the meeting by asking about any recent situations in which Lauren pushed herself to have conversations with unfamiliar peers, extend an invitation, or practice assertiveness. Lauren reported that she had asked her teacher to review her test grade, and the teacher responded positively even though Lauren had been incorrect about the grade. The teacher commented that she was glad Lauren approached her and hoped she would do so again in the future. Lauren proudly told Ms. Hillman that her teacher complimented her diligent work. "So, even though you were wrong in front of the teacher, and your grade remained the same, would you say it was a success?" Ms. Hillman asked. Lauren smiled and said, "I guess you were right that she wouldn't think I was disrespectful." Ms. Hillman was encouraged by Lauren's progress and thought it was a great time to develop Lauren's fear ladder.

"So let's keep the momentum going, Lauren," Ms. Hillman suggested. She explained the rationale for exposures by using the script presented in this chapter. Lauren acknowledged that this approach made sense and said, "This is kind of what we have already been doing with conversations, right?" Ms. Hillman reinforced Lauren's observation and encouraged Lauren to keep up the good work. Ms. Hillman took out the LSAS-CA that Lauren completed when they first met, along with some notes taken during the conversation with Lauren's mother. Together, they created a list of anxiety-provoking situations to work on, including a few additional situations Lauren recently found herself avoiding (e.g., telling a waiter that her order was wrong). Ms. Hillman then asked Lauren to rate the items in order of difficulty. Lauren was indecisive at times, but Ms. Hillman assured her that they would revisit each task before attempting it to gauge whether Lauren was ready to try it. They agreed to meet the following week to start tackling the exposures on Lauren's fear ladder. Since the lowest item was to start a conversation with an unfamiliar peer, which Lauren had practiced in some group sessions, she asked Lauren to continue practicing with less familiar classmates and acquaintances at least once per day. Lauren agreed. See Figure 11.1 for more of Lauren's fear ladder.

Description of Situation	Rating
1. Singing a solo in front of an audience	10
2. Going to a party without my best friend	9
3. Initiating plans with a group of friends or a less familiar friend	9
4. Giving a presentation in history or language arts class	7
5. Auditioning for chorus or musical	7
6. Speaking to an unfamiliar adult or asking my teacher for help	6
7. Giving an opinion in history or language arts in class or in a group project	5
8. Giving the wrong answer to a question in math	4
9. Inviting a close friend to hang out	4
10. Starting a conversation with a classmate	3

FIGURE 11.1. Lauren's fear ladder.

CHAPTER SUMMARY

- The goal of exposure is to disrupt the anxiety cycle by gradually facing situations that have been previously avoided.

- When explaining exposures to students, it is important to emphasize:

  o Confronting anxiety-provoking situations makes us feel more comfortable each time we practice.

  o Exposure is done in a gradual manner, starting with less difficult situations and working up to more challenging ones.

- Steps for creating a fear ladder or fear hierarchy include:

  o Creating a list of feared situations
  o Refining situations to include concrete and specific tasks
  o Rating the subjective difficulty of each task
  o Ensuring a wide range of difficulty levels

- Hierarchies should include tasks that can be performed in school, that target school engagement and classroom participation, and that target core fears of embarrassment/ negative evaluation, including extending invitations.

APPENDIX 11.1

Example—Performance Fears Hierarchy

Description of Situation	Rating
1. Give a speech in front of the whole school to run for class officer	10
2. Give a presentation in class	9
3. Give the wrong answer in class on purpose	7
4. Eat a messy lunch in front of friends	7
5. Choose a group sport in gym (soccer) rather than a solo activity (walk/run)	6
6. Ask an intimidating teacher a question in class	6
7. Volunteer to answer a question in class when unsure of the answer	5
8. Volunteer to read aloud in class	4
9. Volunteer to answer a question in a difficult class (with an intimidating teacher or older students) when confident of the answer	3
10. Volunteer to answer a question in an easy class when confident of the answer	2

Example—Social Fears Hierarchy

Description of Situation	Rating
1. Go to a party where there will be many unfamiliar classmates	10
2. Ask an acquaintance (not close friend) to get together outside of school	10
3. Call an acquaintance by the wrong name on purpose	9
4. Start a conversation with an unfamiliar peer	8
5. Smile at an acquaintance (not close friend) in the hallway	8
6. Start a conversation with an acquaintance (not close friend)	6
7. Ask a friend to get together outside of school	5
8. Initiate a video call (e.g., Facetime) conversation with a close friend	3
9. Ask a stranger for directions/ask for a particular size in a shoe store	3
10. Initiate a text conversation with a close friend	1

Example—Combination of Social and Performance Fears Hierarchy

Description of Situation	Rating
1. Walk around school wearing something embarrassing	10
2. Audition for the school play	9
3. Ask an acquaintance for their phone number or social media account	9
4. Initiate/plan a group activity for friends	7
5. Call a store to ask a question	6
6. Join a new club	6
7. Ask a classmate to work together on a group project	5
8. Send something back or make a special request at a restaurant	4
9. Ask a stranger for directions/ask for a size in a shoe store	3
10. Order in a restaurant	2

Rationale for Exposure Exercises

Why Should We Do Exposures?

Typically, when people are afraid of things, they avoid them! Unfortunately, when we avoid doing things because we feel nervous, shy, or embarrassed, we make it harder on ourselves the next time, and we start to miss out on the things we would really like to do. What tends to happen is that we blow these situations out of proportion in our minds, making them harder to handle in the future. Avoidance prevents us from learning that if we face the situation, it will usually be okay in the end, and we might even enjoy ourselves.

What *Is* Exposure?

Exposure is the opposite of avoidance; it is facing our fears head on, but slowly. Exposure involves gradually entering into situations or intentionally doing the things that cause us anxiety. During exposure exercises, we will start with situations that are manageable and then slowly work our way up to more challenging situations. By gradually easing ourselves into these situations, we learn to feel comfortable instead of feeling nervous. Like anything else, the more we do something, the easier it becomes. Exposures also allow us to test if our fears are realistic or if we might be blowing things out of proportion! To overcome anxiety, we must face our fears and intentionally do things that make us feel nervous and shy, but we will do this in a reasonable and gradual fashion.

My Fear Ladder

Below are spaces for you to list the 10 most difficult situations for you to face. Think of 10 upsetting or fearful situations and rate each one in terms of how upsetting or anxiety provoking it is, on a scale from 0 (not at all) to 10 (extremely upsetting or bothersome). You may use ratings more than once.

Description of Situation	Rating
1. _____	_____
2. _____	_____
3. _____	_____
4. _____	_____
5. _____	_____
6. _____	_____
7. _____	_____
8. _____	_____
9. _____	_____
10. _____	_____

Most

Least

CHAPTER 12

Climbing the Ladder
Exposure Practice in School

At this point students should understand the rationale for exposure and have developed a fear ladder to assist them in gradually facing their fears. It is now time to put the ladders into action by having students start doing the things they have been avoiding. We accomplish this through what we call exposure exercises, challenges, or tasks. Exposure is not as simple as just asking students do something they are nervous about. In fact, there are specific principles that should be followed to maximize the effectiveness of an exposure. These principles include staying in the situation until anxiety is substantially decreased, increasing difficulty in a gradual fashion from one exposure to the next, and a lot of repeated practice. This chapter discusses how to create meaningful exposure tasks, as well as presents important guidelines for implementing them successfully. We also guide school personnel in using the school environment and school groups to enhance the exposure exercises and maximize generalizability of treatment results.

WHAT MAKES AN EXPOSURE EFFECTIVE?

Sticking with It!

One of the most important rules is that students must stay in challenging situations until they feel calmer or their anxiety has substantially decreased (Foa & Kozak, 1986; Foa & McNally, 1996; Lader & Mathews, 1968). A helpful analogy is what happens to our bodies when we enter a cold swimming pool on a hot day. When we first enter a pool it feels very cold and uncomfortable. If we decide quickly that we don't like how it feels and exit the pool, we never learn what ultimately happens: if we stick it out, our body adjusts to the temperature, and we start to feel comfortable. The key point here is that we get used to it! The same thing happens with nervousness and fear. Our bodies calm down because we cannot sustain anxious arousal for long periods of time. Therefore, the second critical idea is that if we tolerate a situation long enough to experience it as less scary or uncomfortable, we learn that the situation is not as bad as it initially seemed and that we can handle it.

There is another vital reason to remain in situations until anxiety decreases. Leaving a situation prematurely, while still anxious, can create more anxiety and make it less likely that students will try entering those situations again in the future. Let's use the example of a teenager named Manuel who was nervous about attending a party. Manuel went to the party but was so uncomfortable that he quickly called his parents to pick him up. Of course, his initial reaction upon leaving the party was relief. However, when reflecting on the party, all Manuel will remember is that he couldn't handle all the negative feelings he experienced while there, and thus the next time he is invited to a party, Manuel will be less likely to attend. It is important that students understand the importance of remaining in situations for a preplanned, reasonable amount of time, or ideally until they feel somewhat comfortable. Whether students are attending a club meeting, social event, or party, they can benefit from determining how long they must remain in the situation ahead of time. Otherwise, the experience may reinforce their anxiety and their belief that they cannot cope with similar situations in the future.

One Step at a Time: Let's Do This Gradually!

Extending the pool analogy, we emphasize that while some people can just dive into the deep end, other people like to go in gradually, one step at a time, allowing themselves to adjust to the temperature at each step. The idea is to highlight that exposures can be done gradually, in small increments and at a pace that is as comfortable as possible for each individual student. This process is guided by the fear ladder or fear hierarchy, which lists feared situations in order of difficulty (Lang & Lazovik, 1963). It should be emphasized that students will start with the easier situations or ones lower on the ladder and gradually move up the ladder one step at a time. When they are comfortable with one step, they will go on to the next, and so on. For many students, several situations may produce roughly similar levels of anxiety. In this case, it can be helpful to skip around the fear ladder somewhat to amass as much practice in as many feared situations as possible. Skipping around the fear ladder somewhat, while being careful to design exposures with a high likelihood of success, can bolster the long-term beneficial effects of exposure and reduce the potential return of fear (Craske, Treanor, Conway, Zbozinek, & Vervliet, 2014; Lang & Craske, 2000). However, for new therapists or counselors who are less comfortable designing exposures, we recommend sticking closely to a model of gradually progressing up a student's fear ladder.

Repeated Practice

For all types of situations, doing an exposure once is not enough to overcome the fear. Most situations will require frequent repetition for a student to experience a decrease in anxiety. The more students practice facing their fears, the less afraid they will be because they will learn they can handle the situation and will feel more comfortable after several attempts.

Therefore, repeated practice is critical. The more we practice, the less nervous and the more confident we will feel! When arranging exposures for repeated practice, it is also helpful to vary aspects of the situations slightly to increase or decrease difficulty and maximize generalization of learning and anxiety reduction in multiple similar circumstances (Craske et al., 2014; Lang & Craske, 2000). For instance, Eric worries about being embarrassed in front of unknown peers. To target this fear of embar-rassment, he performed exposures related to doing embarrassing things in the hallway but varied what he did each time. In the first exposure, Eric walked down the hall between classes with stickers and pieces of

> **The more students practice facing their fears, the less afraid they will be.**

paper stuck in his hair. Later exposures included walking down the hall with toilet paper stuck to his shoe, walking in the hall with his shirt inside out, tripping in the hallway, and dropping his books in the hallway.

GETTING STARTED: THE FIRST EXPOSURE

Given how scary exposures can sound, especially in the beginning, it is important to empha-size the collaborative nature. The role of the school professional is to review the rationale for exposure, guide the selection of an appropriately difficult exercise from the student's fear ladder, provide encouragement in enacting the task, and reflect on learning opportunities that occurred during the exposure. However, it ultimately has to be the student's choice to enter into an exposure. Emphasizing students' control over facing their fears helps enhance their trust in the school professional, as well as in the exposure process. When getting started, we recommend a situation chosen by the student that is low on the ladder and one that you feel can be completed successfully.

THE NUTS AND BOLTS OF IMPLEMENTING EXPOSURES

Step 1: Choosing an Exposure Exercise

When choosing the first exposure, the counselor and student should work together to ensure that the student is capable of handling the task and that the exposure will be a positive expe-rience. Early success is key to continued motivation and momentum. It is better to select a first task that is too easy and will still demonstrate the process rather than a difficult step that the student may have to discontinue before anxiety decreases. As the student gains experience and confidence in moving up the fear ladder, counselors and students can take more risks in choosing more difficult exposures.

Step 2: Break It Down—Get Specific!

To arrange successful exposures and increase the likelihood that students will follow through on completing exposures, counselors and students should be specific when picking exercises to complete. We recommend laying out ahead of time when and where the exposure will take place, what the student will be doing, and who else will be involved (e.g., teachers, peers, other school professionals). When considering an exposure, we also recommend assisting students to identify specific factors or contexts that make the situation more or less difficult so that adjustments can be made if the ladder step seems overwhelming. Factors may include the specific task that a student is doing for her exposure. For instance, one of Davina's fear ladder steps includes reading in front of a group of peers. Davina finds reading a short factual excerpt aloud to a small audience to be the least anxiety provoking. More challenging read-aloud tasks in order of increasing difficulty include reading an easy-to-read poem, reading a more challenging poem (e.g., Shakespeare), and reading something that she wrote herself.

Contexts can also be varied, including the setting, audience, and duration, to name a few. For example, if a student is nervous initiating conversations, it might be helpful to discuss how speaking to someone more familiar or less familiar (e.g., friend, acquaintance) or older or younger (e.g., adult, peer) affects his comfort level. When answering questions in class, there may be certain classes or teachers that are harder than others. Additionally, increasing the time spent in the situation usually makes exposures more anxiety provoking for students (Craske et al., 2014). Having a short conversation with a peer before class is likely to be less challenging than spending an entire lunch period at a table with an unfamiliar peer. Therefore, when facing a particularly intimidating or impairing circumstance, we recommend possibly creating a mini-hierarchy within the ladder steps to further break down the task into smaller steps, as Davina did for her performance tasks. This allows the student to master less anxiety-provoking variations of the ladder step before tackling more difficult scenarios.

Step 3: Preparing in Advance

Because exposures often involve others, we have found that it is important to think about and plan exposures in advance of meeting with students. For example, if you are planning to have the student call different businesses on the telephone, it is advisable to have a list of businesses with their telephone numbers ready for your meeting. If a student is going to ask a teacher to explain a grade he received, it is helpful to know ahead of time whether the teacher is available and where she will be during your meeting. Exposures requiring students to wear something intentionally embarrassing might require agreement with the student ahead of time or school professionals bringing props from home. For public speaking exposures, it is often necessary to assemble a small audience, which requires advanced planning. It can also be helpful to plan for access to a podium, a microphone, a screen for presentations, or use of the auditorium stage to enhance the experience. When preparing, we recommend planning for a few different scenarios to provide flexibility in case a student decides something is too difficult, part of the plan goes awry (e.g., the teacher is absent, the stage is being used), or the student finishes one exposure quickly and there is time to try another.

Step 4: SUDs Ratings

Students are asked to provide subjective units of distress (SUDs) ratings from 0 to 10 (completely calm to absolutely terrified or panicking) before engaging in the exposure, when the exposure exercise ends, and ideally a few times during the exposure. SUDs ratings are expected to decrease by the end of the exposure, although the amount of reduction will vary by student and task difficulty. Students will likely have their own unique barometer of how extreme their anxiety feels to them (i.e., one student might say that a 6 is very nerve-racking while another might consider a 6 to be challenging but manageable). It is important for counselors to gauge what certain numbers mean to their students. Because of this, we recommend that in addition to SUDs, counselors pay attention to students' nonverbal behaviors and physical symptoms of anxiety to assess how challenging the task is for them. For instance, if a student denies that a task is distressing or has a tendency to minimize her anxiety but is shaking and looks like she is about to cry, the counselor may plan an easier exposure for the following exercise.

Step 5: After Exposure

Following exposure practice, the student's expectations prior to the exposure should be briefly compared with the actual outcome of the exposure. Exposures that contradict prior negative expectations enhance students' ability to learn that their feared outcomes are unlikely and negative consequences are not as catastrophic as previously presumed. Students also learn that associated anxiety symptoms are more manageable than they anticipated. Any expected or unexpected positive experiences or opportunities resulting from the exposure should be highlighted. Finally, students should have the opportunity discuss their experience and be praised and reinforced for facing their fears.

INTEGRATING EXPOSURES INTO THE SCHOOL ENVIRONMENT

Conducting exposures at school provides a meaningful opportunity to capitalize on the realistic context to encourage new and challenging behaviors. Exposure practices should take advantage of various school locations and situations (Fisher et al., 2004; Ryan & Masia Warner, 2012). The end-of-chapter appendices provide ideas for various potential exposure exercises that can be completed during sessions or assigned for weekly practice. Some common school exposures include going to the cafeteria to initiate conversations with peers or to purchase and return food, asking questions of the librarian, or visiting the main office to speak to administrative staff. Treatment conducted in school also provides an opportunity to enlist additional school personnel. Because many students experience anxiety talking to authority figures, some exposures might involve interaction with administrators. For example, students might schedule meetings to converse with or to make suggestions or complaints to authority figures. School counselors can facilitate this process by asking school administrators (e.g., principal, dean, assistant principal) to be available for these meetings. In addition, students might deliver the morning school announcements or seek assistance from a teacher they find particularly intimidating. Teachers may participate in classroom exposures involving students arriving unprepared or late to class, reprimanding students in front of others, or assigning students leadership roles for group activities. Finally, students might approach club advisers or coaches to discuss joining clubs or teams. In the context of numerous opportunities available in the school setting, exposure situations can be tailored to each individual student's difficulties (e.g., speaking up in class, joining an activity, approaching a peer in the library or cafeteria).

Compared to traditional clinic settings, treatment at school also allows for the encouragement of social risk taking in a more controlled environment. Adolescents with social anxiety are often hesitant to engage in exposures with potential for negative evaluation or rejection (e.g., inviting a peer to get together, attending a party or dance). Since school counselors are present within the natural school setting, they can encourage and assist students to overcome the anticipatory anxiety involved in attempting more challenging behaviors. This support enhances the likelihood that adolescents will attempt to engage in particularly challenging situations, thus increasing the chance for success and reinforcing future independent action. For example, a school counselor might encourage a student to ask a teacher for extra help, and then assist the student in selecting a teacher who is likely to respond kindly. If this interaction goes well, the student will be more likely to ask for help in the future. Exposures conducted in this way optimize the value of the school environment.

CONDUCTING EXPOSURE IN A GROUP

The school environment has the added benefit of allowing opportunities to conduct exposures in groups with other students, which can be particularly effective and time-efficient. Exposures implemented in groups can involve other members as the audience or as partners with whom to practice conversational skills (see Chapters 7 through 10). Appendix 12.1: Sample Group Exposures includes descriptions for exercises that can be completed by a group of students in session. In addition, student pairs might be sent to various locations and return to discuss their experiences within a group of peers practicing similar exercises. The end-of-chapter appendices collectively provide numerous examples of exposure exercises that can be conducted in the classroom (Appendix 12.2: Sample Classroom Exposures), with peers (Appendix 12.3: Sample Exposures for Engaging with Peers), to support school engagement in clubs or activities (Appendix 12.4: Sample Exposures to Support School Engagement), to challenge students with making social mistakes (Appendix 12.5: Sample Social Mistakes Exposures), and to encourage interactions with adults and safe strangers (Appendix 12.6: Sample Interacting with Safe Strangers Exposures). Peers can also act as supports for each other by attending club meetings or school events together. Because group members are also school peers, relationships beyond the group may be easily facilitated.

PRACTICE, PRACTICE, PRACTICE!

Every time you meet with a student to conduct an exposure exercise, it should end with the assignment of practice exercises for the student to do until the next time you meet. Practice exercises are critical for reinforcing skills and realistic thoughts that were generated through in-session exposures. Assigned practice should include situations inside and outside of school that are similar to what you just accomplished together. Counselors should capitalize on the creativity of their students by engaging them in designing their own homework exposures. This collaboration allows students to feel a sense of mastery and agency in tackling their fears and furthering their treatment. They are also more likely to be motivated to complete practice exercises they designed themselves. Have students check in with you during the week to discuss any difficulties or obstacles they have experienced during practice. Additionally, we recommend that counselors and students briefly review how the practice exposures went at the beginning of the next session. This helps to facilitate any troubleshooting or modification of exercises if they were too difficult or if the student continues to avoid them.

COMMON CHALLENGES IN CONDUCTING EXPOSURES

Students Are Very Resistant to Conducting Exposure Exercises

Some students are eager to face their fears once they understand exposure, but others really struggle to get started. When students are resistant, first review the rationale for why it is important to complete the exposure and stop avoiding. Ask them what will happen if they continue to avoid their feared situations. If this is not sufficient, briefly explore the negative thoughts and predictions that may be contributing to the hesitation. What do they think will happen? Help them challenge these thoughts and, if the reluctance persists, propose a similar exposure that the adolescent finds less daunting. For example, if a student is resistant to the idea of approaching an unfamiliar peer in the cafeteria to start a conversation, a more structured version of this exposure, such as asking the unfamiliar peer to answer survey questions as a mock class assignment, may be an acceptable alternative. Finally, be aware of excessive time spent engaging in cognitive restructuring or discussions about the usefulness of a proposed exposure (e.g., "But I'll never need to ask the librarian for assistance") because these discussions may function as avoidance, squandering time needed for exposure practice. Instead, explain that it is unimportant whether the situation would occur in real life, but rather should be viewed as an opportunity for practice. If the conversation continues, just shift to brainstorming an easier exposure task. Any completed exposure, no matter how easy, is better than successful avoidance! Resistance usually decreases once the student experiences some success with exposures. Reminding students of past successes can also be helpful.

Students Are Using Effective Strategies to Avoid Exposure Exercises

Sometimes students verbally agree to an exposure, but their actions suggest otherwise! They change the topic, talk about their thoughts at length, or continually seek reassurance from you about how the exposure will go. All of these seem like useful conversations, but they are just avoidance in disguise! We recommend validating that the task seems scary but reiterate why you believe the student can be successful facing her fear and quickly find a way to get her started—for example, "I know this seems really difficult, but we both know that the only way to get over the fear is to face it. We already discussed all the reasons why it is likely going to go better than you are predicting. Now let's put it to the test."

The Exposure Caused More Anxiety Than You Anticipated

When helping students practice exposure exercises, keep in mind that they may not be accurate in assigning fear ratings because of their lack of experience with the feared scenario. Therefore, when conducting exposures, it is important to monitor the student's level of distress. If the exposure is much more difficult than expected (e.g., appears to be an 8 out of 10 even though the student had initially rated it lower), modify the task to make the experience more manageable. For example, if a student is extremely anxious reading aloud, ask if he wants to face away from the audience in order to complete the task or reduce the number of people in the audience temporarily. While modifying is important, it is critical that the student complete some version of the original task so as not to reinforce avoidance and negative predictions.

Exposures "Go Wrong" or Have Seemingly Negative Outcomes

We hope that all exposure exercises go smoothly, but inevitably students will engage in a task during which a feared prediction comes true. For example, a peer rejects an invite, a student stutters or makes a mistake during a presentation, or a conversation partner abruptly ends a conversation. While this seems (and feels) disappointing, it can actually be a blessing in disguise. This is the perfect opportunity to engage in realistic thinking, emphasizing that "although it felt bad in the moment, was it really that bad? That was the worst thing that could have happened and you lived through it. Do you think you would be okay if that happened again?" If time allows and the student is willing, try to repeat the exposure to illustrate that the negative outcome was the exception rather than the rule.

Students' Anxiety Is Not Decreasing with Repeated Exposures

One explanation for students' anxiety remaining high during exposures is that the exposure task is too difficult. Try brainstorming an easier version of the task for the student to master before attempting to repeat the original exposure. Another possible reason that anxiety is not decreasing is that the student is engaging in subtle avoidance, such as sticking close to a friend among a group of peers and not saying much. The student may also be engaging in some type of safety behavior, something that the student believes helps her get through the exposure (Lovibond, Davis, & O'Flaherty, 2000; Salkovskis, 1991). For example, Reagan usually checks her reflection in the bathroom mirror to ensure that she looks her best before initiating conversations with her peers. This safety behavior interferes with exposures that involve talking to other students because Reagan attributes success in the task (e.g., good conversation) to the behavior (e.g., checking her appearance and looking good), rather than realizing that most peers are open to conversation and will respond positively regardless of minor flaws. Identifying the presence of safety behaviors is another opportunity to engage in realistic thinking (e.g., "Do you really think it would have gone differently if your hair was a little out of place?") and to reattempt the exposure without the safety behavior. If this is too challenging, it can be a future task to add to the higher part of the fear ladder. Over time and with more practice exposures, these safety behaviors should be gradually faded (Hermans, Craske, Mineka, & Lovibond, 2006; Salkovskis, 1991). Finally, if safety behaviors or avoidance do not seem to be present, just keep practicing! Even if the student is not experiencing a decrease in anxiety after repeating a task, she is still learning from the experience and disproving negative predictions.

LAUREN'S STORY

Over the next several weeks, Ms. Hillman and Lauren met three times individually and once with the group to conduct exposure exercises. The first exposure they attempted was inviting an unfamiliar peer to hang out. Lauren had done this once following a group meeting but had not worked up the courage to try again with any other peer despite her previous success. Ms. Hillman asked Lauren to bring her phone to the session so she could extend some invitations during their meeting. First, Ms. Hillman reviewed the rationale for exposure and guided Lauren through giving it a second thought. Together, they identified two friends Lauren wanted to invite and brainstormed how she could best phrase her invitation. When Ms. Hillman asked Lauren to rate her anxiety, she gave it a 5. She typed out the first text and before sending it reported that her anxiety had increased to a 6. Ms. Hillman asked if she was willing to send it. Lauren agreed and sent the text. Afterwards, Lauren stated, "That was hard, but I'm glad I finally did it." Ms. Hillman asked if she was ready for the next one and reminded her that exposures usually get easier the more you repeat them. Lauren agreed, and as she typed out the second text, she reported some decrease in anxiety before sending it. As Ms. Hillman was asking Lauren about the experience, Lauren received a positive response from the second person she texted, which immediately disconfirmed Lauren's negative expectation that whoever she invites will say no or not respond. In a later session, Ms. Hillman guided Lauren through a similar process to initiate plans with a few less familiar friends.

Given that some exposures had to be conducted outside of school (e.g., going to a party), two individual meetings were focused on assigning and preparing for outside exposures by engaging in challenging of negative thoughts, role-playing, reviewing progress, and problem-solving obstacles. In addition, Ms. Hillman prepared Lauren for classroom exposures (see Lauren's story in Chapter 15, pp. 186–187, for a discussion of classroom-based exposures). Finally, Ms. Hillman reconvened the group to practice giving presentations in front of an audience. She also used the opportunity to help Lauren address her fear of singing a solo by having her practice singing in front of the group. At first, Ms. Hillman asked group members to look down instead of directly at Lauren to decrease the difficulty. Ms. Hillman then suggested that Lauren try again with all eyes on her. Lauren told Ms. Hillman that she wasn't quite ready for a solo, but that she planned to audition for the musical.

"I might need some extra practice sessions when it gets closer." Ms. Hillman invited Lauren to meet with her again in another month to create some practice exposures and to help prepare Lauren for the audition. "I can't believe I'm even considering this," Lauren said. "I never thought I could do it."

CHAPTER SUMMARY

- There are specific principles that should be followed in order to maximize exposure effectiveness:
  - Sticking with it: Students must stay in challenging situations until they feel calmer or their anxiety has substantially decreased.
  - One step at a time: Exposures can be done gradually, in small increments, at a pace that is as comfortable as possible.
  - Repeated practice: Most situations will require frequent repetition in order for the student to experience a decrease in anxiety.
- Steps for implementing exposures include:
  - Choose an exposure exercise that is the right difficulty level. Too easy is better than too hard for very early exposures.
  - Assist students in identifying specific contexts that make the situation more or less difficult so that adjustments can be made quickly if needed.
  - Plan exposures in advance of meeting with students to implement them.
  - Ask students to provide subjective units of distress (SUDs) ratings.
  - Review the student's expectations compared with the actual outcome following the exposure.
  - Assign practice exposures.
- Exposure practice should take advantage of various school locations and situations.
- Conducting exposures in a group is effective and time-efficient. Utilize other group members as audience members or partners.

Sample Group Exposures

Structure group exposures to provide successful experiences, particularly early in treatment. Enlist exposure help from individuals you believe will interact positively with group members and prepare these individuals for the interactions. As often as possible, use same-age peers, as the group members will most likely find these situations both challenging and relevant to their real-world experiences. Sometimes you may need to divide the group in order to accomplish exposures. Some ideas for group exposures are listed below.

PERFORMING FOR THE GROUP

Students perform in front of group members (and peer assistants, if possible). The type of performance depends on the steps in each member's fear ladder, such as reading aloud, singing, giving a presentation, or playing a musical instrument. It can be helpful for students to purposely make mistakes to see that consequences are minor. The "audience" can also provide feedback on nonverbal behaviors that help the student appear more confident.

MAKING A SOCIAL MISTAKE

Prior to a group meeting, arrange with a student to make mistakes in group unbeknownst to other members. After the exposure is finished, disclose that the student made social mistakes on purpose and discuss the group's reactions (e.g., "Did you notice the mistake?" "Did you think badly of him?"). To maintain the student's anxiety during the exposure, do not explain that others will eventually be told the mistakes were planned.

MAKING TELEPHONE CALLS

There are primarily three kinds of calls group members can make.

1. Have students call businesses such as florists, bookstores, or camera stores and ask numerous questions without purchasing anything. This can be helpful for group members who worry about taking people's time or "bothering" others. Be sure that students apply realistic thinking skills (e.g., "It is their job to answer questions").

2. Have students call to place orders (e.g., pizza, Chinese food) or make appointments (e.g., nail salon). A few minutes after placing the order, students call back to cancel. Apply realistic thinking skills (e.g., "people often cancel appointments").

3. Enlist colleagues (typically three to four) to participate in phone calls. Instruct individuals to be friendly and conversational with group members, but to avoid carrying the conversation. During the session, arrange "phone stations" in different parts of the room. Group members call at least two colleagues each and hold conversations to get to know the other person and share informa-

tion about themselves. Students should continue conversations until the group leader ends the exposure (typically 5 minutes). Calls should not be ended just because a student is struggling to maintain a conversation.

SPEED CHATTING

This works best if at least four members are in the group. With fewer members, it is helpful to include peer assistants, if available. Line up two sets of chairs facing one another. The goal is for members to have a conversation with the person sitting across from them for approximately 5 minutes until members are told to "switch." Students on one side then move to new seats so that everyone is now talking to a partner. Keep alert for pairs that are struggling (i.e., both group members have difficulty with the skill, so conversations are not flowing), and consider changing to the next pairing more quickly. In between pairs, ask group members what behaviors (e.g., nonverbal behaviors, kinds of questions) make it easier or more difficult to converse. Provide feedback to the group as appropriate.

Sample Classroom Exposures

Socially anxious students experience significant distress and impairment in the classroom. Many classroom fears include social and performance fears related to interactions with others, participation, or presentations. Due to the importance of school for adolescents, helping socially anxious students engage with peers and teachers in the classroom is critical. Students can work on asking or answering questions, volunteering, or offering opinions during class discussions. Exposures can be varied to adjust the difficulty for students in several ways. Sample exposures are provided.

CLASSROOM PARTICIPATION

- Student asks a question . . .
  - in a subject that is easy **or** hard for the student
  - in a class with many friends **or** few friends **or** older peers
  - in a class with a teacher who seems nicer **or** more intimidating to the student

- Student *answers a question/participates* . . .
  - when the student is confident **or** unsure of the answer
  - in a subject that is easy **or** hard for the student
  - in a class with many friends **or** few friends **or** older peers
  - in a class with a teacher who seems nicer **or** more intimidating to the student

- Student *purposely gives a wrong answer* . . .
  - in a class with many friends **or** few friends **or** older peers
  - in a class with a teacher who seems nicer **or** more intimidating to the student

- Student *volunteers to read aloud* . . .
  - a short factual passage that is easy **or** hard for the student
  - a poem or Shakespearean piece that is easy **or** hard for the student
  - something that the student wrote (e.g., essay, poem)
  - and purposely mispronounces several words
  - in a class with many friends **or** few friends **or** older peers
  - in a class with a teacher who seems nicer **or** more intimidating to the student

- Student *volunteers to write on the board* . . .
  - in a foreign-language class
  - and spells something wrong on purpose
  - in a subject that is easy **or** hard for the student
  - in a class with many friends **or** few friends **or** older peers
  - in a class with a teacher who seems nicer **or** more intimidating to the student

- Student *interrupts the teacher and asks him to repeat what he just said* . . .
  - in a class with many friends **or** few friends **or** older peers
  - in a class with a teacher who seems nicer **or** more intimidating to the student

- Student *provides an opinion or an interpretation in class* . . .

  o that is consistent **or** different from peers in class
  o in a class with many friends **or** few friends **or** older peers
  o in a class with a teacher who seems nicer **or** more intimidating to the student

TALKING WITH TEACHERS

- Student *asks a teacher for extra help* . . .

  o on class concepts **or** homework
  o before school **or** after school
  o who seems nicer **or** more intimidating to the student

- Student *asks a teacher for clarification of a grade* . . .

  o when the student got a high **or** low grade
  o in a class the student is doing well **or** poorly in
  o in a class with a teacher who seems nicer **or** more intimidating to the student

- Student *expresses a preference for where to sit in class if the teacher assigns seats* . . .

  o in a class the student is doing well **or** poorly in
  o in a class with a teacher who seems nicer **or** more intimidating to the student
  o and asks before/after class **or** during class in front of peers

- Student *asks a teacher to provide a job reference or college recommendation letter*

Sample Exposures for Engaging with Peers

Because socially anxious students experience significant distress in social situations with peers, they are often reluctant to get involved with other students. Helping socially anxious students to engage with peers and build relationships is especially important for decreasing social withdrawal and increasing engagement and social support. Therefore, exposures should always include conversations, invitations, and spending time with peers. Below are sample exposures to help students engage with peers. Vary the difficulty of exposures by having students interact with close friends, teammates, friendly acquaintances, less familiar peers, or students in other grades.

INTERACTIONS AND INVITATIONS WITH PEERS

- Student *smiles and says hello* to students who look friendly in the hallway or cafeteria
- Student *starts a conversation in the hallway, before class, after school, etc. . . .*
  - with a friend
  - with a teammate
  - with a friendly acquaintance
  - with an unfamiliar peer
  - with an older student
- Student *invites a friend to do homework together after school*
- Student *invites a peer to join a school club with him*
- Student *purposely hangs around after sports/music practice to talk with peers*
- When talking, student *invites a friend or peer to hang out* (e.g., go to movie, play video games, go shopping, go out to eat, play sports) after school
- Student *asks a peer for her phone number or social media name*
- Student *texts or calls a friend to make plans after school*
- Student *invites a friend to video chat* (e.g., Facetime, Google Hangouts)
- Student *leaves comments or messages for an acquaintance on social media*
- Student *hosts a small get-together at her house*
- Student *throws a birthday party and invites friends, as well as less familiar peers*
- Student *attends a party or school dance with others or alone*

EXPRESSING PREFERENCES AND FEELINGS

- Student *expresses a preference or interest even if he thinks it might not be popular*
  - *"I really like this new book series."*
- Student *purposely disagrees with a friend's opinion*
  - *"I actually think this football team is stronger than that one."*

- Student *offers a suggestion or expresses what she would like to do with a friend*
  - *"I would really prefer to see this movie instead."*
- Student *disagrees with a peer's suggestion for an activity and provides an alternative*
  - *"I would rather not go bowling. How about going to the mall instead?"*
- Student uses an "I" statement to *express positive feelings toward a friend*
  - *"I had so much fun hanging out with you last weekend."*
- Student uses an "I" statement to *express negative feelings toward a friend*
  - *"I felt really disappointed when you never called me back."*

MAKING AND REFUSING REQUESTS

- Student asks a peer *to give him directions to a classroom*
- Student asks a friend/peer/classmate *to copy class notes from when she was absent*
- Student asks a friend/peer/classmate *for help on homework*
- Student asks a friend/peer/classmate *for feedback on his artwork or writing*
- Student asks a friend/peer/classmate *for a favor,* such as . . .
  - to borrow some spare change
  - to borrow a phone to make a call
  - to borrow a book or DVD
  - for the time
  - for her to walk somewhere with the student
  - to run an errand in the school either for or with the student
  - to give a note or item to a teacher for the student
  - for help with a chore or task
- Student *turns down requests for favors from others for 1 week*
  - *"I'm sorry but I can't . . ."*

Sample Exposures to Support School Engagement

Socially anxious students often would like to be more involved in their school community but struggle to know how to go about doing that. School exposures should include helping students to become more engaged by either joining clubs or increasing their participation in after-school activities. Below are sample exposures to help students engage in their school community.

- Student *participates in the school community or school events by* . . .
  - attending a school dance or school fundraiser
  - giving morning announcements or speaking on the loudspeaker
  - submitting artwork or creative writing to the art show or literary magazine
  - submitting an article and asking the school newspaper to run it

- Student *gets involved with a school club by* . . .
  - asking another peer for information
  - asking the club adviser for information or to join
  - asking student leaders to add her to the e-mail list
  - attending a meeting for a club, sport, or activity
  - joining a school club (e.g., debate team, school newspaper, literary magazine, yearbook)
  - asking a club adviser for certain responsibilities (e.g., being in charge of the next fundraiser)
  - pitching an idea for a project or event to a club adviser
  - running for a class or school officer position

- Student *interacts with his coaches or advisers by* . . .
  - expressing a preference to play a certain team position (e.g., shortstop instead of second base)
  - talking with the band or choir director and asking for a solo
  - asking a coach, music director, or other club adviser for help on a certain skill (e.g., pitching, a difficult musical piece, a photography technique)

- Student *interacts with other school personnel by* . . .
  - initiating a conversation with school personnel (note: arrange ahead of time with colleagues if necessary; can also generate some questions ahead of time)
  - making an appointment to speak with administrators/personnel to make suggestions for school improvement (note: let the administrators/personnel know that students will be practicing making a complaint and request that the personnel respond by showing appreciation)
  - asking to interview a teacher, coach, or school administrator for an article or class paper

Sample Social Mistakes Exposures

Students are often extremely worried about the possibility of making mistakes or being embarrassed in social situations. Below are sample exposures that can target some of these core fears of embarrassment and can be done in school settings or assigned for practice in public (e.g., the mall or a store). The number of people who are around can also be varied.

- Student *walks in the hallway, through a public space, or talks to peers* . . .
  - wearing something very unusual for her
  - wearing mismatched clothing
  - wearing no or less makeup than usual
  - with hair all messed up
  - with shirt inside out
  - with toilet paper stuck to shoe or back of pants
  - with food in teeth or stuck to face
- Student *intentionally trips* . . .
  - in a fairly empty **or** crowded hallway/library
  - and drops backpack **or** drops books in the hallway
  - in the cafeteria and drops lunch tray
  - when walking to the front of the class for a presentation
  - during a presentation
- Student *intentionally calls someone by the wrong name* . . .
  - who is a close friend
  - who is an unfamiliar **or** older peer
- Student *yells across the hallway to say hello to someone*
  - who is a close friend **or** who he doesn't know
- Student *intentionally waves at someone he doesn't know*
- Student *intentionally walks into the wrong classroom* . . .
  - in a class with many friends **or** few friends **or** older peers
  - in a class with a teacher who seems nicer **or** more intimidating to the student
- Student *intentionally arrives late to class* . . .
  - in a class with many friends **or** few friends **or** older peers
  - in a class with a teacher who seems nicer **or** more intimidating to the student
- Student *intentionally interrupts someone in a conversation*
- Student *purposely tells a really boring joke to someone* . . .
  - who is a close friend **or** unfamiliar peer **or** older student

- Student *intentionally talks with a mouth full of food to someone . . .*
  - who is a close friend **or** unfamiliar peer **or** older student
  - who is an adult (e.g., teacher, school administrator)
- Student *sprays water under arms before a presentation*
- Student *purposely makes hands shake while drinking or eating something*
- Student *wears her clothes inside out to school*
- Student *sets phone alarm to go off in a movie theater or other quiet location*
- Student *tries to use expired coupons when making a purchase*

APPENDIX 12.6

Sample Interacting with Safe Strangers Exposures

Many socially anxious students have incredible difficulty interacting with strangers (e.g., waiters, store clerks, people over the phone). Below are sample exposures to help students interact with safe strangers. Exposures for outside of the school building should be assigned for homework, and depending on the age of the student, parents should be enlisted for help (e.g., bringing the student to a store or restaurant).

- Student *asks a waiter* . . .
  - for a substitution or modification of a menu item
  - to send food back
  - for the specials of the day
  - what the waiter recommends
- Student *asks a store clerk* . . .
  - where an item is or asks for help finding an item
  - if the store has something in a different size
  - directions to the bathroom
  - directions to a different store
  - for the time
  - to return an item that was previously bought
  - to ring up only half of the items brought to the register
  - to try on jewelry that is inside the display case and then doesn't buy anything
  - to check if they have any more of an item in the back (in her size)
  - to return an item or cancel a transaction
- Student *makes telephone calls* . . .
  - and places a food order—and calls back to cancel for added difficulty!
  - to make an appointment (e.g., nail salon, haircut)—and calls back to cancel!
  - to businesses (e.g., restaurants, florists, bookstores) to ask questions about store hours, inventory, or menus without purchasing anything
  - to businesses and intentionally asks for the wrong store (i.e., calling Best Buy and saying you are trying to reach Home Depot)
  - to strangers chosen by counselors to have a short conversation—enlist other school personnel that the student doesn't know anything about
- Student *contacts businesses, community centers, or nonprofits* . . .
  - by phone or in person to inquire about or apply for volunteer opportunities
  - by phone or in person to inquire about or apply for a job
  - by phone or in person to submit a résumé for after-school or summer jobs
  - to set up an interview for an after-school or summer job

PART III

SUPPLEMENTARY STRATEGIES

CHAPTER 13

Getting Parents Involved
How Can They Help?

Parents have enormous potential for helping their child overcome anxiety by supporting a positive attitude toward facing fears. However, many well-intentioned parents allow or encourage avoidance of anxiety-inducing situations in an effort to shield their child from distress because they are unaware that avoidance strengthens anxiety in the long run. In this chapter, we highlight some beliefs that parents have regarding their child's social anxiety and outline how to educate parents about their own behaviors that may play a role in maintaining their child's anxiety. We then emphasize how to both engage parents and coach them in helping their child overcome anxiety. Specifically, we outline potentially counterproductive strategies that parents often use to temporarily reduce their child's anxiety and offer more effective strategies (Rapee et al., 2008).

HOW DO PARENTS VIEW SOCIAL ANXIETY?

It is important to understand parents' perspectives on their child's anxiety so you can anticipate and address questions or concerns that might arise. The most common parental expectations we have encountered range from beliefs that social anxiety is just a phase to beliefs that shyness is a part of their child's personality that cannot or should not be changed. When frustrated with their child's anxiety, some parents respond by thinking that anxiety is something their child just needs to "get over," while others believe that social anxiety cannot be helped and their child is doomed. As we will discuss, the extreme ends of these perceptions can have negative effects on how parents respond to their child's social anxiety.

"Social Anxiety Is Just a Phase"

We have often heard from parents that social anxiety is a normal part of being a teenager and that their children will "grow out of it" as they mature. For these parents, it is important to differentiate typical self-consciousness from social anxiety. It is certainly true that wanting to gain approval from others, caring a lot about what peers think, and being socially conscious are developmentally appropriate during adolescence. In the absence of social anxiety, however, these common adolescent concerns do not typically cause teenagers to avoid social gatherings and interactions (Heiser et al., 2009). For adolescents with significant social anxiety, worries about negative evaluation go beyond typical self-consciousness, causing them to avoid the types of social encounters that are welcomed by their peers. In fact, while parents of most teenagers complain that their children only want to be with friends and never want to stay home, parents of socially anxious teenagers tell us they beg and plead with their children to make plans and go out. As you begin talking with parents, invite them to elaborate on how social fears limit their children's lives or stop their children from doing the things they would like to do.

Moreover, parents who believe their children's social concerns are a developmental phase often expect that the anxiety will be temporary. Although it is true that some fears may come and go, pervasive social anxiety that interferes with children's willingness to participate in a variety of performance and social situations typically gets worse over time rather than better (Beesdo-Baum et al., 2012; Pine et al., 1998). Therefore, upon encountering these types of parental attitudes about social anxiety, we encourage you to dispel the misconception that adolescents will naturally outgrow their anxiety without intervention. While outgrowing social anxiety may be possible, it is not the typical course we observe from adolescence to adulthood. You may choose to provide information about the stability of social anxiety and the increased risk it poses for the development of depression, substance abuse, and other difficulties later in life (see Chapter 1, pp. 5–6, for details; also see Pine et al., 1998; Wittchen et al., 1999). Intervention can then be presented as a way to address difficulties with social confidence now in order to prevent these more serious problems later. A salient example for parents of high school students is the impending transition to college. While socially anxious high schoolers may be content with their small group of life-long friends, learning and practicing how to establish new relationships will pay off when they need to utilize these skills in college or future jobs. It will be essential for students to participate more actively in classroom situations, perform more confidently in interviews, and take initiative when interacting with professors and other adults. Remind parents that helping their children overcome these fears now will make upcoming challenges more manageable and will allow them to make the most of future opportunities.

"It's Just Her Personality"

Another common perspective of parents is that their child is "just shy," or that it is "just her personality." Often the assumptions consistent with this view are that personality is innate and cannot or should not be changed. It is important to explain to parents that you are in no way trying to change the core of who their child is. It is actually just the opposite. By teaching their child new skills, you are trying to free him from being weighed down by worry and anxiety so that he can feel more comfortable with who he is and less concerned about what others think. We also recommend gently pointing out some of the ways in which anxiety has been limiting the student from reaching his goals (see Chapter 1, pp. 5–6). Emphasizing impairment in academic or athletic achievement is often motivating for parents. Sometimes parents share that they "were the same way" as a teenager. When parents identify with their child's anxiety, say you are pleased that they can understand their child's experience, but then inquire whether they may have benefited from some assistance as a teenager, or if they may have overcome their anxiety more quickly with help. Overall, your goal is to make it clear that social anxiety is something that interferes with the quality of life and healthy development of their child, and that with some effective strategies, significant improvements can be made.

"Get Over It!"

Some parents have difficulty understanding their child's anxiety and have grown impatient, insisting that their adolescent should "just get over it." It is important to understand and empathize with these parents. Imagine how frustrating it might be to constantly push your child or to feel required to do things for her that she should be able to do for herself by adolescence (i.e., intervene with teachers, get the homework when their child is absent, order their child's food, or push their child to invite friends over). Parents often pressure their teenagers to do these things independently and then get angry and become entangled in power struggles when their children refuse. To these teenagers, it isn't as simple as just "getting over it," and parental frustration may only exacerbate their child's anxiety.

In situations like these, we suggest helping parents cultivate or rediscover the empathy they previously had for their child's experience. It may be useful to inquire whether parents have ever experienced anxiety when speaking in public, or whether they have specific fears of heights, insects, or crowded spaces. Ask parents to imagine what it feels like for them when they are faced with a feared situation in order to increase empathy for their child's fear of social situations. It can also be helpful to meet with parents and adolescents together. Have students express how they feel when they are unable to engage in performance or social situations and/or when their parents get angry at them in response. Students will sometimes reveal that it makes them feel like a failure, that they really wish they had the confidence to make the phone call or ask a friend to get together, or that their parents' anger makes them feel criticized or unsupported. If students are unable to express these feelings directly to their parents, it may help for you to provide the explanations and ask for parents' commitment to be supportive even if they cannot completely understand. Clarify for both the teenager and parent that being supportive does not mean the parent will let the child avoid all situations that create some anxiety. Rather, parents can help their child challenge anxious thoughts and can encourage their child to face his fears while empathizing with and encouraging him instead of becoming angry.

"It's Ruining His Life!"

On the opposite end of the continuum, some parents are so distressed by their child's anxiety that they may overestimate its impact. They may feel exasperated because they believe they have exhausted every strategy to help their child overcome anxiety and foresee terrible consequences. If parents have a hard time tolerating their own discomfort when seeing their child in distress, they may do anything to help their child feel better in the moment, which includes coming to the "rescue" and allowing their child to avoid situations that make her anxious. Some parents are eager for assistance from a professional, while others may feel defeated and hopeless. We recommend educating these parents about the components of social anxiety and the effectiveness of cognitive-behavioral strategies (see Chapter 4, pp. 29–32, for details) to instill hope that their child can learn to approach anxiety-provoking situations and conquer her anxiety.

The bottom line is that parents' perspective on their child's anxiety may influence their level of buy-in. Parents who appreciate and understand the impact of anxiety will likely be more engaged and supportive of intervention. Therefore, it is critical to understand the parental attitudes that may interfere and to address them directly. In this way, you can hopefully increase parental engagement and increase the likelihood that students will receive the support they need while facing their fears.

WHAT ARE WAYS TO ENGAGE PARENTS?

Including parents in child anxiety treatment can help maximize improvements in students' overall functioning (Mendlowitz et al., 1999). Their support is valuable for facilitating students' attendance at meetings and treatment-related activities, as well as for increasing students' adherence to treatment strategies and practice exercises (Nock & Ferriter, 2005). Given the importance of parents' support in the intervention process, we encourage creativity and flexibility in determining the best means for involving them. Ideally, we recommend two to three meetings (about 30 minutes each) with parents (Fisher et al., 2004; Ryan & Masia Warner, 2012). With some creativity and advance planning, it may be possible to combine one or more of these meetings with other events that would normally bring parents to school (e.g., back-to-school night, college advising). If you are working with more than one student at a time, such as when implementing group interventions, it might be efficient to invite a few parents to come together to discuss these common topics as a group. While this may be logistically difficult, it ultimately saves time, and parents often appreciate the opportunity to exchange experiences and ideas with other parents facing similar challenges. While in-person meetings are preferable, we understand that this is not always feasible. In these cases, we recommend offering the option of scheduled telephone calls or using e-mail to provide important educational information about social anxiety (e.g., Handout 4.1), recommended parent strategies (see Handout 13.1: Tips for Parents of Anxious Children), or homework assignments for parents to do with the child.

"Did I Cause My Child's Anxiety?"

Throughout your initial conversations with parents, it is common for them to ask questions about the causes of social anxiety. This may be because many parents blame themselves or believe they have "done something wrong." If this occurs, carefully explain that anxiety is caused by a combination of interacting factors, including a genetic vulnerability and experiences over time that reinforce avoidance because it decreases anxiety in the short term. It helps to tell them that good parents naturally want to protect their children but that sometimes too much protection is too much of a good thing, because it keeps children from learning that they can handle things on their own.

> **Parents' interest and engagement in treatment is important and beneficial for their child.**

Additionally, praise parents for becoming involved and emphasize that parent interest and engagement in treatment is important and beneficial for their child. Emphasize that although their adolescent may always be a little on the anxious side, the good news is that we can teach students effective ways to manage their anxiety and help parents learn how to support their child's efforts.

PARENT EDUCATION ABOUT SOCIAL ANXIETY

At the start of your work with students, it is beneficial to provide parents with psychoeducation about social anxiety similar to the information you provided to the students. In the first parent meeting, describe the three components of social anxiety and explain the interconnection of physical, cognitive, and behavioral symptoms. You want to make sure that parents understand how these symptoms interact to maintain and intensify anxiety in their children (see Handout 4.1). We recommend that you directly connect these symptoms to the rationale for strategies you will be teaching their child to use when confronting social anxiety. More specifically, to address catastrophic thinking, you will be teaching adolescents to evaluate negative predictions more realistically (see Handouts 6.1–6.7), which will increase the likelihood that they will enter into situations they have avoided. In addition, you will be teaching students social skills (e.g., initiating conversations, speaking to adults and teachers) and guiding them in practicing these skills to promote confidence in their ability to handle social situations. Finally, and most importantly, you will support them in gradually entering situations they are avoiding (see Handout 11.1 for exposure rationale and Handouts 12.1–12.6 for examples of exposure situations). Through varied and repeated exposures, students will learn that feared scenarios do not typically occur (Craske et al., 2014). In time, social and performance situations will not cause as much anxiety and distress as they do now, and students will feel more capable of managing social interactions. All of this information can usually be covered in one initial meeting.

WHAT HAVE PARENTS BEEN DOING TO DEAL WITH THEIR CHILD'S ANXIETY?

As part of your second contact, we recommend asking parents how they usually respond to their child's anxiety so you can tailor instructions for individual parents. Provide some scenarios that you know are difficult areas for their child. Probe parents with questions such as "What do you say and do when your daughter tells you she is nauseous the morning before a presentation, performance, or big game?," "What do you say and do when your son tells you he has decided to stay home from a party that you know he was excited about attend-

> **Parents often permit or enable avoidance in an effort to rescue their child from anxiety.**

ing?," or "How do you handle it when your child receives comments on a progress report about not participating in class?" Your goal in asking questions is to gather information to help parents strategize. Parents have usually tried several approaches that were unsuccessful and now feel helpless.

They are often permitting or even enabling their child's avoidance (e.g., making the child's decisions, speaking to various coaches and teachers, allowing the child to remain home from school events). Look both for instances where parent behavior allows the child to avoid and instances where the parent encouraged their child to face her fears.

Once parents discuss ways they handle anxiety, gently ask parents to consider how some of their responses might be maintaining or exacerbating the child's anxiety. In order to minimize defensiveness and blame, it is important to empathize. Highlight how these unhelpful strategies that allow avoidance of anxiety make sense on the surface because they are consistent with parents' natural instincts to protect their child. It can also be helpful to say that these strategies might work well with other children but are not the best fit for anxious teenagers. To aid you in your work with parents, the following sections outline some strategies you are likely to hear from parents and briefly explain how they contribute to anxiety. Be sure to also praise parents when they actively support and encourage their child to independently face feared social situations. Balancing the conversation by pointing out both helpful and unhelpful strategies that parents have previously used can help parents feel like equal partners in the treatment, rather than feeling blamed or criticized for their style of parenting.

UNHELPFUL STRATEGIES THAT PARENTS SOMETIMES USE

Permitting or Encouraging Avoidance

This is the most critical behavior to attempt to change. If you have limited time with parents, focus your attention on this one. Understandably, when parents observe their children experiencing anxiety and having uncomfortable physical symptoms they want to eliminate the anxiety as fast as possible. In addition, anxious children often seem timid or give the impression that they cannot handle various situations. Therefore, parents may feel the urge to protect or rescue them by taking over in difficult situations. Parents may let adolescents "off the hook" and remove the expectation that they face their discomfort. It may be easier to allow a child to stay home from a party or to support his decision to quit the school play, rather than tolerate the distress these situations induce. Permitting avoidance may be particularly likely to occur when parents feel unprepared to help their children cope with anxious feelings.

Unfortunately, when parents go to great lengths to eliminate *any* distress, discomfort, or potential failure through overprotection, there can be unintended negative consequences for their children (Festa & Ginsburg, 2011). For instance, allowing teenagers to miss certain school events or discouraging them from trying out for a new sport prevents them from learning appropriate skills for behaving in these situations and confronting emotions like disappointment and embarrassment. This parental behavior sends a message to children that evaluative situations are dangerous or threatening. Furthermore, it implies that the consequences of failing are unacceptable, rather than a necessary byproduct of trying new things and learning through experience. It is essential that parents learn that while avoidance is an effective strategy for reducing anxiety in the short term, it is highly problematic in the long term. Avoidance becomes negatively reinforced, meaning that because it so immediately and effectively reduces anxious thoughts and feelings, it often becomes a favored strategy for dealing with anxiety. Children who consistently avoid feared situations never learn that these situations will get easier over time and that they have the skills to cope with them.

Being Overly Directive

Because parents are often trying to minimize their children's distress, some parents tend to step in and take over for their child in anxiety-provoking situations. They may tell their child exactly what to say (e.g., when speaking to various adults, extending an invite to a friend) in various interpersonal interactions. Excessively controlling children's interactions is similar to overprotective parenting in that it prevents children from confronting their fears and is associated with child anxiety (McLeod, Wood, & Weisz, 2007). Again, this behavior robs adolescents of the opportunity to learn how to problem-solve or handle difficult situations on their own and to learn from feedback and experience. Parental overinvolvement and excessive direction also imply that parents do not believe the child can competently manage the situation. In the long run, adolescents may internalize this message and become overly reliant on their parents to solve problems for them.

Providing Excessive Reassurance

Anxious teenagers often ask parents for reassurance that everything will go "okay" when anticipating situations. Seemingly counterintuitive, this type of reassurance seeking actually maintains or increases anxiety (Cougle et al., 2012). If you ask students, they will say that telling an anxious teenager that he will be fine, or that there is nothing to be afraid of, is ineffective. It usually does not help or only temporarily decreases anxiety. The even bigger problem is that the more reassurance a child receives, the more he requires and the more dependent he becomes on parents for coping with anxiety-provoking situations. Reassurance seeking (and reassurance giving) is actually associated with more anxiety later. Like the parenting behaviors described above, providing excessive reassurance prevents adolescents from learning to cope more independently with anxiety and interferes with the development of autonomy and self-confidence.

WHAT SHOULD PARENTS DO INSTEAD?

The third meeting should focus on providing helpful strategies for assisting teenagers to overcome anxiety. If you have only one meeting with parents, prioritize teaching parents these helpful strategies. The main message we convey is that the best way for parents to help their anxious teenagers is to encourage them to face their fears so they can develop the confidence to face challenging situations and learn that they can handle them. Increased autonomy leads to the development of more effective coping and problem-solving skills, which are essential for nurturing independent adolescents capable of making a successful transition to young adulthood. Specifically, we recommend the following parent strategies summarized in Table 13.1 and presented below to replace the unhelpful techniques discussed in the preceding section.

Prevent Avoidance and Model Facing Fears

As explained earlier (see Chapters 4, 11, and 12), it is critically important that parents encourage their socially anxious adolescents to face feared situations in order to learn through experience that anxiety eventually dissipates and that they can handle these situations.

> **Parents should encourage socially anxious adolescents to face feared situations.**

Once parents understand this concept, inquire about impairment caused by their child's anxiety and invite them to provide additional fear ladder or exposure goals, and to brainstorm ways of addressing those situations to help students climb their ladder. For example, parents can suggest that their child call a relative, speak to a store clerk, order for himself at a restaurant, or invite a friend over. In addition, they can help their child identify spontaneous opportunities as they arise.

It is important to emphasize parents' role as supportive coaches who make suggestions, remind their child about important points (anxiety will subside over time), and provide reinforcement for effort, while making it clear that the adolescent is in charge and has the ultimate choice about facing her fear. We advise against creating a power struggle around

TABLE 13.1. Alternative Parent Strategies to Try

Unhelpful strategy	Try this instead
Permitting or encouraging avoidance	Prevent avoidance and model facing fears
Being overly directive or overprotective	Tolerate negative emotion and prompt problem solving
Providing excessive reassurance	Assist with giving it a second thought

facing fears and making it an aversive experience. If the child is very resistant, what we have found helpful is to teach parents to empathize and say, "I know this step feels too hard. What do you think you can handle?" This may lead to practicing exposure in a slightly less difficult situation that the child feels more ready to confront and that will build confidence for the next step. When a child pushes himself past his comfort zone, remind parents to praise him, but clarify that they should reinforce effort rather than outcomes that are out of the child's control. For example, if a peer says no to a movie invitation, a parent might express how proud he is of the child for being brave and asking. Moreover, we recommend that parents intentionally model how they face their own fears and describe their experience to their child. For example, a parent might describe to a teenager how she was anxious about applying for a new job, calling a friend she hadn't spoken to in a while, or giving an important presentation at work, but how she managed to do it anyway, highlighting how it went better or was easier than initially expected.

Tolerate Negative Emotion and Encourage Problem Solving

Asking parents to become less protective in certain situations is difficult because it requires them to go against their instincts and learn to tolerate their own and their children's feelings of anxiety and distress. It is important to emphasize to parents that while anxiety can feel temporarily unpleasant, it is not harmful and rather necessary. We want them to learn that anxiety should no longer trigger or justify avoidance. It is okay to experience anxiety. In fact, it can be used as a cue to explore the predictions about upcoming situations that are causing the anxious feelings and do something about them. Rather than helping adolescents eliminate anxiety by removing them from difficult situations and doing things for them, we encourage parents to support their child in solving problems. Adolescents can generate their own solutions and choose the best one by weighing the pros and cons—with guidance of course! For example, a parent could encourage an adolescent to think of possible solutions for addressing a disappointing grade. It may also be helpful for parents to role-play the chosen solution with their child ahead of time (e.g., talking to the teacher). This approach is more beneficial to the adolescent's development than the parent becoming overly involved and contacting the teacher directly to discuss the grade, bypassing the student completely.

Assist with Giving It a Second Thought

Instead of providing excessive reassurance that there is "nothing to worry about," we want parents to teach their children to help themselves by using anxiety as a signal to explore and challenge their own negative assumptions (see Chapters 5 and 6). We are not suggesting that parents should be insensitive. Rather, the first step we recommend is for parents to communicate empathy for their child by validating their thoughts and feelings about an anxiety-provoking situation. For example, we encourage parents to say things like "I understand that this is difficult for you" or "I know you feel scared." Parents can then provide encouragement and support with statements such as "I know you feel scared, but I am confident that you can face this." Parents may also offer to guide students through the steps of "giving it a second thought": "Do you think your thoughts about this are realistic?," "Can we look at this another way?," "What are some questions you can ask yourself about this situation?"

COMMON CHALLENGES WHEN INVOLVING PARENTS

Parents Are Overly Anxious Themselves

Anxious children often have parents who also experience anxiety. In these cases, it is possible that parents are less likely to encourage adolescents to confront their fears because they also have exaggerated predictions and expect negative outcomes from social situations. It is important to discuss how the parent's own anxiety influences his parenting and the consequences of overprotection of his child. It will be important to monitor whether parental anxiety is interfering with a student's progress and to address it. In some cases, it can be helpful for the student to teach parents the skills he is learning and to have them practice as well. However, anxious parents can be limited in their ability to use these skills effectively. In cases where you cannot manage a parent's anxiety, it may be important to suggest that the parent seek her own treatment, especially if the parent's own anxiety is interfering with her ability to allow the child to experience distress when entering challenging situations.

Parents Are Unable to Tolerate Their Child's Anxiety While Facing Fears

There are situations in which a parent feels too concerned about a child experiencing distress, disappointment, or rejection to allow her to take any social risks and may even inadvertently discourage it. They may continue to allow the child to avoid social encounters or to do things for the child that she finds difficult. In this situation, we have found it useful to speak to parents about what this will mean for their child in the future. In addition, we have used the scenario of having them imagine that their child is diabetic instead of anxious. We ask parents if they would give in and allow their child to avoid ever testing her blood sugar because of the discomfort of a needle prick. Parents respond to this question with an enthusiastic "NO!," understanding that temporary discomfort is critically important for preventing worse consequences later. We explain that giving in and allowing students to avoid situations that make them anxious can also have worse consequences such as increased anxiety, more social withdrawal, or depression.

LAUREN'S STORY

Around the time of the first group meeting, Ms. Hillman had another phone conversation with Lauren's mother to present a detailed overview of the strategies she had been working on with Lauren. Ms. Hillman had reached out to parents of all the students in the group to try and arrange for all the parents to come in person for a group parent education session.

Unfortunately, she was unable to coordinate a group meeting with each parent's schedule. She elected to contact each parent by phone instead.

Ms. Hillman presented Lauren's mother with explanations and examples of the CBT triangle, realistic thinking, social skills training, and exposures. She also answered questions that Lauren's mother had about how to interact with Lauren at home in anticipation of anxiety-provoking situations. Ms. Hillman learned that Lauren's mother was very understanding and empathic toward Lauren's anxiety but noted that she also had a difficult time tolerating Lauren's distress and sometimes encouraged her to avoid situations that seemed "too hard." "I'm probably a little anxious myself," Lauren's mother shared.

Ms. Hillman emphasized the importance of approaching rather than avoiding anxiety-provoking situations. She reiterated the rationale for exposures and confronting fears. Ms. Hillman also coached Lauren's mother on each of the steps for giving it a second thought so that she could use this strategy to encourage Lauren to enter difficult situations rather than avoid them. Ms. Hillman e-mailed Lauren's mother Handout 6.6: Challenging Thoughts and encouraged her to practice using it with Lauren. Ms. Hillman also sent Lauren's mother a copy of Handout 13.1: Tips for Parents of Anxious Children.

Following this conversation, Ms. Hillman kept Lauren's mother in the loop about what they were practicing with periodic e-mails. Ms. Hillman and Lauren's mother also e-mailed back and forth with updates on Lauren's accomplishments in and out of school with respect to completing tasks on her fear ladder. The day before Lauren had plans to attend a party without her best friend, her mother called Ms. Hillman for some extra coaching.

CHAPTER SUMMARY

- Involving students' parents in learning strategies to decrease anxiety increases the likelihood that students will receive appropriate support.

- It is critical to gain an understanding of parents' perspectives on their child's anxiety to address any perceptions that may interfere with students' progress.

- Be flexible when engaging parents (in-person meetings, telephone calls, online communication, providing literature).

- Provide psychoeducation about social anxiety and the rationale for the strategies you are teaching students.

- It is critical for parents to understand that although avoidance provides temporary relief, it will worsen anxiety and cause more significant limitations in the long run.

- Helpful strategies for parents of anxious adolescents include preventing avoidance, refraining from rescuing their child in difficult situations, modeling facing fears, tolerating their child's negative emotion, prompting their child to problem-solve, and encouraging their child to realistically evaluate his negative predictions and confront his fears.

Tips for Parents of Anxious Children

- **Communicate empathy.** Let your child know you understand it is difficult to face fears. Review with him why facing his fears is important for accomplishing *his* goals, and remind him that facing fears will get easier the more he practices.

- **Prevent avoidance** of feared or anxiety-provoking situations as much as possible:
  - *Look for opportunities* for your child to practice pushing past comfort zones.
  - *Encourage,* but don't force it—get her agreement to challenge herself by facing her fear and remind her why it is important in the long term.
  - If he doesn't agree, try to *find a way to make it a bit easier*—see what he will agree to, and encourage small, gradual steps.

- **Reward and praise effort** rather than results when your child attempts something she is anxious about or previously avoided.

- **Model non anxious, brave behavior.** Let your child know when you are anxious about something but are facing it anyway. Share strategies that are helpful for you and tell him how you challenge your anxious thoughts.

- **Tolerate your own anxiety** when watching your child in distress. Resist your natural parental urge to rescue when your child is anxious, and remind yourself and your child that repeated practice makes things easier.

- **Prompt problem solving** by asking your child to brainstorm her own solutions. Allow your child to choose a course of action by evaluating the pros and cons of different approaches and then allow her to carry out her plan independently (e.g., asking a teacher to review a low grade).

- Help your child engage in **realistic thinking** rather than providing reassurance. Try some of the following questions:
  - "What is the evidence that this thought is really true?"
  - "What is the probability that will happen?"
  - "What are some other possible explanations?"
  - "If the thought is accurate, what is the worst that could happen? And could you live through that?"

CHAPTER 14

School Social Events and Peer Assistants

We have described how conducting intervention at school provides many meaningful opportunities for socially anxious students to practice facing feared situations, such as participating in the classroom and interacting with teachers. However, despite the many advantages of the school environment, it can be difficult to create opportunities for students to practice navigating unstructured social situations with peers, especially if you have been working with students individually. One way to accomplish this is to plan and implement social events either at school or, if possible, outside of school. This chapter recommends different types of activities that may be valuable for students with social anxiety and provides ideas for including school peers, such as other students with anxiety or peer assistants.

WHY ARE SOCIAL ACTIVITIES IMPORTANT?

Many students have told us that knowing how to act during unstructured group social events (e.g., when they do not have a specific task or goal) is among the most anxiety-provoking situations they encounter. Implementing social events provides students with realistic opportunities to practice social skills and promotes skill generalization. Unstructured social activities also allow for exposure to several commonly avoided situations (e.g., attending a social event without friends, initiating conversations with unfamiliar peers, performing in front of others) and allow students to practice individually tailored challenges (e.g., making small talk, making minor social mistakes, being captain of a team) that may be difficult to simulate within a typical school day (Fisher et al., 2004; Ryan & Masia Warner, 2012). In addition, if you have not been able to do so, social events provide an opportunity to actively observe students in anxiety-provoking situations, which can inform your choice of additional behaviors to target for change (e.g., the student does not look friendly or does not approach others).

WHAT TYPES OF SOCIAL ACTIVITIES ARE HELPFUL?

Any activity that promotes social interaction with peers and that teenagers consider enjoyable is valuable. We recommend trying to organize between two and four gatherings. These activities can be held during school, after school, or on the weekends—whatever is feasible for you and the students. We have found that holding an informal pizza lunch during the school day can be the most manageable option and tends to be well attended. Other ideas for school activities might be various games or sports played in the school gym or on outside fields, such as basketball or volleyball. Lip-sync contests, interactive board games (e.g., charades, Pictionary), relay races, and various icebreakers can be fun as well. It is always desirable to have food such as pizza or other snacks and drinks. Food can make the event feel more fun and realistic, gives students something "to do," and also allows socially anxious students to practice eating in front of others, which can be anxiety provoking for some.

Choose enjoyable activities that promote social interaction.

If you are able to plan a social event outside of school, possibly in a community location on a weekend, we recommend starting with something structured and familiar to all like bowling. Bowling has inherent structure because it allows for predictable interaction, with each student taking a turn, and provides for a communal focus and topic for conversation. Using a more structured activity as the initial event tends to be less intimidating and provides more support for students who may be less practiced in certain social skills. As students progress, later social events should be less structured (e.g., going to a restaurant, having a board-game party at school) to challenge students to use their skills. We have found that rollerblading, laser tag, and picnics are good ways to promote positive interaction. Additionally, indoor amusement centers or arcades can be effective as settings for later social events after students are already familiar with other group members. These types of large unstructured venues, however, can create a challenge for counselors when trying to ensure that students are engaged with peers and not only playing games alone. It can be beneficial to enforce the "buddy rule" that is common for school trips and inform students that they should not be alone at any point. The only type of activity to avoid would be something that does not encourage interaction, such as attending a movie or a play. Appendix 14.1: Recommendations for School Social Events outlines several potential activities for counselors to consider.

WHAT SHOULD I TRY TO ACCOMPLISH AT A SOCIAL EVENT?

The primary task of the school personnel running the social events is to actively ensure that every student is engaged. Particularly at the first event, the role of the group leader is to encourage interaction between group members. However, at later events, we recommend that group leaders try to limit their presence to facilitating interaction only when a student is having particular difficulty. It can be helpful to provide each student with specific assignments prior to the event, such as starting three conversations or finding out one thing about each person there. However, it is likely that you will need to encourage students to approach others while in the situation. We strongly advise that all direction be provided in a very subtle and discreet manner to avoid embarrassing students. For example, ask a student to help you with something so you can speak with her privately without others suspecting the reason you are pulling her aside. You may also facilitate interaction without singling students out by nudging students together—for example, by assigning pairs of students to be partners and changing partners a couple of times during an event. Students can be sent to do various tasks together, like setting up a game or finding a place for the group to sit. We strongly recommend incorporating exposures in every kind of social event. Group leaders may encourage students to order the food at the event, offer food or drinks to others, divide up players to make teams, and approach unfamiliar peers. However, keep in mind that social events will cause differing levels of anxiety for each student, so assign additional exposures accordingly. Students who are already at the top of their fear ladder by attending the event (or who were extremely hesitant to attend) may only require assignments that facilitate interaction (e.g., initiate conversation), while those experiencing moderate levels of anxiety should be pushed to do more (e.g., assume a leadership role, be first to perform, order food).

SHOULD I HAVE OTHER SCHOOL PEERS AT A SOCIAL EVENT?

One worthwhile strategy to ensure success and enhance engagement at social events is to involve prosocial, friendly school peers. We recognize that arranging for additional peers to attend can be logistically difficult and thus recommend capitalizing on existing peer leadership programs when possible. Many schools have peer leader or peer assistant programs. Peer assistants are usually helpful, friendly, and good-natured students who have been identified by school personnel and have undergone a rigorous selection process (e.g., teacher recommendations, personal essays, interviews).

When peer assistants are included, their primary role is to create a positive experience for nervous students at social events. Peer assistants "grease the wheels" by bringing enthusiasm and energy to the events and ensuring that all students are engaged in conversation and integrated into group activities. Peer assistants can also facilitate peer support within the school environment through assistance with exposures and skills practice, such as by bringing a group member to join a school club or by talking with a group member in the cafeteria or hallways.

> **Prosocial peer assistants "grease the wheels" by bringing enthusiasm and energy to social events.**

Although peer assistants are typically adolescents who are sensitive to the feelings of others, we urge you to be extremely cautious about the confidentiality of the students with whom you are working. First, we recommend briefly interviewing all potential peer assistants before involving them in social events or exposures. During the interview, we suggest asking about their participation in extracurricular activities, how they respond to bullying, and what they would do if they noticed a student sitting by himself during an activity. In our experience, the best peer assistants are not necessarily the most extroverted students but rather students who are caring and empathic. Second, we have made it a rule not to provide any specific information about students' difficulties to peer assistants or to ever use the words "social anxiety" with peer assistants. Rather, we usually say that we are conducting a school program aimed at enhancing future success through training in assertiveness, public speaking, and interacting with new people. We then explain that we are starting this training with students on the shyer side.

We recommend showing the students you are working with the list of peer assistants who may be included. This allows socially anxious students to feel more comfortable and prepared for early social events. It also gives students the opportunity to "veto" some of your peer assistant recommendations. Students may not want particular peer assistants involved for any number of reasons related to confidentiality concerns or prior interactions with the peer assistants. For instance, a student might not want one of his teammates to know that he is participating in your school's program. Additionally, socially anxious students who have previously been victimized by other peers may have concerns if your chosen peer assistants are friends with students who have teased or bullied them.

Finally, our most important suggestion is that, whenever possible, aim to use student helpers who have experienced social anxiety and with whom you have previously worked and had success. If schools have a yearly intervention program, counselors can invite back the members from the prior year to be peer assistants. Not only can these prior members understand and empathize with your current students, but they are often proud and excited to be involved as peer assistants. Inviting prior members to be peer assistants has the added bonus of supporting continued skill development and school engagement after you are no longer working with a particular student.

HOW SHOULD I ENCOURAGE HESITANT STUDENTS?

Social events are often logistically easier to arrange when working with students in groups because group members are already familiar with the other students who will be attending. However, with some creativity and planning, counselors may successfully involve multiple students who are each receiving individual intervention. In either case, as you might expect, most students are hesitant to attend social events, particularly the first one. They are nervous, uncertain of what it will be like, and probably expecting the worst. When discussing social events with students, begin by reviewing the rationale for attending. We suggest telling students that they may experience anticipatory anxiety before the event and brainstorming with them some strategies for managing the anxiety. Your goal is for students to attend the event despite feeling anxious. In particular, devoting some time to helping students identify and challenge anxious thoughts is recommended. As the event approaches, students can review their challenging questions and realistic thoughts, either independently or with a parent (hopefully one who is ready to prevent avoidance). For extremely avoidant students, it might be helpful to pair them with another student or peer assistant so they can carpool and arrive together. Another option may involve introducing hesitant students to others who will be attending the event in advance.

In our experience, it is also helpful to address concerns regarding confidentiality. Some students may be too anxious to ask about this, but almost all are wondering about it. We recommend asking each student for a commitment to keep the event and their true reason for being there confidential, which most are motivated to do. It can also be helpful to remind students that everyone there is in the same boat, so if they want to keep it private they should assume others do as well. Choosing a venue that is less public, traveling to a neighboring town or scheduling the event during a time when other school peers are less likely to be present (e.g., during the school day) may increase participation by group members who are particularly concerned about confidentiality. Additionally, to increase students' comfort and address confidentiality concerns when outside of school, it can be helpful to give the group a club name (e.g., Peer Leadership Club) and have school personnel accompany the students as club advisers.

Although these strategies will increase students' comfort, it is our experience that for social events outside of school, you will need parental support to bring students to the event despite their resistance. Reaching out to parents in advance, priming them to expect their child's anxiety and efforts to avoid, and asking parents to commit to bringing their child anyway can increase the likelihood that students will attend the event.

To maximize buy-in and support from parents or guardians, it is important that they understand the benefits of participating in these activities. Parents may need a reminder that the best way to help their child overcome anxiety and become more engaged at school is to face these difficult, unstructured social situations. We have found it helpful to integrate our explanation of the value of social events with education surrounding parent strategies for helping children overcome anxiety (e.g., preventing avoidance, gradually facing fears; see Chapter 13). Attending a school-sponsored event with a trusted school professional who understands anxiety is advantageous as a first step in gradually facing this fear. Providing parents with specific details, such as dates and locations, allows them to plan ahead with their child to ensure that students are available to attend. Giving this information directly to parents also reduces opportunities for miscommunication or avoidance by the student. In environments where enlisting parental support is difficult, it may be advisable to stick to social gatherings at school either during the school day or immediately after.

WHAT CAN I EXPECT AT A SOCIAL EVENT?

One important note to remember—these social events are also anxiety inducing for the school personnel running them! At first you might have a silent group of students staring into space with everyone looking miserable. At times you may feel as if you are torturing them. Remember that even when socially anxious students look uncomfortable, they often want to be there. Stay strong and be persistent. Keep talking and get involved in the game or activity. With some warmth and encouragement, the students will begin to loosen up and interaction will increase so that you can fade into the background. In our experience, social events inspire positive change and increase confidence.

Social events are a safe way for students to start putting themselves out there with desirable consequences. Students often say the best part of working with us was the social events, and their feedback almost always mentions that they wish there were more of them. At first we found this to be shocking since they looked so miserable at times! However, this is the core of social anxiety and what sets it apart from other social difficulties. Adolescents with social anxiety desperately want to socialize and have friends; they just feel too paralyzed by fear to go for it and risk being disliked or rejected. Learning through experience that positive outcomes are more likely than negative ones can be a real game changer for them. It is important to remember that they truly desire social interaction and relationships, but anxiety interferes. You are helping them take healthy steps to overcome their fears even though it may seem difficult at the beginning.

> **Students often want more social events!**

LAUREN'S STORY

During the last group meeting (see Chapter 10, pp. 113–114), Ms. Hillman told Lauren and the other students that she planned to meet with them once as a group outside of school. Ms. Hillman and another school counselor who had been working with a couple of students on reducing anxiety decided to coordinate a social event. Between them, there were six students they were currently meeting with and four students with whom they had previously implemented these strategies successfully. The counselors met with the four previous students individually to make sure they would have a respectful, positive attitude about being a peer assistant and helping other students. The counselors then arranged a date for the group members and peer assistants to go bowling. The local bowling alley was convenient, relatively inexpensive, and provided sufficient structure for a first social event.

Ms. Hillman convened the group for a brief 10-minute meeting to provide information about the social event, respond to questions, and challenge unrealistic negative predictions about the event. She also spent a few minutes with each student individually to identify at least one specific exposure to implement at the social event. Lauren committed to asking the employee at the desk which lanes were assigned to the group. She also decided to exchange her bowling shoes for a different size. For added difficulty, Ms. Hillman encouraged her to exchange the shoes more than once.

The day of the event, the counselors were expecting five of six students and four peer assistants. Ms. Hillman received a call from one student's father an hour before the event. He informed her that his son was refusing to attend and asked Ms. Hillman for advice about how to encourage his child to face his fears. Ms. Hillman provided coaching to the father, and the student eventually agreed to attend. Lauren and the other students arrived, looking nervous and reserved. Lauren did not ask the employee for the lane assignment but remembered to request a new shoe size. Once the game was under way and snacks were ordered, Ms. Hillman discreetly reminded the peer assistants to initiate more conversations. Over time, everyone appeared to relax a bit. Although Lauren initially stuck pretty close to another student who had been in her group, she began initiating a conversation with some of the unfamiliar peers about halfway through the event. Ms. Hillman made sure to discreetly praise each student's efforts at the end of the event. The counselors agreed that it was a challenging but worthwhile event!

CHAPTER SUMMARY

- Social events are essential because they provide opportunities for students to practice social skills and allow for exposure to several commonly avoided situations.

- We recommend that two to four social gatherings be held either at school or in the community (e.g., at a bowling alley) during school hours, after school, or on the weekends, depending on what is most feasible.

- School personnel running the social events should encourage interaction between students and incorporate student exposures when possible.

- Enlist prosocial peer assistants to attend social events to help engage students and create a positive environment. We strongly recommend enlisting students whom you have previously helped overcome similar issues.

- Even when students look uncomfortable and need encouragement at social events, they often want to be there and report that social events were their favorite part of the intervention.

Recommendations for School Social Events

This list is just a handful of suggestions for school counselors to refer to when planning social events with students. Many activities below can be paired together, and food is encouraged at social events. We recommend that counselors work with students to choose activities that will be enjoyable to those attending, taking into consideration their ages, interests, and suggestions. Counselors are encouraged to use community or Internet resources for additional ideas. The only rule is that the chosen activity must promote social interaction!

- *Bowling*—because of its inherent structure, bowling can be a good first activity
- *Ice skating or roller blading*
- *Group painting activities* (e.g., paint-a-pot parties)
- *Laser tag*
- *Miniature golf*
- *Trivia*
- A *pizza party with games or activities*
- A *picnic with outdoor games or activities*
- *Pumpkin/apple picking or pumpkin carving*
- *Interactive games* (e.g., Catch Phrase, Taboo, Pictionary, charades)
- *Team sports* (e.g., volleyball, soccer, basketball, badminton)
- *Field games or icebreakers* (e.g., human knot, potato sack races, water balloon tosses, egg tosses, egg on spoon races, dizzy bat races, obstacle courses, relay races)
- *Lip-sync or karaoke contests*—may be particularly challenging for students with significant performance fears
- *Arcades or party gyms*—these venues are often enjoyable for students, but can be a challenge for counselors to ensure that students do not end up playing games alone
- *Mall scavenger hunts*—can serve as additional exposures. Counselors can assign teams and create tasks that encourage students to make social mistakes or interact with safe strangers (e.g., asking a cashier for a particular item in a store)

CHAPTER 15

Classroom Strategies for Teachers

Throughout this book we have discussed how school counselors and other professionals who work outside the classroom can implement meaningful intervention for social anxiety within the school setting. Equally important is what teachers do in the classroom. Of course, academic instruction is a school's main priority. However, implementing simple classroom strategies that address students' social and emotional needs can promote school engagement and help students reach their academic potential. Because social anxiety often interferes with academic success, and because the classroom setting involves several challenging scenarios (see Chapter 2, pp. 14–15), the assistance of teachers can maximize the benefits of school-based services. As individuals with direct access to students' classroom behaviors, teachers have an essential role in identifying students with social anxiety and in executing real-time intervention strategies right in the place where difficulty occurs (Fisher et al., 2004; Ryan & Masia Warner, 2012). In this chapter, we review the importance of teachers' ability to recognize social anxiety. We then discuss how school counselors can enlist the help of teachers in facilitating skills practice in class, encouraging peer socialization, and promoting school engagement. By supporting socially anxious students with classroom-based strategies, teachers can play a key role in helping students to generalize new skills and make progress in overcoming social anxiety.

HOW CAN I SUPPORT TEACHERS IN RECOGNIZING SOCIAL ANXIETY?

As discussed in Chapters 1 and 3, social anxiety in children and adolescents can be difficult to detect and often goes unidentified by parents and school professionals. Teachers, however, are in a good position to identify social anxiety because the classroom provides several social and performance situations that more clearly expose students' fears. The key is helping teachers know what to look for! First and foremost, teachers must be trained in recognizing behavioral signs of anxiety. We recommend that counselors provide teachers with basic psychoeducation related to anxiety (see Chapter 4 for review), possibly during one or two faculty meetings. As an alternative to in-school faculty meetings during the school day, counselors might also host a professional development seminar or workshop. This may be particularly desirable when educational meetings or workshops can be counted toward continuing education requirements for teachers. The first meeting should include information related to common observable signs of social anxiety in the classroom (see Handout 15.1: Common Observable Signs of Social Anxiety in the Classroom), as well as discussion of the main intervention strategies effective for social anxiety. Make sure teachers know how to refer students to you for individual support or for participation in a group program if you intend to run one. The more teachers know about the services being offered in school, the more likely they are to help students access those services!

As part of the initial contact, we recommend that counselors encourage teachers to pay particular attention to students (1) who are reluctant to participate in class, (2) who do not seem to interact much with their peers during noninstructional or unstructured classroom time, (3) who exhibit anxious or avoidant behaviors around presentations or group work, (4) who regularly avoid requesting help or asking questions even when their classroom performance indicates an academic need, or (5) whom the teacher might classically label as "shy." In addition to these behavioral signs, socially anxious students may on occasion express their anxiety to teachers in subtle ways. Counselors can prime teachers to pay attention to how questions such as "Can I go last for the presentation?," "Can I write a report instead of presenting?," or "Can I work alone instead of with a group?" might be communicating fears of public speaking or worries about working with peers. Additionally, when students only ask teachers questions about course material after class rather than during the lesson, this may indicate fears of embarrassment or fears of being judged by peers for not understanding the material. Encourage teachers to probe students for more information about potential social anxiety. Questions such as "What are you afraid might happen if you participate in this class debate?" or "What is the worst possible outcome of giving this class presentation?" can help continue the conversation. Helping teachers know what to look for and how to gather more information allows them to identify those students who might need some extra encouragement and support.

TRAINING TEACHERS TO SUPPORT ANXIOUS STUDENTS

The second meeting should focus on classroom strategies for helping students face their fears. You can also speak to teachers individually on a case-by-case basis. We recommend explaining how socially anxious students usually describe some classes as more anxiety provoking for them than others. While several of the factors that impact students' perceptions will be out of the teacher's control (e.g., composition of the peers in the class, students' preexisting skill in the subject area), there are steps that teachers can take to foster a supportive and inclusive classroom environment and encourage students to face their fears. We recommend discussing with teachers how they might facilitate participation and engagement in their classroom. Like parents, sometimes well-meaning teachers are unknowingly permitting avoidance or are pushing students in ways that actually increase their anxiety. It is important to communicate to teachers which strategies are unhelpful and train them to employ helpful strategies more systematically.

UNHELPFUL STRATEGIES THAT TEACHERS SOMETIMES USE

Permitting Avoidance

Sometimes well-meaning teachers will allow students to avoid things that are difficult for them because they recognize the student's anxiety and want to be empathic. For instance, teachers may allow socially anxious students to write a report instead of giving an individual oral presentation. Teachers might also avoid calling on a socially anxious student in class because they know answering questions makes the student nervous. Other times, teachers may not recognize a student's behavior as avoidance and may unknowingly reinforce it. For example, a teacher may not recognize that a socially anxious student only asks questions before or after class. The teacher might praise the student for coming for extra help instead of urging the student to ask the question during class when other peers are present. Teachers should be informed that while allowing students to avoid challenging tasks makes the student feel better in the short term, avoidance actually increases anxiety over time as fears and avoidance become further reinforced.

Providing Excessive Reassurance

As discussed in Chapter 13, it is common for anxious teenagers to ask for reassurance. In school, this may present as students sending in assignments or presentations early, asking if everything "looks okay." Students may bring completed homework assignments to their teachers before school to check their answers for fear of giving a wrong answer in front of peers during class. Additionally, when students communicate anxiety or fear about classroom requirements (e.g., presentations), teachers can easily fall into the trap of providing anxious students with excessive reassurance. Counselors should inform teachers that while reassurance may make a student feel better for that one assignment, it actually maintains the student's anxiety over time (Cougle et al., 2012). Recommend that teachers stay away from relying on reassuring statements like "It'll be okay" or "You'll do fine," because these statements do not help students understand their anxiety or plan to face their fears.

Overzealous Inclusion and Praise

On the other end of the spectrum, some teachers will go out of their way to call on anxious students in an effort to encourage greater participation. While supporting classroom engagement is generally recommended, singling out students or relying on the "popcorn method" in class (i.e., calling on students randomly rather than having students raise their hands) can have the unintended result of making that class terrifying for the student! Instead, provide teachers with strategies to gently encourage participation in ways that gradually increase in difficulty and promote successful student engagement. Another strategy that sometimes backfires is when teachers single out socially anxious students for excessive public praise on a job well done, thinking that it will be positively reinforcing for the student. For some very anxious teenagers who just want to blend in, excessive public acknowledgment can have the unintended consequence of actually embarrassing them (and making them want to disappear into their chair!). Instead, encourage teachers to use more subtle forms of reinforcement, such as a warm smile, a written note, or quick verbal praise (e.g., "Nice job").

FOSTERING A SUPPORTIVE CLASSROOM ENVIRONMENT

Communicate to teachers that your goal is to give them the most effective strategies for engaging anxious students in the classroom and to train them in systematically supporting students in facing their fears. Specifically, we recommend presenting the following strategies to replace the unhelpful ones discussed above, and we encourage counselors to provide teachers with straightforward written materials for reference, such as Handout 15.2: Classroom Strategies to Help Socially Anxious Students.

Actively Empathize with Anxious Students

Adolescents with social anxiety often believe that no one else understands them and they experience significant embarrassment related to their social discomfort. When trusted and supportive adults like teachers take the time to get to know them, anxious students are more likely to open up and acknowledge their fears. Instead of reassurance, recommend that teachers communicate empathy during individual conversations by describing a student's emotion and validating her experience with reflective statements like "Public speaking can be really scary," "You are worried about this group project," or "You're afraid of what your classmates think when you don't understand." Explain how opening up conversations with gentle empathic statements and asking students to articulate their fears prompts students to recognize their own reactions to feared situations. Consistent empathy from a teacher also creates a safe space where students can talk about their anxiety and use their teacher for support in facing their fears in the classroom. When discussing empathy, it is also helpful to remind teachers to refer students who are struggling to the school personnel who are prepared to offer in-school intervention.

Help Students Face Their Classroom Fears

In describing how teachers can help students face their fears, counselors should remind teachers how patterns of avoidance maintain anxiety rather than reduce it. Additionally, explain how repeated, gradual exposure to feared circumstances is the most effective strategy to reduce anxiety. We recommend that counselors emphasize for teachers that their role in helping students face their fears will primarily fall in the domains of classroom participation (i.e., asking questions in class, answering questions in class, participating in class discussions) and classroom presentations. Encourage teachers to draw on conversations with their socially anxious students and to use their creativity to flexibly adjust assignments or activities to make tasks either more manageable or more challenging, depending on the student's needs. It is helpful to assure teachers that this does not mean they must adjust their curriculum and requirements to allow socially anxious students to avoid presentations or skip anything that is challenging. In fact, you are recommending the exact opposite! Rather than allowing students to completely avoid something that is hard for them (e.g., answering questions in class), you will be providing teachers with specific tiered strategies to help students experience success in challenging tasks.

Asking Questions in Class

Socially anxious students often avoid asking questions in class because they fear sounding stupid. Explain that there are tiered steps teachers can take with socially anxious students to help them start spontaneously asking questions in class. Initially, a teacher may provide the student with a question that is commonly asked about the topic being discussed or lesson of the day. Next, the teacher may inform the student of what material will be covered so the student can prepare a question in advance to ask at a planned time in the lesson. The teacher and student can also plan for the student to ask questions during independent or group work when peers might not be paying as much attention but are still present, until eventually the student practices asking questions more spontaneously in front of the whole class.

Answering Questions in Class

Answering questions is another difficult challenge for socially anxious students who fear getting an answer wrong and making a fool of themselves. Provide teachers with a similar tiered model to assist with answering questions. A teacher may first provide the student with a question and its answer before class so that when the teacher asks the question, the student can participate with confidence. This will allow him to practice speaking up in class first without the fear of being incorrect. The teacher can then gradually increase difficulty by providing the student with only the question he will be asked without providing the answer, until eventually the student is only provided the general topic of the day. The stated goal should be that eventually the student starts volunteering to answer questions in class without any assistance from the teacher. For a short time, this may look like the student is only participating when he is confident of the answer, but teachers should continue to encourage students to answer questions when they are less sure or not confident at all.

Participating in Classroom Discussions

A common report card comment for socially anxious students is that they "need to work on class participation," and participating in classroom discussions is a key part of that. To assist students in contributing to classroom discussions, teachers often have several strategies. We recommend highlighting for teachers some of the following ideas and asking them to share additional strategies they have found successful. First, teachers can pose a discussion question to the class and have students initially discuss their thoughts with classmates sitting next to them. Afterwards, the pairs can be asked to share their thoughts about the topic. After sharing with their partner, a socially anxious student might work up to being the spokesperson for the pair or a small group. Teachers might also assign particular roles in group projects to reduce the likelihood that a socially anxious student either does not participate at all or ends up carrying the majority of the workload. To challenge a socially anxious student to practice assertiveness skills, recommend that teachers assign her to be a group leader for a project.

Furthermore, many teachers skillfully use online discussion boards to assist students with participation, and it can be helpful to highlight the benefits of such technology. Students might be required to pose questions or respond to other students online before class. Explain to teachers that in order to help generalize this participation into the physical classroom setting, teachers can then require students to expand on a question or comment during in-class discussions the following day. This allows socially anxious students to gauge their classmates' thoughts and ideas about a topic to prepare for how they would like to respond in class. As with asking and answering questions, the goal is for students to eventually participate in classroom discussions spontaneously. With these strategies, however, teachers can allow students to set smaller goals for participation, as long as the student continually demonstrates progress by increasing participation throughout the year.

Classroom Presentations

Presentations are also a significant stressor for many students with social anxiety. To help socially anxious students face this fear, we recommend allowing students opportunities to practice their presentation beforehand. For in-class group or paired presentations, teachers may include a short practice session the day before, during which the class can break into their groups and rehearse. For individual presentations, we recommend that teachers pair students up to practice their presentations in front of only one or two peers first. This helps to make presentations feel more manageable by having students work up a miniature fear ladder that gradually increases in difficulty without allowing an opportunity to avoid the presentation all together. For students with extreme social anxiety, suggest that a teacher allow the student to briefly practice her presentation individually with the teacher before or after school prior to giving it to the whole class.

Additional Strategies

Some students also fear walking into a classroom full of students or performing in front of their peers, for example by volunteering to write on the whiteboard or to help the teacher with a demonstration. They may be anxious about other students watching them or about being the center of attention, because they fear public embarrassment. To help a student get used to peers watching him, we recommend that the teacher and student plan for him to walk in 2–3 minutes late to class or to leave the class in the middle to go to the bathroom. To draw even more attention to a student, teachers might also arrange with a student to volunteer for a demonstration or to complete a problem on the board. To initially make this task more manageable for some students, teachers can provide the student with the question and answer that she will be writing on the board. Remind teachers that this type of support should be faded over time until participation and classroom engagement is more spontaneous and flexible.

Encourage Socialization with Prosocial Peers

We recommend next explaining to teachers that some fears can be difficult to target directly, such as interacting socially with other peers during classroom downtime or group activities. These types of unstructured interactions are especially challenging for students with social anxiety, but they are incredibly important for increasing exposure to social situations and challenging negative cognitions related to anxiety. We recommend telling teachers that to the extent that they are aware of the social dynamic in their classroom, they can provide socially anxious students with opportunities to meet and make friends with prosocial or patient peers. One simple but sly technique is to mindfully seat socially anxious students next to friendly, kind peers. Varying the seating chart periodically also allows socially anxious students to engage with a variety of classmates.

Encourage teachers to also intentionally assign pairs and groups for projects or presentations in a similar fashion, rather than letting students choose their own arrangements. Like varied seating arrangements, assigning groups creates opportunities for socially anxious students to interact with different (and preferably kind and sociable) peers. Additionally, many students feel a lot of anxiety when they must form their own groups. Particularly at the beginning of the school year, teacher-assigned groups can alleviate some anticipatory fears about not having a group to work with and some of the pressure associated with asking peers to join a group. As the school year progresses and socially anxious students interact with more classmates, teachers may begin to include opportunities for students to find their own groups or choose their own seating arrangements.

Reinforce Brave Behavior

Many teachers are aware that one of the most effective ways to shape behavior is through positive reinforcement. Quite simply, if students do something that you like, tell them so they want to do it again! For adolescents, this most often consists of verbal, labeled praise. Explain to teachers that for socially anxious students, teachers should specifically praise them when they take risks and face their fears. Encourage teachers to include written notes on assignments being returned in class, such as on project or presentation grading rubrics. They might also send the student an encouraging e-mail if they notice increased class participation. Additionally, explain to teachers that giving intentional verbal praise in class can be helpful for reinforcing socially anxious students, but caution them against going overboard and accidentally embarrassing the student. Providing an illustrative example can also be helpful. For instance, Juan took a risk in chemistry class and answered the teacher's question even though he was visibly unsure of his answer and prefaced his response with "I might be wrong, but . . ." His teacher noticed his brave behavior and praised him: "That's right, Juan. Thank you for taking a chance even though you weren't sure. Excellent work."

We recommend emphasizing for teachers the importance of being specific about which behaviors they are praising. In the example above, highlight how Juan's teacher didn't thank him for getting the answer right. She thanked him for participating even when he was unsure. Juan just happened to be correct on that question. We recommend drawing attention to the fact that praising students is easy when their achievement is high, but it can be more of a struggle to reinforce students when they answer incorrectly.

> **Praise students for effort, not outcome!**

Especially for socially anxious students who have perfectionistic expectations or who fear embarrassment, explain to teachers that rewarding student efforts and attempts is incredibly important. You can ask teachers to rewrite what the exchange between Juan and his teacher might have looked like if he had answered incorrectly. Because his teacher praised his efforts rather than his answer, it actually does not need to be very different. She might have said, "That's *not quite* right, Juan, *but* thank you for taking a chance even though you weren't sure. Excellent work." Explain that by adding only three words, Juan's teacher could communicate that the answer was incorrect and still praise him for his efforts. Helping teachers shift the ways they praise students can help them positively reinforce socially anxious (and *all*!) students. We recommend encouraging teachers to apply the motto "Praise effort, not outcome!"

PUTTING IT ALL TOGETHER: WHAT DOES IT LOOK LIKE?

We recommend that counselors provide teachers with an example of what it might look like to systematically help a student face her fears. Using the story of Harper below can help illustrate how to implement these recommended strategies:

Harper was a socially anxious sophomore in high school. In advance of a particular presentation, Harper asked her teacher, Ms. Simmons, if she could write a research paper instead of giving a short 5-minute presentation. Ms. Simmons *recognized* Harper's social anxiety and chose to *empathize* with her first. Ms. Simmons reflected back, "It sounds like you are feeling nervous about talking in front of the class." By reflecting back Harper's anxiety, Ms. Simmons was able to open up a conversation about anxiety, ways of coping, and strategies they could use to make presenting easier without allowing Harper to avoid the presentation all together. She understood that if she allowed Harper to simply avoid the presentation, Harper's anxiety around presentations would only increase in the long term. Instead of letting Harper write a paper, Ms. Simmons helped Harper to *face her fears* and gave her the opportunity to practice the presentation with only one student ahead of time.

The day before the presentations, Ms. Simmons set aside 10 minutes in class and paired students up to practice their presentations one last time. Ms. Simmons purposely paired Harper with Ebony, a particularly *positive and prosocial peer*. In practicing, Harper was able to challenge some of her anxious thoughts, such as "Everyone will think my topic is stupid" and "I will completely mess up." Having experienced some success, Harper was able to move up her fear ladder and complete her presentation in front of the whole class. After Harper completed her presentation in class, Ms. Simmons praised her by saying, "That was a very interesting topic, Harper. Thank you for sharing with us." Additionally, Ms. Simmons wrote a personal note on Harper's grading rubric *reinforcing her brave behavior:* "I'm proud of you for pushing yourself to present this to the whole class even though you were nervous about it."

SUPPORTING SCHOOL ENGAGEMENT

Teachers also play a crucial role in developing the school culture and encouraging student engagement with opportunities outside of the classroom. In many schools, it is the teachers who act as coaches and volunteer their time as advisers for extracurricular activities. We recommend highlighting that because of their generous involvement teachers are uniquely positioned to foster and support school engagement for socially anxious students, who are often either not involved or minimally involved in the greater school community. As teachers recognize the talents and interests of their students, encourage them to make a conscious effort to invite socially anxious students to join certain clubs, connect students with advisers of other groups, or nominate students for leadership positions within different activities. For instance, an English teacher might recognize a talented writer in his class: "Antwon, the last poem you wrote was beautiful. I'd love for you to submit it to the next edition of the literary and art magazine, and I'd love to have you join the editorial staff." Similarly, a physical education teacher might praise a student's athletic ability or work ethic: "Carolyn, I saw the effort you put in while running laps today. I'd love that kind of work ethic and persistence on the track team. Please consider trying out."

Reaching out to students and fostering their talents is something that teachers do on a daily basis already. We recommend highlighting this and expressing appreciation for their hard work, while emphasizing how, for a socially anxious student who fears taking risks or being judged by others, the personal invitation from a teacher can be a crucial step in helping her pursue her interests. Teachers should be encouraged to provide socially anxious students with genuine praise for their achievements and efforts, and then link those strengths to new opportunities for the students to try. We also find it helpful to suggest that teachers connect socially anxious students to a peer in a club or recommend attending activities with a friend. Teachers who are club advisers can also introduce socially anxious students in initial meetings or assign them to a particular club project with a prosocial peer. In this way, teachers can be supportive of students and help set them up for success while still requiring them to take action to face their fears.

COMMON CHALLENGES TO ENGAGING TEACHERS

It Is Difficult to Schedule Faculty Meetings

While we recommend faculty meetings or professional development workshops to best communicate information to teachers, we encourage counselors to be creative in disseminating information based on what is feasible in their schools. Instead of a faculty meeting, some might video-record informational or training presentations to disseminate via e-mail or online school web pages. At a minimum, however, counselors may provide teachers with educational documents including brochures or handouts, such as Handout 15.1 and Handout 15.2 provided with this chapter. In addition, when working with an individual student, it can be especially beneficial to reach out to that student's teachers to provide them with tailored classroom strategies for that particular student.

Teachers Report They Are Too Busy

With increasing curriculum demands and increasing requirements for standardized testing, some teachers may report that they are already too busy or that they cannot realistically implement strategies to help their students. In these instances, it is beneficial to highlight the academic strategies related to classroom participation and presentations, as well as to focus on how these strategies are designed to improve students' academic performance. For teachers who are incredibly resistant, we recommend emphasizing recognition of social anxiety and referring students to counselors when teachers notice students having difficulties.

LAUREN'S STORY

With Lauren's permission, Ms. Hillman checked in briefly with her history, language arts, and math teachers. They all agreed that Lauren was an excellent student but that she was hesitant to speak up and difficult to get to know. Ms. Hillman shared that Lauren is extremely anxious about class presentations, which all the teachers had already noticed. In an individual conversation with Lauren's history teacher, the teacher explained, "I usually give my students the option of writing an essay instead of presenting and Lauren always chooses the essay." Ms. Hillman told Lauren's teacher that she had been working with Lauren to practice presentations and gently explained the importance of encouraging presentations rather than allowing avoidance. She asked the teacher whether she would permit Lauren to initially give a presentation to her individually for practice and feedback, followed by a presentation in front of the class. The teacher agreed and asked what else she could do to help. Ms. Hillman said that Lauren was making an effort to participate more in class and asked if, as a first step, the teacher would assist Lauren by providing questions that would be posed in class with their answers ahead of time. This would help Lauren get used to speaking up in class, and she could then proceed to answering questions with less certainty and more limited preparation. Ms. Hillman then had similar conversations with the language arts and math teachers regarding participation. She provided all teachers with Handout 15.1 and Handout 15.2 as a reference. Although one teacher was not receptive and said she did not have the time to provide questions ahead of time, Lauren reported positive responses to her increased participation and better interactions with all teachers.

CHAPTER SUMMARY

- Unhelpful strategies that teachers sometimes use for dealing with student social anxiety include permitting avoidance, giving excessive reassurance, or providing overzealous praise.

- By *recognizing* social anxiety and actively *empathizing* with students, teachers can create and foster a supportive classroom environment where students can face their fears.

- Rather than allowing socially anxious students to completely avoid challenges, teachers can adjust assignments to make tasks more manageable so students can *face their fears*.

- Intentionally *pairing students with prosocial peers* gently provides socially anxious students opportunities to meet and make friends, and practice interacting with classmates.

- *Positively reinforcing brave behavior* increases the likelihood that socially anxious students will engage in classroom and social interactions.

- Teachers can *support school engagement* by inviting socially anxious students to join activities, connecting them with group advisers, or nominating them for various positions.

Common Observable Signs of Social Anxiety in the Classroom

Teachers are in a good position to identify social anxiety because the classroom provides several social and performance situations that more clearly expose students' fears. The key is knowing what to look for! Below are common observable signs that could be indicative of social anxiety in your students.

- Avoids eye contact with teachers or peers

- Appears quiet and speaks softly or mumbles, making it difficult to hear

- Limited or reluctant participation in class (e.g., does not raise hand, ask questions, provide opinions, or contribute to discussions)

- Does not talk or exhibits discomfort when talking to peers during class downtime

- Appears particularly nervous or does not provide opinions during group projects
  o Might make avoidant requests: "Can I work alone instead of with a group?"

- In group projects, difficulties with assertiveness may be demonstrated by not taking leadership positions or unfairly carrying the majority of the workload

- Appears particularly nervous during presentations or avoids them altogether (i.e., does behind-the scenes work on group presentations so others take speaking roles)
  o Might make avoidant requests: "Can I go last for the presentation?" or "Can I write a report instead of presenting?"

- Will not ask a teacher for help or assistance with schoolwork even when experiencing noticeable difficulties

- Exhibits physical symptoms (e.g., shaky hands, shaky voice, sweating, or flushed face)

Classroom Strategies to Help Socially Anxious Students

- **Actively empathize with students:** Let your student know you understand it is difficult to face fears. Review with her why facing her fears is important for accomplishing *her* goals, and remind her that facing fears will get easier the more she practices.

- **Help students face their classroom fears:** Rather than allowing a socially anxious student to avoid tasks that are hard for him, work with the student to adjust tasks to make them more manageable. Below are some suggestions. Frame these challenges as ways to begin approaching, rather than avoiding, feared situations.
  - **Asking questions in class:** Provide students with questions or help them plan questions to ask at specific times.
  - **Answering questions in class:** Provide students with answers or the questions they will be asked in advance so they can get used to raising their hand and speaking in front of the class.
  - **Participating in classroom discussions:** Allow students to discuss in small groups or pairs first, or use online discussion boards, to facilitate classroom engagement.
  - **Classroom presentations:** Allow students to practice presentations in advance.
  - **Walking into the classroom late:** Plan with the student to walk in late or leave the classroom in the middle of the lesson.
  - **Volunteering for various classroom tasks:** Plan with a student to volunteer for a classroom demonstration or complete a problem on the board in front of the class. Make the task easier by giving her the answer, if needed.

- **Encourage socialization with prosocial peers:** Mindfully seat students next to friendly, kind peers to encourage socialization or pair them with prosocial peers for group work.

- **Reinforce brave behavior:** Provide socially anxious adolescents with verbal, labeled praise when they display brave behavior. This can be in the form of subtle verbal praise during class, written notes on assignments, or e-mails. Remember: **Praise effort, not outcome!!!**

- **Support school engagement:** Invite students to join clubs or school activities and facilitate their engagement by introducing them to the group, pairing them with friendly group members, or assigning them specific tasks or roles in the group.

PART IV

OTHER PRACTICAL AND CLINICAL CONSIDERATIONS

CHAPTER 16

The Nuts and Bolts of Helping Anxious Students at School
Putting It All Together

This chapter is intended to serve as a practical how-to guide for implementing the strategies described throughout the book. We provide instruction about the logistical aspects of procedures that are not discussed in previous chapters, including enlisting support within the school environment, obtaining buy-in from students and parents, forming groups, organizing meetings, maintaining and addressing confidentiality, and taking advantage of the school environment for optimizing interventions. The bulk of this chapter focuses on suggestions and tips for delivering intervention strategies in a group format because this modality may be the most optimal for students with social anxiety and is probably the most time-efficient for counselors. While the initial formation of a group can be logistically challenging, once established, groups require less time and effort because they allow you to work simultaneously with multiple students and provide convenient access to peers for practicing social skills and other strategies. However, general guidelines that may be employed with both group and individual implementation are provided.

ENLISTING SUPPORT FROM WITHIN THE SCHOOL

School Administrators

Groups are routinely used for supporting students in schools. School counselors, psychologists, and social workers are expected to facilitate various types of groups (e.g., social skills, peer leadership, children of divorce, grief/loss). Yet, with many competing demands for personnel resources and student instructional time, you might experience some resistance from school administrators when requesting to provide a group for students with social anxiety.

As discussed in Chapters 1, 2, and 15, administrators and other stakeholders may not initially understand or appreciate the extent to which social anxiety can negatively impact students and their school experience. Therefore, the first step in enlisting support from school administrators is to educate them on the value of implementing school intervention for socially anxious students. This can be achieved by providing psychoeducation about social anxiety and its associated impairment and long-term consequences (e.g., educational underachievement) as described in the chapters mentioned above. We suggest highlighting the ways in which social avoidance interferes with academic performance and school engagement. It might be helpful to explain that the intervention teaches skills to address these specific problems, such as participating in class, speaking in front of peers, approaching teachers for help, collaborating with classmates, joining school activities, and speaking to school personnel such as principals, teachers, and counselors. In addition, counselors may want to provide school administrators with empirical articles that demonstrate the effectiveness of cognitive and behavioral strategies for social anxiety (See Fisher et al., 2004; Masia Warner et al., 2005, 2007, 2016). Depending on your school's administrative structure and policies, to whom you pitch the program and how you should present it may vary. Some counselors may find that a formal presentation to a team of administrators or a written proposal about running a group is necessary, while others may be able to schedule one individual, informal meeting with a direct supervisor or administrator.

> **Emphasize practical and academic benefits of your school-based program.**

Teachers and School Staff

Once you have gained approval from school administrators to implement the program, it is critical to obtain buy-in from teachers and other school professionals (e.g., counselors, paraprofessionals, administrative assistants, coaches) who have daily interaction with students. These professionals are essential resources for identifying students who may benefit from intervention. In addition, teachers who understand the benefit of school social anxiety treatment are more likely to cooperate if you wish to administer social anxiety screening measures (described in Chapter 3) during the class period for a particular subject or if you need to meet with students during class time. Furthermore, fostering acceptance and enthusiasm within the school environment will produce helpful allies when it comes time to design and implement meaningful exposures.

As discussed in Chapter 15, we suggest requesting time during a faculty meeting or professional development activity to introduce the rationale for helping students with social anxiety and to inform faculty that you will be forming a group. Again, highlighting the tangible ways that intervention will improve engagement and performance in the classroom will go a long way in convincing teachers that this program is worth any potential inconvenience it may cause. This initial meeting is also a good opportunity to describe the type of student who may benefit from the program. Have teachers brainstorm which of their students may fit this profile and solicit nominations of students. You may also wish to communicate the specific ways in which you will ask teachers to be involved, emphasizing that you will limit the burden as much as possible. Many teachers will welcome this collaboration because they want to engage socially anxious students but have been at a loss regarding how to do so. When this occurs, offer some suggestions outlined in Chapter 15 or provide them with a copy of the chapter. However, expect that some teachers may be skeptical at first, especially if you are asking to usurp class time. It is important to keep in mind that teachers have many other pressures that may supersede dealing with students who often sit in the back of the room quietly and avoid eye contact. Yet, we have found that most teachers change their views once they have observed students becoming more engaged in their classrooms. Often, these teachers will share positive experiences with others at school, adding to the significance and credibility of your efforts.

OBTAINING BUY-IN FROM PARENTS AND STUDENTS

Communicating with Parents

Once you have earned the support of school administrators and colleagues and determined that a particular student might benefit from intervention, we suggest first reaching out to the student's parents. Depending on your school policy, you may require explicit parental consent in order to provide this type of intervention. Therefore, it is advisable to learn whether parents will be agreeable before presenting the option to students. Additionally, because these students will be very anxious about discussing their social fears with you and may try to avoid doing so, having supportive parents who encourage them to participate may increase the likelihood that the student will agree.

Communication with parents may include telephone calls, letters, e-mails, or invitations to in-person meetings to explain that students have indicated some difficulties in social situations during school (e.g., classroom, lunchroom) and may benefit from a school program that you will be offering. It is critical to present these strategies to parents in a way that emphasizes the academic benefits of learning skills related to public speaking, class participation, and school engagement. For example, when promoting these intervention strategies, use phrases such as "In this program, your child will learn how to be more confident in performance situations such as public speaking, will learn how to better advocate for herself and her academic needs, will become more comfortable in social situations, and will practice assertiveness skills." Presenting the everyday, practical skills and benefits may help students and parents to invest in the process of treating social anxiety and to feel more comfortable about some missed class time. Chapter 13 provides additional detail for educating parents about social anxiety and the advantages of intervention. Over time as more students benefit from this program in your school and as more families become aware of your school's resources for helping their child, parents may contact you to refer their child when they recognize his struggles with social anxiety.

Parents will likely have many logistical questions or concerns about how student participation will affect academic commitments even when they fully buy into the program and potential benefits for their child. For example, they may have concerns about their child missing class time or about their child not having time to participate in other after-school activities. They may also worry about confidentiality and stigma, namely whether school staff and peers will be aware of students' participation, and what that might mean for their child (e.g., will their child be teased for participating?). Anticipating and adequately addressing these concerns is crucial for obtaining buy-in from parents. Suggestions on how to address scheduling and confidentiality concerns are presented later in this chapter.

Getting Commitment from Students

Now it is time to talk to your students! We recommend meeting with students individually so that you can tailor your discussion to their specific anxiety symptoms, and so that they feel comfortable asking questions and expressing concerns or fears they may have. Provide education about social anxiety and a description of what their participation will involve. It can be helpful to review the impairment that students previously identified on screening measures or through the assessment process. Then, highlight how this program's strategies will address their specific concerns (e.g., making new friends, being able to try out for a role in the school play, interviewing for a job or college admission).

After presenting an overview, gauge how students are feeling about the prospect of participating. Expect students to respond with a range of reactions. Some will be relieved and eager to accept help, while others will deny that they find social situations challenging and may be tough to win over. Most students will find the idea of a group more anxiety provoking than meeting with you individually. However, some will appreciate the opportunity to meet peers experiencing similar struggles.

For students who appear hesitant, we recommend acknowledging their fear and predicting that discussing their social anxiety in a group of peers will be difficult and uncomfortable. However, remind them that every group member will be nervous and unlikely to judge them because they are experiencing similar feelings. It may also help to inform students that they will not be expected to speak up in the initial meetings, although increasing participation will be encouraged over time. This is a good analogy for the program as a whole, in that it is effective by pushing students outside of their comfort zone, albeit in a very gradual manner.

If students are still reluctant or noncommittal, we suggest obtaining a commitment to attend three to four meetings to gain a better idea of what the intervention would entail. You may want to emphasize that "sampling" the program will allow them to make a decision based on experience rather than fear of the unknown. The reason we recommend encouraging attendance at more than one or two meetings is because students will hopefully feel more comfortable as they become more familiar with you and the other group members. The first couple of meetings tend to be the most awkward because most students are nervous and few participate. It may also be helpful to offer students the opportunity to meet with you individually a couple of times prior to the start of the group to increase their comfort level with discussing their social fears. Keep in mind that you should try to schedule the first group soon after gaining students' commitments because if too much time passes, their anxiety may convince them that they no longer wish to participate. In other words, strike while the iron is hot! (See Appendix 16.1: Sample Script for Gaining Commitment from a

Student for a sample conversation in which a school professional encourages a student to commit to trying the group.)

PUTTING A GROUP TOGETHER

We understand that you may or may not have the luxury of carefully selecting which students would function well together in a group. However, we have found it helpful to consider the following factors when forming a group.

Number of Students

We recommend small groups of approximately four to six students per group. This is the ideal number for each member to get adequate time and attention while allowing for group discussion, feedback, and role-play partners. It is wise to invite a slightly larger number of students (seven to eight) to join in anticipation that some will decline participation from the beginning and others may decide to discontinue after a few meetings.

Age of Students

A narrow age range is preferable. As a general rule, 1 or 2 years in either direction is advised (e.g., 9th and 10th graders). We advise against having freshmen and seniors in the same group whenever possible because they face different social situations and may perceive the group as irrelevant to them. For instance, seniors may be more focused on job interviews or navigating the transition to college, while freshmen are still adjusting to high school. Furthermore, younger students may experience much older students as intimidating.

Student Gender

We suggest avoiding situations in which there is only one student of a specific gender in the group. However, you may also consider gender on a case-by-case basis, as some students have told us that they actually feel more comfortable or less judged around students of another gender.

Anxiety Severity

We recommend varying the level of severity and impairment in any given group. That is, we suggest mixing students who have mild to moderate anxiety, or who only experience anxiety in performance situations, with the students who are struggling with more severe and pervasive social anxiety. A group with this composition is beneficial for students on both ends of the continuum. Students with milder symptoms will feel helpful and more confident, and more anxious students will observe peer models who may already be facing some fears despite distress. Having students with varying levels of anxiety severity also helps the group as a whole to function better because some of students will be more talkative and willing to take risks. In our experience, even when the most anxious students do not appear to be actively participating, they are usually engaged and learning vicariously through other students. Hearing students describe similar experiences and observing them face their fears can be motivating.

ORGANIZING GROUP MEETINGS

Once your group is formed, it is time to begin scheduling meetings!

Where?

This may seem silly to mention, but it is important to reserve an appropriate room for group meetings. The most important consideration is that the room be private, meaning students or staff will not frequently pass by in the hallway or look inside. We have sometimes had to cover windows with paper temporarily to increase privacy. There should also be adequate space to move around, as we want to encourage physical movement and realistic role plays. Desks are not necessary, but if you use a classroom we recommend arranging the desks in a circle or other configuration that does not resemble a traditional classroom. If you are meeting with students individually, it is fine to simply use your office if it meets the privacy criteria.

How Often?

The number of meetings required to implement all the strategies described in this book will vary based on your experience and the composition of your group. As a general guideline, we suggest 10 to 14 group meetings along with one or two individual meetings with group members to construct students' fear ladders (see Chapter 11). If feasible, we also suggest one to two meetings with parents (see Chapter 13) and two to four social events (see Chapter 14). At least five to six group meetings should be devoted to conducting exposures. We suggest aiming for weekly meetings when possible, although some weeks will inevitably be missed due to holidays, snow days, or testing periods. Toward the end of the program, consider spacing out groups so that you are meeting every other week to allow more time for students to practice outside of group.

When?

In general, we recommend holding group meetings for the length of one class period during the school day rather than after school for several reasons. First, students are more likely to attend meetings during the day, partially because daytime meetings are more difficult for nervous students to avoid than are after-school meetings where students can head home quickly after the bell rings. Given that you will have their course schedule, you will also know where students are in the building and will be able to remind them of their weekly group more easily. Additionally, some students have important commitments after school that they cannot or will not want to miss, while others may have logistical concerns related to transportation. Finally, it is also easier to plan exposure exercises that take advantage of the school environment during the course of the day.

Obviously, some students (as well as school administrators and teachers) will be hesitant to lose instructional time. If you are meeting with students individually rather than in a group, it should be possible to schedule meetings during that student's nonacademic periods. Keep in mind that, while convenient, lunch is not advisable because we do not want students to miss social opportunities. When running groups, we have rotated the meeting period each week so that students are not consistently missing the same class. This model limits missed instructional time and also helps to maintain confidentiality because students' classmates are less likely to notice excessive absences from any particular class. However, if this is not acceptable to your school community, you may want to explore forming a school club that meets after school.

How Will Students Remember?

Providing a group schedule at or before the first meeting is useful, especially for parents. Students will still require weekly reminders that are subtle and will not be experienced as stigmatizing. We suggest using whatever mode of communication is typical for your school. In our experience, written guidance passes delivered during homeroom have worked well. Students receive these types of passes for a variety of reasons, including scheduling future-semester courses, so they usually do not draw unnecessary attention to group members. If you are meeting after school, we still recommend sending subtle reminders or passes on the day of the meeting during homeroom or during last period to encourage attendance.

ADDRESSING AND MAINTAINING CONFIDENTIALITY

Addressing group rules and expectations is important in any group, but acknowledging the specific concerns that socially anxious teenagers may have about participating in a group is critical. Given the complexities of maintaining confidentiality in a group that is run within the school setting, you should discuss confidentiality with students when you initially invite them to join the group, and devote time to reviewing these issues at the first group meeting. Adequate attention must be paid to the following general issues, even if specific guidelines may vary based on your individual school policies.

What Will Others Know?

Students will be concerned that others will know they are participating, will worry about what types of details will be disclosed, and will question what others' impressions will be. When groups take place during the school day and students are missing instructional time to participate, the students' teachers and usually an administrator (e.g., the principal) must be aware that they are participating because they will require an excused absence. However, you may clarify to concerned students and parents that specific details about the students' activities during the group, for example, what specific situations are on their fear ladder, will not be shared with these adults. Students may also be concerned about peers noticing that they are absent from classes on a regular basis. It can be helpful to assist students in challenging how realistic these fears are as well as brainstorming some possible responses if questioned by peers.

Will Group Members Talk about Each Other Outside of Group?

As in other groups, all students must commit to keeping what others say and do within the group confidential. Each student must feel safe and free to be vulnerable in expressing his fears in order to take risks and confront feared situations. We recommend having each student sign a confidentiality contract that reflects this commitment, and have provided one option for counselors to use (See Handout 16.1: Confidentiality Contract). Some counselors may wish to create their own customized confidentiality contract that addresses issues unique to their school or their group members.

Always emphasize and adequately address group confidentiality.

We also recommend addressing what students may tell their parents about the group. The guiding principle is that students can talk to anyone they want about what they are personally learning or doing in group as an individual but should not mention other group members by name or talk about what others are doing in the group. Generally, we have found that because socially anxious students are so concerned about their own privacy, they are not likely to discuss other group members or the activities of the group.

How Will Students Interact with Each Other Outside the Group?

Students sometimes want to know how group members should act toward each other in the school setting outside of the group in order to maintain confidentiality about group membership. Within a school setting, it is more likely than not that students will know other group members before starting the program. They may even be in groups with friends, acquaintances, or teammates. Encourage students who regularly spend time with one another outside of the group to maintain their usual relationship while refraining from talking about the group or other group members outside of your actual meetings. In large schools where students may not know other group members prior to beginning the program, some students may worry that if they say hello to another group member in the presence of other peers, someone may ask how they know each other. A discussion at the beginning of the program about how members "know each other" can be helpful to address these concerns. Students can decide on any "story" they want, but encourage generic statements like "We met after school," as these are usually sufficient and easier to remember than a long, complicated or made-up story.

How Will Students Interact with Group Leaders Outside the Group?

Students may also worry about how they should interact with you as the group leader outside of the group. In large schools, students may have concerns about their peers questioning how the student knows you. In small schools, however, students may be very familiar with all the school counselors who provide scheduling help each semester, and so how they "know" you will not be their main concern. Rather, they may be afraid that you will approach them about the group when they are with peers or that you will somehow disclose their participation to their friends. A good solution is to tell students that you will not greet them unless they greet you first and that you will never discuss the group or their participation in the group with them in public (e.g., hallways, lunchroom) or when other peers are present. Students may have additional questions or concerns depending on your school culture, which we recommend you adequately address based on the guiding principles above.

EXPOSURES IN THE SCHOOL ENVIRONMENT

Now that you are past the awkward first meetings and have taught students important skills, it is time to start planning exposures! Below are some logistical tips for implementing the types of exposures discussed in Chapter 12 that optimize use of the school environment.

Know Where People Are!

This may sound obvious, but knowing where specific people are when you are planning an exposure will save you precious time and prevent missed opportunities. For example, if you have prepped a student to go speak to her physics teacher and she has finally worked up the courage to do so, you want to make sure that your student can easily find her teacher. We have found it invaluable to have a master schedule that includes listings of all classes, rooms, and teaching assignments throughout the day. This information will allow you to choose a teacher who will be easily accessible at the time you need them before you begin the exposure. This also allows for flexibility when you need to adjust the difficulty level of an exposure or quickly find a Plan B!

Plan Ahead!

We advise speaking with teachers ahead of time to ensure they will be available and accessible. This also allows you to prepare the teacher for the exposure, given that early on you may want the teacher to respond extremely positively to your anxious student. Planning ahead is also useful if you want your student to speak with administrators, coaches, or other school adults. You may also need to plan ahead to reserve specific areas of the school, such as the auditorium to practice public speaking, the music room for a student to play her instrument, or the cafeteria to role-play a lunch situation. Advance planning is necessary for carrying out a variety of other exposures and can include bringing a list of store phone numbers to make phone calls, written materials for students to read aloud, or props for wearing something embarrassing. Groups are hectic and time flies, so help yourself by managing the logistical aspects ahead of time whenever possible.

Phones Allowed!

Some exposures, such as calling stores or businesses, will require the use of a telephone. More specifically, some exposures will require students to use their cell phones in order to text friends, extend invitations, or post on social media. Therefore, it is important for you to let students know that you would like them to bring their phones and use them when instructed during exposures. Most students would be thrilled to hear that phones are allowed during your meetings; however, you may find that some students "forget" their phones or have other excuses related to phones not being allowed because they are avoiding the exposures associated with the phone. Of course, be sure to gain approval from school administrators prior to these exposure sessions and assure students that special circumstances have been arranged for group.

CHAPTER SUMMARY

- Obtain permission and support from school administrators by providing psychoeducation about the practical and academic benefits of treating social anxiety.

- Proactively address parent and student fears about confidentiality and missed classwork to increase buy-in and participation in the program.

- Consider practical information when creating groups of students, such as the number of students, age of the students, student gender, and anxiety severity.

- Be sure to carefully plan where, how often, and when groups will meet. Remind students of scheduled groups in advance of meeting times.

- Always begin a group program with a conversation about the group rules for confidentiality.

- Plan logistical details of exposures in advance, such as where important personnel (e.g., teachers) will be, and remind students that phones are allowed!

Sample Script for Gaining Commitment from a Student

SCHOOL PROFESSIONAL: Now that you know a little bit about the group and how it would help you to feel more comfortable in social and performance situations like [add specific situations], what are your thoughts about participating?

STUDENT: I'm not sure.

SCHOOL PROFESSIONAL: Is there anything specific you are worried about?

STUDENT: I don't know.

SCHOOL PROFESSIONAL: I know it might seem uncomfortable to join a group of unfamiliar peers, since you've told me that speaking to peers makes you really nervous. I can understand that it is tough to talk to them in general, never mind to share personal things, like how you are sometimes uncomfortable in social situations. Is this part of what makes you unsure about participating?

STUDENT: Yes.

SCHOOL PROFESSIONAL: That makes sense. But it is important for you to remember that everyone in the group is in the same boat. So if anyone understands how you feel, it's them. I don't think they will be judging you because they feel the same way.

STUDENT: Yeah, I guess that's true. How many people are going to be in the group?

SCHOOL PROFESSIONAL: We are still talking to everyone that we think might be a good fit for the group, so I'm not 100% sure, but we usually include about four to six students.

STUDENT: What grade are they in? Am I going to know them?

SCHOOL PROFESSIONAL: We will have juniors and seniors in this group. And I don't know, you might recognize a couple. Unfortunately, I can't tell you who is going to be in the group because it's my job to keep the group confidential. Just like I wouldn't tell anyone that you were thinking of participating. The only way to find out is to come to the first group meeting.

STUDENT: Ugh, I wish I could know for sure.

SCHOOL PROFESSIONAL: I know, but remember how we talked about how that is part of the process? The best way we know to help teenagers feel less anxious is by having them slowly and gradually face the situations that make them the most nervous.

STUDENT: Yeah, but it is still going to be really hard.

SCHOOL PROFESSIONAL: You're right, it is going to feel difficult at first. But remember, you're the one who told me that you want to get better at this so that you can be prepared to make new friends going forward, like in college.

STUDENT: True . . . So if I decide to do it, how does it work? I don't want anyone outside of the group to know about this.

SCHOOL PROFESSIONAL: Good question. We will be meeting once per week during the school day. Groups will take place during a different period each week so that you don't miss the same class more than a couple of times. We will provide you with a schedule ahead of time and will send regular guidance passes to your homeroom each day we have a meeting.

STUDENT: So I will be missing class? What about my teachers?

SCHOOL PROFESSIONAL: The principal and your teachers will know that you are participating in a guidance program, but that is it. We will not share details about what you say or do in the group, unless you want us to.

STUDENT: No, I don't want them to know.

SCHOOL PROFESSIONAL: Okay. Is there anything else you want to ask me about?

STUDENT: I guess that is it.

SCHOOL PROFESSIONAL: So what do you think?

STUDENT: I guess I will come check out the first meeting and see what it's like.

SCHOOL PROFESSIONAL: That's great, I'm proud of you for pushing yourself to make the hard choice. I think it will be worth it. Can I suggest one thing though?

STUDENT: What?

SCHOOL PROFESSIONAL: Can we make a deal that you will come to at least the first three meetings before making a final decision?

STUDENT: Why three?

SCHOOL PROFESSIONAL: Just because I think the first meeting will probably feel somewhat uncomfortable for you. But as we talked about, these things usually feel easier the more we get used to doing them. Also remember that everyone is going to feel nervous that first day, including me!! So I wouldn't want you to judge it based on that first meeting.

STUDENT: Okay, I'll try.

SCHOOL PROFESSIONAL: Okay, great. I think you're making a good decision about this. I really think it is going to help you meet some of your goals about college. I will let you know when we finalize the schedule.

Confidentiality Contract

1. This instrument is a contract for confidentiality among the members of the group whose purpose is to increase confidence in social or performance situations.

2. Each member of this group acknowledges the need to keep personal information shared in the group, including names of other group members, **private**.

3. For the purpose of this group, any information provided by a group member to the group about him- or herself should be considered personal and private information.

4. In order to become a group member and retain membership, each member must agree to protect this private information. Information gathered about other members of the group cannot be shared with anyone else. That information shall remain with the member and not be shared with any other person.

5. If you agree with these procedures, please acknowledge this by signing below:

_____   _____

Student signature   Date

_____   _____

Group leader signature   Date

CHAPTER 17

Applying Intervention Skills to Other Anxiety Concerns

Anxiety disorders often occur together or in clusters (Merikangas & Swanson, 2009). There-fore, adolescents with social anxiety may endorse other types of fears or general worries that co-occur with social concerns. In addition, once their social anxiety improves, some-times other anxieties may linger, become more central, or also require attention. The good news is that many of the strategies described in this book can be utilized to address other types of anxiety. While this book focuses on treating social anxiety in school, this chapter provides an overview of how to apply the main techniques, namely realistic thinking and exposure, to help students with other fears and worries. Understanding how these skills can be applied to other anxiety presentations provides school personnel with additional tools for addressing a variety of student concerns. We briefly review some common presentations of anxiety at school and highlight feasible, specific strategies that can be implemented within the school setting. This chapter is not designed to be a comprehensive review of treatments for all anxiety disorders; rather it describes additional anxious behaviors that are likely to cause impairment in the school setting, such as specific phobias, generalized anxiety and worry, test anxiety, and school refusal. We also discuss referring students to community resources when additional treatment or more intensive services are required.

HOW IS ANXIETY SIMILAR ACROSS DIFFERENT TYPES OF FEARS?

As discussed in Chapter 4, fear and anxiety are normal biological processes that help us to detect and respond to danger by motivating us to escape or fight back. Physical changes associated with anxiety (e.g., heart racing, sweating, pupil dilation, increased respiration) prepare our bodies for this fight-or-flight response (Stratakis & Chrousos, 1995). Anxiety can be adaptive at low to moderate levels because it compels us to act. Our ability to plan details and concentrate on a task improves when we experience some anxiety (Selye, 1974). For instance, being a little nervous about a test may motivate a student to study and help to ensure that she remains focused during the exam. Some increased anxiety in the face of pressures such as academic demands can be expected in adolescence, just as some anxiety during social situations is developmentally normative. However, too much anxiety can interfere with functioning, as in the instance when a student has so much test anxiety that he cannot concentrate during exams, doubts his answers, and subsequently performs poorly.

As discussed in Chapter 4, when we are faced with frightening situations or feared circumstances, our thoughts, behaviors, and physical/emotional feelings influence one another in an ongoing cycle that fuels anxiety. Negative thoughts increase anxious feelings and behavioral avoidance. Uncomfortable physical sensations lead to negative thoughts and motivate avoidance of situations associated with those sensations. Persistent avoidance, in turn, strongly reinforces both negative thoughts and physical symptoms. This "CBT triangle," introduced in Chapter 4 and reproduced in Figure 17.1, is not unique to social anxiety. Rather, it is a general model of the anxiety cycle and applies to all types of fears. The specific feared stimulus may differ across types of anxiety (e.g., fear of animals, fear of social situations), but negative thoughts, anxious arousal, and avoidance behaviors will still be present and function in a similar cyclical manner. High rates of co-occurrence among anxiety disorders help to illustrate how different types of anxiety all share the same features of distress in response to feared stimuli.

Anxiety disorders commonly co-occur!

Understanding this co-occurrence is particularly important for school professionals because if a student presents with one type of anxiety (e.g., social anxiety), she is more likely to present with another type (e.g., generalized anxiety, specific phobia) as well. Understanding how the CBT triangle is consistent across anxious presentations allows school personnel to use the treatment strategies described in this book (i.e., realistic thinking and exposure) flexibly in order to help students interrupt the anxiety cycle in a variety of contexts.

APPLYING INTERVENTION STRATEGIES FLEXIBLY

Throughout this book we have focused on addressing countless fears related to a variety of social and performance situations through strategies of realistic thinking and exposure. As

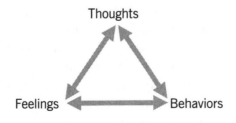

FIGURE 17.1. The CBT triangle.

counselors become attuned to recognizing physical and behavioral presentations of social anxiety, it will also become easier to identify students' signs of anxiety in other contexts. Once they are aware of the numerous anxious thoughts that can creep up in social and performance situations, and of the many opportunities and situations both within and outside school that can be used for potential exposures, we hope that school professionals will brainstorm how they might use exposures flexibly and creatively to address other types of student fears. Below we review and highlight the primary intervention strategies for a number of fears and worries.

Just as the CBT triangle is an essential foundation for social anxiety intervention, psychoeducation that includes the anxiety cycle is applicable to any student whose functioning is impaired by fears or anxiety. Regardless of whether fears are specific, general, or social in nature, begin by teaching students how their thoughts, feelings (physical and emotional), and behaviors (avoidance!) interact to maintain their anxiety. Help students to plug their own physical sensations of anxious arousal, their anxious thoughts, and their unique patterns of behavior into the CBT triangle to illustrate how their anxiety (any type) is maintained or increasing over time.

As students become familiar with their anxious thoughts, use realistic thinking strategies (see Chapter 6) to teach them to challenge anxious thoughts with questions such as "What is the likelihood that this feared outcome will happen?," "What usually happens in this situation?," and "If this did happen, would I be able to cope with it?" After students challenge their thoughts, help them replace their negative thoughts with more realistic ones. Remember that the goal is not to get students to always think positively; rather, we want students to be accurate and realistic in order to encourage approach rather than avoidance of anxiety-provoking situations.

Because avoidance is the behavioral hallmark of anxiety, facing fears through exposure is crucial for helping students overcome a myriad of fears and challenges (see Chapters 11 and 12). In order for students to develop a fear ladder and face their feared situations, it is first necessary to get a sense of what types of fears they are experiencing. Does your student have specific fears related to one particular circumstance or does he have many general worries? You may find it useful to administer a questionnaire to help identify potential fear targets. Two screening measures reviewed in Chapter 3, the Multidimensional Anxiety Scale for Children (MASC 2; March & Parker, 2004) and the Screen for Child Anxiety Related Emotional Disorders (SCARED; Birmaher et al., 1997, 1999), can be given in their entirety (rather than just the social subscale) to provide relevant information for understanding students' anxiety. Once you've identified your student's feared situations, work together to build a fear ladder and design exposures that help the student directly challenge those fears (see Chapter 11). Coach students to identify their negative thoughts, rate their SUDs before, during, and after the exposures, and then evaluate whether their negative feared outcomes came true. If the outcomes did come true, have the students explain how they coped with their anxiety (see Chapter 12 for details).

> **Use realistic thinking and exposures flexibly to address a variety of student fears.**

HOW CAN I ADDRESS COMMON PRESENTATIONS OF ANXIETY IN SCHOOL?

Below we review some common presentations of anxiety and related disorders. In most schools, it would not be feasible for school professionals to intervene with all anxieties and fears that students have. Thus, we focus on fears that specifically occur in school and cause impairment for students in an academic setting.

Specific Fears and Phobias

What Do Specific Fears and Phobias Look Like?

Many children and adolescents will express fears of specific objects or experiences throughout their development (e.g., fear of the dark in childhood). For many, these fears are transient and do not cause significant distress or impairment in functioning. However, when a specific fear of an object or situation is experienced as significantly intense and irrational, and when it causes significant distress and impairment for an individual, it is known as a specific phobia. Common phobias include fears of animals (e.g., dogs, spiders), fears of the natural environment (e.g., heights, thunderstorms), fears of specific spaces or situations (e.g., planes, elevators, closed spaces), or fears of other types of stimuli (e.g., loud sounds, medical and dental procedures).

While counselors could potentially treat various types of phobias in school, it may be more appropriate to refer a student to outside community services if a specific phobia is noticed but not directly impairing the student's academic abilities. For instance, it would not likely be feasible to treat a high school student's phobia of flying in planes during the school day. Occasionally, however, you may notice students who have specific phobias that impact them during school and for whom swift intervention would be extremely beneficial. For instance, a student with an animal phobia or a phobia of seeing blood or needles may struggle with dissections or watching videos during an anatomy, biology, or health science class. In that case, it may be useful to briefly intervene with that student during school. Similarly, a student with a phobia of fire may experience distress when required to use a Bunsen burner during chemistry class.

How Can I Address Specific Fears and Phobias?

Once the feared stimulus has been identified, treating a specific phobia with realistic thinking and exposures is often fairly straightforward, though it may still be challenging to convince a student to engage in exposures. For instance, Clara was a student who was specifically afraid to use the school elevator because she worried that it would break down with her inside. When she was injured and had knee surgery following a soccer game, she unfortunately needed to use crutches and take the elevator for 6 weeks at school. At that time, her phobia of elevators became sufficiently impairing to cause problems at school. By working closely with her school counselor, Clara learned to challenge her anxious thoughts by replacing them with realistic thoughts, such as "This elevator has never gotten stuck before. Even if it does get stuck, there are many people who would notice that I was missing and would be able to get me out. Even if it does get stuck, I won't be trapped forever." For exposures, she and her counselor practiced standing in front of the elevator and watching it, then practiced stepping on and off quickly while the door was still open, and then practiced stepping on and allowing the door to close briefly, until finally Clara could ride the elevator the two floors she needed.

Generalized Anxiety and Worry

What Does Generalized Anxiety Look Like?

Some students may seemingly worry about everything, acting like "little adults" or "worrywarts." Students who present with excessive worries that are not confined to one specific fear or event but rather span a wide range of life circumstances may have generalized anxiety. Adolescents may have excessive concern regarding their competence in sports or other activities or their grades and academic achievements. These students are often perfectionistic in their work and set unreasonably high expectations for themselves. They tend to worry about their grades on every test or assignment or their ability to complete all their work on time, even when they consistently perform well in school. These adolescents may find it necessary to redo homework assignments multiple times, excessively check their work, obsess about when graded work will be returned, cry over what others would consider a good grade, and constantly seek reassurance from teachers related to grades or the accuracy and quality of work. When pressing a student on what the specific catastrophic feared outcome is, school counselors may be surprised to find out that an anxious A student spends 6 hours on homework each day because she is worried about failing out of school, not being admitted to a good college, or not being able to find a job in the future. For generally anxious students, their worry and reassurance seeking is an attempt to avoid these feared catastrophic outcomes.

In addition to academic concerns, students with generalized anxiety also worry about things that are mostly out of their control such as the future, relationships between other people, their family's finances, the health and safety of their loved ones, natural disasters, or world events. At the core of these worries is a fear of uncertainty and feeling out of control. These students crave predictability and routine, often presenting as rigid or inflexible. They may quickly become agitated or unraveled when they are faced with spontaneous decisions or changes in their schedule or expectations, and this distress is likely to be out of proportion to the severity of the actual situation. As you may expect, this can lead to chronic nervousness or tension. For example, students with this type of anxiety may be thrown off by a fire drill because it disrupts what they planned to accomplish during a class period, or by a makeup game scheduled on short notice because it will interfere with how they planned to use their after-school time. Regardless of the current focus of the worry, overall their concerns are experienced as all-consuming and difficult to stop. Additionally, when considering what would happen if a feared outcome did come true, students with generalized anxiety often underestimate their own ability to cope with the outcome, instead assuming that they would be helpless or lose control.

How Can I Address Generalized Anxiety and Worry?

Some students with general, nonspecific worries may have trouble identifying exactly what makes them anxious. When delivering psychoeducation to these students, teach them to use their body cues as signs of anxiety to pinpoint what their thoughts and beliefs are in the moment. Sometimes, avoidance can also be difficult to detect among students with generalized fears because it can be subtle. Typically, avoidance for these students manifests as procrastination, rumination (replaying worries without trying to figure out how to resolve a situation), distress that functions as distraction, or sleep difficulties and other physical complaints that then lead to missed opportunities to engage in valued activities.

When discussing realistic thinking with students with generalized anxiety, it is important to focus on the probability of their most extreme feared outcomes (e.g., failing out of school, never being able to find a job) because they are often unlikely to happen. Additionally, challenge students to realistically think about their ability to cope with the negative outcome if it were to come true. Because students often worry about a chain of events (e.g., "If my assignment is not perfect, I'll get a bad grade, I'll fail this class, and I won't be able to go to college and get a good job"), counselors can help them think about each link of the chain as a thinking error and help them to challenge each part (e.g., "I have never failed an assignment or class before and I usually do well," "Even if I fail this assignment, my class average will still be a B, which is passing," "Other students have failed assignments and even courses before, and they still graduated and went to college," "Not everyone who has a job did well in school. I will probably be able to get a job in the future").

As with social anxiety, when adolescents are presenting with generalized worries, many of their fears will occur at school because this is where they spend the most time and likely experience the most distress related to their performance and perfectionism. Thus, focusing school exposures directly on the fears and impairment experienced at school can be greatly beneficial for generally anxious students, even when they also have other non-school-related worries (e.g., health and safety of family). Oftentimes, students will be able to translate the skills they learn related to realistic thinking and exposure in school to their feared circumstances outside of school. Exposures for generally anxious students in school can focus on fears such as "If I am not perfect or if I make a mistake, I will not get into the college of my choice." For exposures, students may turn in an assignment without checking it over or proofreading; or they can intentionally insert typos or grammatical errors into a paper they submit. Additionally, students can purposely answer questions wrong on their homework assignments, complete homework in a sloppy or disorganized way, or purposely neglect a small homework assignment (e.g., reading a chapter, one day's daily math homework). Counselors can even arrange with a teacher to have the student turn in a significant class assignment or project late. For in-class exams, exposures might include students limiting their study time for a large test or purposely not studying for a small quiz. Students who are perfectionistic about time may also purposely show up late to class.

Involving teachers is important—for example, allowing students to lose only partial credit for work not completed, providing a pass on the first infraction, or allowing students to retake a quiz they did not study for as an exposure if they score below a certain grade. It is critical to strike a balance between allowing some natural consequences to occur and illustrating that the consequences are manageable. Depending on the situation, such as how many of these types of exposures are conducted and parents' attitudes toward the students' grades and anxiety, you may want to explain your rationale to parents or encourage the student to discuss it with them ahead of time.

Test Anxiety

What Does Test Anxiety Look Like?

While test anxiety is not technically classified as an anxiety disorder, it is often one of many worries for students experiencing generalized anxiety disorder. Given how much this particular feared circumstance can impair students in school, strategies for dealing specifically with test anxiety are important. While many students may become slightly nervous before important exams or if they are unprepared, some students experience severe test anxiety. In these cases, students may feel like their mind goes blank or that their thoughts are racing when they sit down to take a test. They experience difficulty concentrating and may be distracted by negative thoughts about past performance on exams or future catastrophic consequences of potential failure. Certain stimuli such as movement or noises from other students or a ticking clock can feel overwhelming. Even if these students are unable to recall important information during the exam, they can often accurately report most of the answers when they leave the test and are not under the demands of a testing situation. This highlights just how much anxiety interferes with their performance.

How Can I Address Test Anxiety?

When practicing realistic thinking with students with test anxiety, help them to identify their negative thoughts that occur before, during, and after the exam. Help students recognize that if they think, "I'm going to fail this test," "I always do poorly on tests," "If I don't get an A, it means I am dumb and a failure," or "If I do poorly, it will ruin my grade, I'll fail the class, and I then won't get into college," of course they will be nervous! Use challenging questions (e.g., "What is the evidence that for that?") and practice replacing the negative thought with a more realistic thought such as, "I usually do well on tests," "This test is only a small part of my overall grade," or "I spent time preparing and I know the material well." Remember, the goal is to practice *realistic* thinking to reduce anxiety. Students do not need to think overly positive thoughts such as "I'm definitely going to get a 100%" in order to reduce their anxiety. In fact, this kind of thinking can lead to disappointment or more anxiety when students do not live up to overly positive, unrealistic predictions, especially perfectionistic students. If students gravitate toward overly perfectionistic or unrealistic replacements when revising their negative thoughts, guide them to be more realistic instead. For instance, to help tackle some perfectionistic pressures that students might have about their test performance, try practice statements such as "I don't need to get every question perfect. I can still do well even if I get a few questions wrong."

Additionally, building and working up a fear ladder related to testing situations is important. Certain temporary accommodations in school may be necessary for students to systematically work on exposing themselves to anxiety-provoking examinations. At first, you will likely need to work with teachers to find ways to make completing tests less anxiety provoking. For instance, a student's fear ladder may include items such as taking a test with extended time, taking a test in smaller classrooms or individually with the teacher, and taking a test facing a clock so he can see how much time he has left. You can slowly increase the difficulty by decreasing the time the student is provided until it is the same amount of time as the regular class (e.g., 45 minutes). You might also have students start the test with a full class but agree to allow them to finish the test afterwards with a teacher in a small room if they run out of time. Ultimately, the goal is not to allow students to always have accommodations because that would be a form of avoidance. Rather, it is to provide students with systematic strategies that effectively address anxiety until they are reacclimated to the main classroom environment with less distress during typical testing.

School Phobia and School Refusal

What Do School Phobia and School Refusal Look Like?

The terms "school phobia" and "school refusal" are often used interchangeably to refer to students who refuse to attend school regularly. School phobia and school refusal may manifest as missing full days or frequently arriving late or leaving early, despite parents' efforts to force students to attend. As with test anxiety, it is important to understand that school refusal does not qualify as a stand-alone anxiety disorder in DSM-5 (American Psychiatric Association, 2013). Rather, it is a *behavior* that may be present in the context of many difficulties. Students who refuse to attend school are attempting to avoid something that occurs as part of the school day, so it is critical to determine what that something is. Adolescents may refuse school for a multitude of reasons, often, but not necessarily, due to anxiety. For example, adolescents may refuse school because they have social anxiety, test anxiety, or separation anxiety (fear of something bad happening to themselves or their parents while they are apart). They may also have frequent stomach pain, diarrhea, or constipation and feel nervous about needing to use the bathroom repeatedly or fear that other students will notice. On the other hand, students may be refusing school for entirely different reasons. For example, they may be depressed, experiencing increased difficulty in learning due to ADHD or other specific learning disabilities, or may not meet criteria for any disorder but are avoiding school because they are being bullied.

How Do I Address School Phobia and School Refusal?

The first step in addressing school refusal is to identify and treat the underlying problem driving the avoidance behavior. Depending on the reason behind school avoidance, you may need to refer your student to a mental health provider in the community (see the next section, pp. 214–216). Often, addressing the core concern will result in reduced school avoidance. However, when the behavior has lasted a while or the core fear is pervasive throughout the school day (e.g., severe social anxiety), it may be necessary to create a fear ladder to gradually reintegrate the student into the school setting. For example, fear ladder items can include: come to the school on a day that school is closed or during a staff development day, come to the school on a regular day but spend time in a counselor or nurse's office or another "easy" place, attend "easy" classes only, attend an increasing number of class periods, attend a half day, attend a full day. Often, these fear ladder steps reflect accommodations that may be at odds with school policy. Therefore, it may be helpful to educate school administrators about students' anxiety and gradual exposure. These students typically want to reengage in school but find it too difficult and overwhelming, and they are responsive to a collaborative and gradual approach. For a more comprehensive review of intervention for school refusal consistent with this approach, we recommend the following resources by Kearney and colleagues. (See the reference section for full information.)

- *Helping School Refusing Children and Their Parents: A Guide for School-Based Professionals* by Christopher A. Kearney (2008)
- *Getting Your Child to Say "Yes" to School: A Guide for Parents of Youth with School Refusal Behavior* by Christopher A. Kearney (2007)
- *School Refusal Behavior in Youth: A Functional Approach to Assessment and Treatment* by Christopher A. Kearney (2001)

REFERRING STUDENTS TO OUTSIDE TREATMENT

This book was designed to help school personnel provide intervention for students' social anxiety within the setting where the anxiety occurs. We have also given school personnel strategies for recognizing anxiety and assisting students with various fears that are likely to be observed in the school setting. It is our hope that counselors will use these strategies to effectively intervene for students with social anxiety. We also hope that school professionals capitalize on the information in this book to increase identification and early intervention for students struggling with other anxiety issues as well. Given that this book is not a comprehensive manual to train counselors to treat *all* anxiety disorders, we feel it is pertinent to address the issue of referring students for outside treatment. In addition, students with anxiety often present with co-occurring issues such as depression, self-injury, substance use, eating disorders, histories of trauma and traumatic symptoms, or significant obsessive and compulsive symptoms that may require intensive treatment in the community.

What Are Conditions That Warrant Referral to Community Providers?

When necessary, we encourage referrals to community services, including but not limited to treatment by psychologists or psychiatrists, or other existing treatment programs. This may be indicated when a counselor becomes aware of multiple or extremely pervasive anxiety disorders, or of additional impairing circumstances requiring more intensive intervention. Below, we briefly outline some anxiety and anxiety-related disorders that we believe are appropriate for referral to a specialized cognitive-behavioral provider in the community.

Panic Attacks or Chronic Physical Complaints

Anxiety is often accompanied by panic attacks or chronic physical complaints such as stom-achaches, gastrointestinal distress, or headaches. A panic attack is an abrupt rush of anxiety or intense fear peaking within minutes, including intense physiological symptoms such as a racing or pounding heart, shortness of breath, trembling or shaking, sweating, and nausea or intestinal distress and thoughts related to fears of dying, losing control, or going crazy. Panic attacks can be cued, such as when facing a particular situation that a student fears (e.g., a presentation, an important test) or they can be uncued and happen seemingly "out of the blue." Because panic attacks are aversive and frightening, students may seek medical attention or leave the situation in order to reduce the physical anxiety symptoms. We advise school professionals to refer these students to outside providers because treatment of panic attacks and anxiety with chronic physical complaints requires exposure related to the physi-cal symptoms, called interoceptive exposure (Craske & Barlow, 2006) and collaboration with physicians to ensure that medical conditions have been ruled out.

Separation Anxiety

While separation anxiety is more common among school-age children and often resolves by adolescence (Kessler et al., 2012), it may still be present in high school settings. Students with separation anxiety fear that something bad will happen to them or to their parents when they are not together, for example, when the student is in school. Separation anxiety may be a core fear underlying school refusal. It may also manifest as avoidance of walking home from school alone, staying home alone, or sleeping separately from parents. Students with separation fears tend to avoid sleepovers, overnight school field trips, and summer camp. Some students may be able to separate from their parents in these situations but experience significant distress and negative cognitions, or exhibit significant checking behavior, such as frequently texting or calling parents when they are not together. While it is appropriate and helpful for school professionals to assist students with separation anxiety when it occurs at school, we recommend an additional referral to a community provider because much of the fear ladder will have to be implemented at home and in close collaboration with parents.

Obsessive–Compulsive Disorder

Obsessive–compulsive disorder (OCD) is much more than the fear of germs or doing things in multiples of certain numbers, as commonly portrayed in the media. OCD is characterized by recurrent obsessions and compulsions that are time-consuming or significantly interfere with normal routine, academic functioning, or relationships. Obsessions are unwanted and intrusive ideas, thoughts, or images that enter someone's mind and cause significant distress. The most common obsessions among youth have themes of contamination, aggression, sym-metry, religion, and sex. Compulsions are defined as repetitive behaviors or mental acts that prevent or reduce anxiety or distress. Compulsions most common among young people are excessive washing, repeating or undoing, checking, touching, counting, ordering/arrang-ing, and hoarding (Swedo, Rapoport, Leonard, Lenane, & Cheslow, 1989). Obsessions and compulsions are functionally related—compulsions are performed in an attempt to reduce the distress and anxiety brought on by the obsessions (Foa & Franklin, 2001). Compulsions are negatively reinforced over time by their ability to reduce or "neutralize" the anxiety created by obsessions (Piacentini & Langley, 2004). The recommended treatment for OCD is exposure and response prevention (ERP). ERP relies on CBT principles similar to those described in this book, including exposing individuals to circumstances that normally provoke anxiety and compulsive behaviors. However, it also involves blocking rituals and compulsive behaviors to remove the negative reinforcement effect of the compulsion. We recommend that school personnel be mindful of potential obsessive and compulsive behavior by students and refer these students to mental health providers with a specialization in OCD and ERP. For additional information and resources related to OCD, we recommend visiting the website for the International OCD Foundation (*https://iocdf.org*).

How Do I Identify Appropriate Providers in the Community?

We recommend that school professionals develop a list of available local mental health service providers who deliver effective evidence-based services. It may be difficult to discern whether providers are trained in CBT and an exposure-based approach to treatment, so we suggest reaching out to local providers to hear whether their approach sounds similar to strategies described in this book. You may also search for referrals by national professional organizations such as the Anxiety and Depression Association of America (ADAA; *www.adaa.org*) and the Association for Behavioral and Cognitive Therapies (ABCT; *www.abct.org*), or regional professional organizations. We also advise you to elicit feedback from families who have had successful experiences with community providers in order to build your referral list.

Students can simultaneously seek intervention in the community while receiving evidence-based supports in school. After referring students, we recommend active collaboration with students' external treatment providers to ensure that they are receiving necessary individualized support at school and to offer assistance in implementing valuable school-based exposures.

CHAPTER SUMMARY

- Multiple anxiety disorders often co-occur, and adolescents with social anxiety may present with additional specific fears or general worries.

- Psychoeducation, realistic thinking, and exposure strategies can be adapted and used flexibly to help students address various fears and worries within the school environment.

- Common types of anxiety that may impair students in school include specific phobias, general worries related to academic achievement or school performance, test anxiety, and school refusal.

- School personnel are encouraged to make referrals to appropriate community services and to collaborate with students' treatment providers to ensure that students receive the supports they need.

CHAPTER 18

Keep It Up!
Ways to Maintain Student Progress

By this time, you will have proudly watched your students take some steps to limit the impact of social anxiety on their lives and gain more confidence interacting with others. Congratulations on the progress you and your students have made together! By understanding social anxiety and using the strategies in this book to think more realistically, enhance their social skills, and face their fears, students can learn how to stop allowing social anxiety to negatively affect their experiences and lives. However, as with any new skills, continued practice is required to strengthen the skills and make them more habitual. This chapter focuses on how to sustain students' progress once they have successfully acquired these skills and you have stopped meeting with them regularly.

WHEN WILL I KNOW
MY STUDENTS HAVE MADE ENOUGH PROGRESS?

If you are like most other counseling professionals, you may always feel that there is more to do or other goals you would like to help your students achieve. However, progress may be sufficient if students have experienced a meaningful decrease in social anxiety and can enter into most situations they have previously avoided. You may want to use one of the social anxiety assessment tools we outlined in Chapter 3 to get a sense of students' current anxiety level or discuss the following questions with your students to determine how they are currently doing and whether they have made a significant change in their quality of life.

- Did they make a couple of new friends or develop deeper friendships with acquaintances?
- Are they regularly seeing friends outside of school?

- Do they feel comfortable contacting a friend to ask her to do something?
- Are they able to participate in class or speak to a teacher when they have a question?
- Can they give a presentation when necessary?
- Have they been able to join a school club or sport that they have been interested in?
- Do they look friendly and are they able to start conversations with others?
- Are they able to assert themselves when necessary?
- Are they able to think more realistically and see that there are other possible interpretations to their typically negative ones?
- Are they able to do most things they want to do, or that are important to them, with manageable anxiety?

If your answer to most of these questions is yes, your students have probably learned the strategies you have taught them, and it may be time for them to try and make further progress on their own. It is not realistic to think that social anxiety will go away completely, and it does not have to. Rather, we want students to understand that, even though they may still feel anxious in certain social situations, they can no longer allow anxiety to stop them from doing the things they would like to do. In fact, we want them to do just the opposite—we are asking them to purposely do those socially healthy things that still make them uncomfortable or involve some social risk.

HOW DO I WRAP THINGS UP?

We recommend having one or two concluding meetings with students to review progress and prepare for the future. The first goal is to understand students' perspectives on this experience by having them reflect on the process and identify the changes they have made. Next, we recommend predicting when setbacks may be likely to occur, followed by a discussion about identifying warning signs and developing a plan for addressing a future increase in social anxiety (Fisher et al., 2004; Ryan & Masia Warner, 2012).

Having Students Take Stock

It is important to help students process their experience so that their hard work and accomplishments are acknowledged and reinforced. Often, anxious students have trouble giving themselves credit for the positive strides they have made. Acknowledging and taking ownership of progress will increase students' confidence that they can overcome similar challenges in the future. It also emphasizes that often the biggest gains come from the hardest challenges. We recommend giving the following prompts to guide this discussion and providing students with Handout 18.1: What Have I Learned?

1. "What were the most difficult experiences you had while trying to overcome your social anxiety?"
2. "Which strategies did you find most and least helpful?"

3. "What was your favorite strategy or new skill?"
4. "What do you see as your biggest accomplishments and changes?"
5. "What areas would you like to continue working on? Are there situations you are still avoiding or entering with dread?"
6. "What plans can you make to address those remaining areas?"

You can either do this individually or in a group. If you have a group of students you are working with at the same time, we have found it rewarding for them to give informal presentations covering these topics. You can even make this into a special ceremony and reserve a room at school (possibly with a small stage) and conduct a "mini-graduation." The students can give short speeches and be presented with a small gift (e.g., Starbucks gift card). You might also want to include a celebratory cake or other food to mark their success.

Talk about Setbacks

Although you certainly do not want to put a damper on all that students have accomplished, you do want to make sure they have realistic expectations going forward. Of course, we all like to think that when we have mastered something, it will stay with us forever. However, it is important to let students know that you expect they will still experience social anxiety and that it is not completely gone. Without this knowledge, they may become discouraged or hopeless if anxiety returns and they are not expecting it. We recommend predicting that although their anxiety currently feels more manageable, there are times when it will reemerge and seem to be taking over again. They may feel nervous, shy, and anxious again in the future and experience days when they want to avoid things they have been doing regularly with little difficulty. For example, students might find themselves nervous again before a party, school activity, or the first day of school, and this might be surprising or discouraging to them. They should understand that this is normal and expected and can be addressed.

Such setbacks are common and should not be cause for alarm. Increases in anxiety may be related to lack of sleep or changes in eating, menstruation, or alcohol or drug use. Setbacks can also be triggered by life events or stressors, such as physical illness, injury, death of loved ones, divorce of parents, termination of significant relationships, or receiving a bad grade. Anxiety can also worsen when students experience increased pressure or demands like midterms or final exams.

The return of fear in these situations is often very gradual and students may not even notice it until they find they are starting to avoid certain social situations again. Additionally, students will be entering into significant life transitions, such as starting college or beginning a new job. These transitions, along with the new responsibilities, people, and relationships that they bring can be particularly challenging and may be associated with acute

> **Prepare students to proactively identify and address setbacks.**

increases in anxiety for some. Anticipating the return of anxiety allows students to be prepared and catch setbacks early on before they become significantly impairing. Therefore, it is important to teach students to be aware of warning signs.

Discuss Warning Signs of Increased Social Anxiety

Each person will have her own reactions to alert her that social anxiety is on the rise, and it will certainly be important for students to get to know their individual response. Some common examples of warning signs to educate students about are:

1. An increase in physical symptoms when in social situations (e.g., stomachaches, pit in stomach, feeling hot, sweating)
2. An increase in negative predictions of what will happen when anticipating social gatherings and what the consequences will be (e.g., I will sound boring, I won't know what to say, I will mess up)
3. Increased worries about what other people will think or how others will react to them
4. An increase in withdrawal and avoidance (e.g., staying home from places, difficulty making eye contact, leaving social situations early or quickly, making excuses or rationalizing why you can't go to social events)

It is natural to lose some confidence and to feel more anxious at times. We recommend that counselors spend time discussing warning signs with students and teaching them to recognize and acknowledge the symptoms. Probably one of the easiest ways to do this is to instruct them to list what situations they have started to avoid. If they are avoiding situations or experiences that are important to them or that they desire to be part of, their anxiety is likely on the rise. We recommend instructing students to start working on confronting their fears as soon as possible, even if they have to start with relatively easy situations and go from there. It is also helpful to remind students that if they were able to overcome anxiety once, they will be able to do it again if they are willing to face it, especially because they now have all the skills they need. School personnel may choose to have students review and complete Handout 18.2: My Anxiety Warning Signs to help them identify specific indicators that they need to increase their skill usage.

HOW TO HANDLE A RETURN OF SOCIAL ANXIETY

Don't Beat Yourself Up

The first rule to review with students is that if they notice an increase in anxiety and avoidance, they should try not to be hard on themselves. They may feel discouraged that entering into certain situations has become more difficult or they may experience an overall loss of confidence. However, it is critical to keep a realistic (rather than anxious) mindset. How students think about a minor setback can influence whether it continues and becomes worse. We recommend prompting students with examples and working through a thought exercise outlining what they would do if they experienced a resurgence of anxiety. Draw on their skills such as realistic thinking. For example, if you were having difficulty starting conversations again and you thought, "Oh no, I am right back where I started," how would you feel and what would you do? Many people would feel a sense of doom and have negative thoughts like "I am a failure," "I will never get better," "It is happening all over again," "All the hard work I did was a waste." Feeling discouraged about a setback will make it less likely that students will take the necessary steps to get back on track. If you predict for students that they will experience setbacks at various times such as when sick or during exams or after a fight with a friend, it may be easier for them to say to themselves, "I knew this would happen, but it's not a big deal. It's because I was stressed out from all my tests." Therefore, we recommend predicting setbacks, reviewing how thoughts can influence students' ability to get back on track, and encouraging them not to beat themselves up. Instead, preemptively make a plan to identify which skills to start practicing more regularly.

Identify What Skills to Start Practicing Again

When students are experiencing increased anxiety, it is usually because they have slowly returned to their old habits. It is important to help them think about which skills were initially helpful and whether they have stopped practicing them. Have they practiced challenging their thoughts concerning the likelihood that negative outcomes will actually occur? Have they been pushing themselves to generate more realistic interpretations? They should also consider whether they have been doing a lot of things others have asked of them despite preferring not to do so. If this is the case, maybe it is time for them to start practicing refusing requests and being assertive. Students may also ask themselves whether they have been challenging themselves to try new social situations on a regular basis, or whether they have fallen into old patterns of avoidance? You want to make sure students understand that it is important to keep confronting their fears, or anxiety may worsen. Remind them that they will never learn a situation is probably not as bad as they think it is if they don't try it. Following this discussion, you may want to recommend that students make a list of skills that would be helpful to practice more regularly.

Get Back on the Horse

The ultimate rule to instill in students is this: When they notice themselves becoming anxious or nervous about social situations or avoiding them, it means that it is time to try to push themselves and enter the situation. *From now on, anxiety should be used as a signal for approaching, not avoiding.* True growth only comes when we place ourselves in situations where we feel uncomfortable. If we live our lives only doing things within our comfort zone and never experiencing discomfort, we will never grow or change as people. Encourage students to push themselves at times when it is difficult to confront their fears.

Social anxiety should be a signal for approaching, not avoiding!

The truth is that to fully overcome their social anxiety, experiencing discomfort and confronting their fears has to become a routine part of their lives.

Summarize a Plan for Students to Stay Well

Experiencing a return of anxiety symptoms can be scary for students. All the steps described in this chapter can help students to anticipate it, be prepared to identify the warning signals, and to have a plan for what to do when it happens. Provide students with a summary of the steps to take if they notice an increase in anxiety and have them elaborate on their plan with Handout 18.3: My Plan to Stay Well.

1. "Write down your warning signs ahead of time so you are aware of them and can identify them when they occur. Examples of warning signs may include avoiding answering questions in class, infrequently initiating conversations, and increased worry about what others think during school events."
2. "If you notice an increase in anxiety symptoms, do not beat yourself up. If it is because you have not been sleeping well, try to get a good night's rest. If you have had a lot of exams, be patient. Wait for the exams to be over and then take stock of the situation."
3. "Write down the skills you may have stopped practicing, such as doing exposures on a regular basis, asking open-ended questions, initiating conversations, and questioning the probability of negative events."
4. "List specific steps to perform, such as conducting regular planned exposure exercises, initiating three conversations per day for the next week, and inviting someone to get together."

BOOSTER SESSIONS

One of the best things about helping students with anxiety in the school setting is that you are there with them in one of their most challenging environments. In fact, in our 2016 study of 138 adolescents with social anxiety treated at school (Masia Warner et al., 2016), we found that having intervention delivered by school counselors to whom students can have continued access may have enhanced students' treatment compliance and supported further treatment gains even after the intervention program had ended. Therefore, because we know that students will likely continue to have some difficulties, we recommend continuing to check in with them from time to time. As discussed in Chapter 14, one effective but informal way to check in with your students and support their progress is by inviting your students back to participate as prosocial peers in social events the following year. This increases opportunities for your students to keep practicing their skills and maintain reductions in their anxiety.

To more formally check in with your past students, you could continue to meet with them once a month or once every other month, depending on your schedule and how the student is doing. At these meetings, we recommend that you monitor her anxiety symptoms and how often she has been using her skills and entering into difficult social situations. You can use one of the social anxiety rating scales (i.e., MASC 2, LSAS-CA) that we recommended in Chapter 3 to assess the level of her symptoms at each visit. This would help determine if her symptoms are staying the same, worsening, or improving. If you determine that her anxiety is worsening, we recommend reinstating more regular meetings to practice relevant skills or to plan and conduct some exposures at school. Similarly, if you had conducted intervention in group settings, you might invite all the students back for a group "reunion" where they can discuss how they are doing now, seek support and skills practice, and revise their plan for maintaining progress, if needed.

CHAPTER SUMMARY

- Progress may be sufficient if students have experienced a meaningful decrease in social anxiety and can enter into most situations they had previously avoided.

- Have students take stock of their progress, recognize the skills they have practiced, and give themselves credit for the positive strides they have made.

- Discuss potential future setbacks for students and help them identify warning signs of increased anxiety.

- Have students develop a plan for actions to take and skills to practice if they notice increased anxiety.

- Consider providing booster sessions throughout the year or regularly assessing how students are doing after they have stopped meeting with you in order to maintain student progress.

What Have I Learned?

You have worked hard and accomplished a lot! It is time to take stock and recognize your achievements. Take ownership of your progress and reflect on what you've learned!

1. **What were the most difficult experiences you had while trying to overcome social anxiety?**

   _____

   _____

   _____

   _____

2. **Which strategies did you find most and least helpful? Why?**

   _____

   _____

   _____

   _____

3. **What was your favorite strategy or new skill? Why?**

   _____

   _____

   _____

   _____

4. **What do you see as your biggest accomplishments and changes?**

   _____

   _____

   _____

   _____

5. **What areas would you like to continue working on?**

   _____

   _____

   _____

   _____

My Anxiety Warning Signs

Each person will have his or her own reactions to alert him or her that social anxiety is on the rise. Think about your own anxiety response and how you will know when it's time to dig your heels back in and start practicing! Check off boxes for warning signs that apply to you or add your own!

1. **Have I experienced an increase in physical symptoms when in social situations?**
   - ☐ Stomachaches, butterflies in the stomach, or needing to use the bathroom
   - ☐ Racing heart, heart palpitations, or tightness in the chest
   - ☐ Heavy breathing or shortness of breath
   - ☐ Sweating or blushing
   - ☐ Muscle tension or shakiness (e.g., hands or voice)
   - ☐ Headaches or dizziness
   - ☐ _____

2. **Am I making negative predictions or worrying about negative social consequences?**
   - ☐ "I know it will go badly."
   - ☐ "If I make a mistake it will be the end of the world."
   - ☐ _____
   - ☐ _____
   - ☐ _____

3. **Am I worrying about what other people will think or how others will react to me?**
   - ☐ "I have to be perfect or everyone will laugh at me."
   - ☐ "No one will want to talk to me."
   - ☐ _____
   - ☐ _____
   - ☐ _____

4. **Am I avoiding people and places or withdrawing because I am anxious?**
   - ☐ Staying home from places or leaving situations early
   - ☐ Making excuses or rationalizing why I can't go to social events
   - ☐ Difficulty making eye contact or talking to others
   - ☐ Avoiding participating in class (e.g., asking/answering questions, giving opinions)
   - ☐ _____
   - ☐ _____
   - ☐ _____

My Plan to Stay Well

Experiencing a return of anxiety symptoms can be scary! Make sure you have a plan for what to do if you notice that you are becoming anxious. Create your own checklists for questions 1 and 2 below and use the lists provided for questions 3 and 4, plus any items you may want to add.

1. *Review warning signs:* **My major warning signs are . . .**

   ☐ _____

   ☐ _____

2. **If I notice an increase in anxiety symptoms, *I will not beat myself up!* What else might be going on for me right now that might account for my increased anxiety?**

   ☐ _____

   ☐ _____

   ☐ _____

3. **Skills I may have stopped practicing are . . .**

   ☐ Realistic thinking

   ☐ Doing exposures on a regular basis

   ☐ Initiating or maintaining conversations

   ☐ Extending invitations

   ☐ _____

   ☐ _____

   ☐ _____

4. **What I will do now is . . .**

   ☐ Challenge my thoughts and replace them with more realistic alternatives

   ☐ Do something that makes me nervous each day

   ☐ Ask or answer three questions in classes each day

   ☐ Initiate three conversations each day

   ☐ Invite a friend to get together each week

   ☐ _____

   ☐ _____

   ☐ _____

   ☐ _____

References

Alfano, C. A., Beidel, D. C., & Turner, S. M. (2006). Cognitive correlates of social phobia among children and adolescents. *Journal of Abnormal Child Psychology, 34*(2), 182–194.

American Psychiatric Association. (2013). *Diagnostic and statistical manual of mental disorders* (5th ed.). Arlington, VA: Author.

American School Counselor Association. (2016). ASCA National Model: Executive Summary. Available at *www.schoolcounselor.org/asca/media/asca/ASCA%20National%20Model%20Templates/ANMExecSumm.pdf.*

Anctil, T. M., Klose Smith, C., Schenck, P., & Dahir, C. (2012). Professional school counselors' career development practices and continuing education needs. *Career Development Quarterly, 60*(2), 109–121.

Anderson, E. R., & Hope, D. A. (2009). The relationship among social phobia, objective and perceived physiological reactivity, and anxiety sensitivity in an adolescent population. *Journal of Anxiety Disorders, 23*(1), 18–26.

Anti-Bullying Bill of Rights Act. Public Law 2010, Chapter 122, New Jersey legislature.

Armbruster, P., & Lichtman, J. (1999). Are school based mental health services effective?: Evidence from 36 inner city schools. *Community Mental Health Journal, 35*(6), 493–504.

Beck, A. T., & Emery, G. (1985). *Anxiety disorders and phobias: A cognitive perspective.* New York: Basic Books.

Beesdo-Baum, K., Knappe, S., Fehm, L., Höfler, M., Lieb, R., Hofmann, S. G., . . . Wittchen, H. U. (2012). The natural course of social anxiety disorder among adolescents and young adults. *Acta Psychiatrica Scandinavica, 126*(6), 411–425.

Beidel, D. C. (1991). Social phobia and overanxious disorder in school-age children. *Journal of the American Academy of Child and Adolescent Psychiatry, 30*(4), 545–552.

Beidel, D. C., & Turner, S. M. (2007). Clinical presentation of social anxiety disorder in children and adolescents. In *Shy children, phobic adults: Nature and treatment of social anxiety disorder* (2nd ed., pp. 47–80). Washington, DC: American Psychological Association.

Beidel, D. C., Turner, S. M., & Dancu, C. V. (1985). Physiological, cognitive and behavioral aspects of social anxiety. *Behaviour Research and Therapy, 23*(2), 109–117.

Beidel, D. C., Turner, S. M., & Morris, T. L. (1995). A new inventory to assess childhood social anxiety and phobia: The Social Phobia and Anxiety Inventory for Children. *Psychological Assessment, 7*(1), 73–79.

Beidel, D. C., Turner, S. M., & Morris, T. L. (1998). *Social effectiveness therapy for children: A treatment manual.* Unpublished manuscript, Medical University of South Carolina.

Beidel, D. C., Turner, S. M., & Morris, T. L. (1999). Psychopathology of childhood social phobia. *Journal of the American Academy of Child and Adolescent Psychiatry, 38*(6), 643–650.

Beidel, D. C., Turner, S. M., & Morris, T. L. (2000). Behavioral treatment of childhood social phobia. *Journal of Consulting and Clinical Psychology, 68*(6), 1072–1080.

Beidel, D. C., Turner, S. M., Young, B. J., Ammerman, R. T., Sallee, F. R., & Crosby, L. (2007). Psychopathology of adolescent social phobia. *Journal of Psychopathology and Behavioral Assessment*, 29(1), 46–53.

Birmaher, B., Brent, D. A., Chiappetta, L., Bridge, J., Monga, S., & Baugher, M. (1999). Psychometric properties of the Screen for Child Anxiety Related Emotional Disorders (SCARED): A replication study. *Journal of the American Academy of Child and Adolescent Psychiatry*, 38(10), 1230–1236.

Birmaher, B., Khetarpal, S., Brent, D., Cully, M., Balach, L., Kaufman, J., . . . Neer, S. M. (1997). The Screen for Child Anxiety Related Emotional Disorders (SCARED): Scale construction and psychometric characteristics. *Journal of the American Academy of Child and Adolescent Psychiatry*, 36(4), 545–553.

Black, J. J., Tran, G. Q., Goldsmith, A. A., Thompson, R. D., Smith, J. P., & Welge, J. A. (2012). Alcohol expectancies and social self-efficacy as mediators of differential intervention outcomes for college hazardous drinkers with social anxiety. *Addictive Behaviors*, 37(3), 248–255.

Blakemore, S. J., & Choudhury, S. (2006). Development of the adolescent brain: Implications for executive function and social cognition. *Journal of Child Psychology and Psychiatry*, 47(3–4), 296–312.

Carrigan, M. H., & Randall, C. L. (2003). Self-medication in social phobia: A review of the alcohol literature. *Addictive Behaviors*, 28(2), 269–284.

Chen, Y. P., Ehlers, A., Clark, D. M., & Mansell, W. (2002). Patients with generalized social phobia direct their attention away from faces. *Behaviour Research and Therapy*, 40(6), 677–687.

Christner, R. W., Forrest, E., Morley, J., & Weinstein, E. (2007). Taking cognitive-behavior therapy to school: A school-based mental health approach. *Journal of Contemporary Psychotherapy*, 37(3), 175–183.

Clark, D. M. (2005). A cognitive perspective on social phobia. In W. R. Crozier & L. E. Alden (Eds.), *The essential handbook of social anxiety for clinicians* (pp. 193–218). Hoboken, NJ: Wiley.

Clark, D. M., Ehlers, A., Hackmann, A., McManus, F., Fennell, M., Grey, N., . . . Wild, J. (2006). Cognitive therapy versus exposure and applied relaxation in social phobia: A randomized controlled trial. *Journal of Consulting and Clinical Psychology*, 74(3), 568–578.

Clark, D. M., & Wells, A. (1995). A cognitive model of social phobia. In R. G. Heimberg, M. R. Leibowitz, D. A. Hope, & F. R. Schneier (Eds.), *Social phobia: Diagnosis, assessment, and treatment* (pp. 69–93). New York: Guilford Press.

Colognori, D., Esseling, P., Stewart, C., Reiss, P., Lu, F., Case, B., & Masia Warner, C. (2012). Self-disclosure and mental health service use in socially anxious adolescents. *School Mental Health*, 4(4), 219–230.

Cougle, J. R., Fitch, K. E., Fincham, F. D., Riccardi, C. J., Keough, M. E., & Timpano, K. R. (2012). Excessive reassurance seeking and anxiety pathology: Tests of incremental associations and directionality. *Journal of Anxiety Disorders*, 26(1), 117–125.

Craske, M. G., & Barlow, D. H. (2006). *Mastery of your anxiety and panic: Therapist guide*. New York; Oxford University Press.

Craske, M. G., Treanor, M., Conway, C. C., Zbozinek, T., & Vervliet, B. (2014). Maximizing exposure therapy: An inhibitory learning approach. *Behaviour Research and Therapy*, 58, 10–23.

Cuming, S., & Rapee, R. M. (2010). Social anxiety and self-protective communication style in close relationships. *Behaviour Research and Therapy*, 48(2), 87–96.

Donker, T., Griffiths, K. M., Cuijpers, P., & Christensen, H. (2009). Psychoeducation for depression, anxiety and psychological distress: A meta-analysis. *BMC Medicine*, 7(1), 79.

Erath, S. A., Flanagan, K. S., & Bierman, K. L. (2007). Social anxiety and peer relations in early adolescence: Behavioral and cognitive factors. *Journal of Abnormal Child Psychology*, 35(3), 405–416.

Evans, S. (1999). Mental health services in schools: Utilization, effectiveness, and consent. *Clinical Psychology Review*, 19(2), 165–178.

Festa, C. C., & Ginsburg, G. S. (2011). Parental and peer predictors of social anxiety in youth. *Child Psychiatry and Human Development*, 42(3), 291–306.

Fisher, P. H., Masia-Warner, C., & Klein, R. G. (2004). Skills for social and academic success: A school-based intervention for social anxiety disorder in adolescents. *Clinical Child and Family Psychology Review*, 7(4), 241–249.

Foa, E. B., & Franklin, M. E. (2001). Obsessive– compulsive disorder. In D. H. Barlow (Ed.), *Clinical handbook of psychological disorders* (3rd ed., pp. 209–263). New York: Guilford Press.

Foa, E. B., Franklin, M. E., Perry, K. J., & Herbert, J. D. (1996). Cognitive biases in generalized social phobia. *Journal of Abnormal Psychology*, 105(3), 433–439.

Foa, E. B., & Kozak, M. J. (1986). Emotional processing of fear: Exposure to corrective information. *Psychological Bulletin*, 99(1), 20–35.

Foa, E. B., & McNally, R. J. (1996). Mechanisms of

change in exposure therapy. In R. M. Rapee (Ed.), *Current controversies in the anxiety disorders* (pp. 329–343). New York: Guilford Press.

Ginsburg, G. S., Kendall, P. C., Sakolsky, D., Compton, S. N., Piacentini, J., Albano, A. M., . . . Keeton, C. P. (2011). Remission after acute treatment in children and adolescents with anxiety disorders: Findings from the CAMS. *Journal of Consulting and Clinical Psychology, 79*(6), 806–813.

Ginsburg, G. S., La Greca, A. M., & Silverman, W. K. (1998). Social anxiety in children with anxiety disorders: Relation with social and emotional functioning. *Journal of Abnormal Child Psychology, 26*(3), 175–185.

Grover, R. L., Ginsburg, G. S., & Ialongo, N. (2007). Psychosocial outcomes of anxious first graders: A seven-year follow-up. *Depression and Anxiety, 24*(6), 410–420.

Heimberg, R. G., Brozovich, F. A., & Rapee, R. M. (2010). A cognitive-behavioral model of social anxiety disorder: Update and extension. In S. G. Hofmann & P. M. DiBartolo (Eds.), *Social anxiety: Clinical, developmental, and social perspectives* (2nd ed., pp. 395–422). San Diego, CA: Academic Press.

Heiser, N. A., Turner, S. M., Beidel, D. C., & Roberson-Nay, R. (2009). Differentiating social phobia from shyness. *Journal of Anxiety Disorders, 23*(4), 469–476.

Henderson, L., & Zimbardo, P. (1998). *Trouble in river city: Shame and anger in chronic shyness.* Paper presented at the American Psychological Association 106th National Conference, San Francisco, CA.

Herbert, J. D., Gaudiano, B. A., Rheingold, A. A., Myers, V. H., Dalrymple, K., & Nolan, E. M. (2005). Social skills training augments the effectiveness of cognitive behavioral group therapy for social anxiety disorder. *Behavior Therapy, 36*(2), 125–138.

Hermans, D., Craske, M. G., Mineka, S., & Lovibond, P. F. (2006). Extinction in human fear conditioning. *Biological Psychiatry, 60*(4), 361–368.

Herzig-Anderson, K., Colognori, D., Fox, J. K., Stewart, C. E., & Masia Warner, C. (2012). School-based anxiety treatments for children and adolescents. *Child and Adolescent Psychiatric Clinics of North America, 21*(3), 655–668.

Hofmann, S. G. (2007). Cognitive factors that maintain social anxiety disorder: A comprehensive model and its treatment implications. *Cognitive Behaviour Therapy, 36*(4), 193–209.

Hofmann, S. G., Albano, A. M., Heimberg, R. G., Tracey, S., Chorpita, B. F., & Barlow, D. H. (1999).

Subtypes of social phobia in adolescents. *Depression and Anxiety, 9*(1), 15–18.

Individuals with Disabilities Education Improvement Act of 2004, 20 U.S.C. § 1400 et seq.

Johnson, J., Rochkind, J., & Ott, A. (2010). Why guidance counseling needs to change. *Educational Leadership, 67*(7), 74–79.

Katzelnick, D. J., Kobak, K. A., DeLeire, T., Henk, H. J., Greist, J. H., Davidson, J. R., . . . Helstad, C. P. (2001). Impact of generalized social anxiety disorder in managed care. *American Journal of Psychiatry, 158*(12), 1999–2007.

Kearney, C. A. (2001). *School refusal behavior in youth: A functional approach to assessment and treatment.* Washington, DC: American Psychological Association.

Kearney, C. A. (2005). *Social anxiety and social phobia in youth: Characteristics, assessment, and psychological treatment.* Dordrecht, The Netherlands: Springer Science & Business Media.

Kearney, C. A. (2007). *Getting your child to say "yes" to school: A guide for parents of youth with school refusal behavior.* New York: Oxford University Press.

Kearney, C. A. (2008). *Helping school refusing children and their parents: A guide for school-based professionals.* New York: Oxford University Press.

Kendall, P. C., Settipani, C. A., & Cummings, C. M. (2012). No need to worry: The promising future of child anxiety research. *Journal of Clinical Child and Adolescent Psychology, 41*(1), 103–115.

Kessler, R. C. (2003). The impairments caused by social phobia in the general population: Implications for intervention. *Acta Psychiatrica Scandinavica, 108*(Suppl. 417), 19–27.

Kessler, R. C., Avenevoli, S., Costello, E. J., Georgiades, K., Green, J. G., Gruber, M. J., . . . Sampson, N. A. (2012). Prevalence, persistence, and sociodemographic correlates of DSM-IV disorders in the National Comorbidity Survey Replication Adolescent Supplement. *Archives of General Psychiatry, 69*(4), 372–380.

Kessler, R. C., Berglund, P., Demler, O., Jin, R., Merikangas, K. R., & Walters, E. E. (2005). Lifetime prevalence and age-of-onset distributions of DSM-IV disorders in the National Comorbidity Survey Replication. *Archives of General Psychiatry, 62*(6), 593–602.

Kessler, R. C., Foster, C. L., Saunders, W. B., & Stang, P. E. (1995). Social consequences of psychiatric disorders: I. Educational attainment. *American Journal of Psychiatry, 152*(7), 1026–1032.

Kessler, R. C., Stang, P., Wittchen, H. U., Stein, M., & Walters, E. E. (1999). Lifetime comorbidities between social phobia and mood disorders in the

US National Comorbidity Survey. *Psychological Medicine, 29*(03), 555–567.

Kessler, R. C., Stein, M. B., & Berglund, P. (1998). Social phobia subtypes in the National Comorbidity Survey. *American Journal of Psychiatry, 155*(5), 613–619.

Lader, M. H., & Mathews, A. M. (1968). A physiological model of phobic anxiety and desensitization. *Behaviour Research and Therapy, 6*(4), 411–421.

Lang, A. J., & Craske, M. G. (2000). Manipulations of exposure-based therapy to reduce return of fear: A replication. *Behaviour Research and Therapy, 38*(1), 1–12.

Lang, P. J. (1968). Fear reduction and fear behavior: Problems in treating a construct. In J. M. Shlien (Ed.), *Research in psychotherapy* (Vol. 3, pp. 90–103). Washington, DC: American Psychological Association.

Lang, P. J., & Lazovik, A. D. (1963). Experimental desensitization of phobia. *Journal of Abnormal and Social Psychology, 66*(6), 519–525.

Lovibond, P. F., Davis, N. R., & O'Flaherty, A. S. (2000). Protection from extinction in human fear conditioning. *Behaviour Research and Therapy, 38*(10), 967–983.

Lucock, M. P., & Salkovskis, P. M. (1988). Cognitive factors in social anxiety and its treatment. *Behaviour Research and Therapy, 26*(4), 297–302.

March, J. S., & Parker, J. D. (2004). The Multidimensional Anxiety Scale for Children (MASC). In M. E. Markish (Ed.), *The use of psychological testing for treatment planning and outcomes assessment* (3rd ed., Vol. 2, pp. 39–62). Mahwah, NJ: Erlbaum.

March, J. S., Parker, J. D., Sullivan, K., Stallings, P., & Conners, C. K. (1997). The Multidimensional Anxiety Scale for Children (MASC): Factor structure, reliability, and validity. *Journal of the American Academy of Child and Adolescent Psychiatry, 36*(4), 554–565.

Masia, C., Beidel, D. C., Albano, A. M., Rapee, R. M., Turner, S. M., Morris, T. L., & Klein, R. G. (1999). *Skills for academic and social success.* Available from Carrie Masia Warner, PhD, NYU Child Study Center, 1 Park Avenue, 8th floor, New York, NY 10016.

Masia Warner, C., Colognori, D., Brice, C., Herzig, K., Mufson, L., Lynch, C., . . . Ryan, J. (2016). Can school counselors deliver cognitive-behavioral treatment for social anxiety effectively?: A randomized controlled trial. *Journal of Child Psychology and Psychiatry, 57*(11), 1229–1238.

Masia Warner, C., Fisher, P. H., Shrout, P. E., Rathor, S., & Klein, R. G. (2007). Treating adolescents with social anxiety disorder in school: An attention control trial. *Journal of Child Psychology and Psychiatry, 48*(7), 676–686.

Masia Warner, C., & Fox, J. K. (2012). Advances and challenges in school-based intervention for anxious and depressed youth: Identifying and addressing issues of sustainability. *School Mental Health, 4*(4), 193–196.

Masia Warner, C., Klein, R. G., Dent, H. C., Fisher, P. H., Alvir, J., Marie Albano, A., & Guardino, M. (2005). School-based intervention for adolescents with social anxiety disorder: Results of a controlled study. *Journal of Abnormal Child Psychology, 33*(6), 707–722.

Masia Warner, C., Klein, R. G., & Liebowitz, M. R. (2003a). *The Liebowitz Social Anxiety Scale for Children and Adolescents* (LSAS-CA). Available from Carrie Masia Warner, PhD, NYU Child Study Center, 1 Park Avenue, 8th floor, New York, NY, 10016.

Masia Warner, C., Storch, E. A., Pincus, D. B., Klein, R. G., Heimberg, R. G., & Liebowitz, M. R. (2003b). The Liebowitz Social Anxiety Scale for Children and Adolescents: An initial psychometric investigation. *Journal of the American Academy of Child and Adolescent Psychiatry, 42*(9), 1076–1084.

McLeod, B. D., Wood, J. J., & Weisz, J. R. (2007). Examining the association between parenting and childhood anxiety: A meta-analysis. *Clinical Psychology Review, 27*(2), 155–172.

Mellings, T. M., & Alden, L. E. (2000). Cognitive processes in social anxiety: The effects of self-focus, rumination and anticipatory processing. *Behaviour Research and Therapy, 38*(3), 243–257.

Mendlowitz, S. L., Manassis, K., Bradley, S., Scapillato, D., Miezitis, S., & Shaw, B. E. (1999). Cognitive-behavioral group treatments in childhood anxiety disorders: The role of parental involvement. *Journal of the American Academy of Child and Adolescent Psychiatry, 38*(10), 1223–1229.

Merikangas, K. R., He, J. P., Burstein, M., Swanson, S. A., Avenevoli, S., Cui, L., . . . Swendsen, J. (2010). Lifetime prevalence of mental disorders in US adolescents: Results from the National Comorbidity Survey Replication– Adolescent Supplement (NCS-A). *Journal of the American Academy of Child and Adolescent Psychiatry, 49*(10), 980–989.

Merikangas, K. R., He, J. P., Burstein, M., Swendsen, J., Avenevoli, S., Case, B., . . . Olfson, M. (2011). Service utilization for lifetime mental disorders in US adolescents: Results of the National Comorbidity Survey– Adolescent Supplement (NCS-A).

Journal of the American Academy of Child and Adolescent Psychiatry, 50(1), 32–45.

Merikangas, K. R., & Swanson, S. A. (2009). Comorbidity in anxiety disorders. In M. B. Stein & T. Steckler (Eds.), *Behavioral neurobiology of anxiety and its treatment* (pp. 37–59). Berlin: Springer Verlag.

Mesa, F., Beidel, D. C., & Bunnell, B. E. (2014). An examination of psychopathology and daily impairment in adolescents with social anxiety disorder. *PLOS ONE, 9*(4), e93668.

Mesa, F., Nieves, M. M., & Beidel, D. C. (2011). Clinical presentation of social anxiety disorder in adolescents and young adults. In C. A. Alfano & D. C. Beidel (Eds.), *Social anxiety in adolescents and young adults: Translating developmental science into practice* (pp. 11–27). Washington, DC: American Psychological Association.

Moyer, M. (2011). Effects of non-guidance activities, supervision, and student-to-counselor ratios on school counselor burnout. *Journal of School Counseling, 9*(5), 1–31.

Nelson, E. C., Grant, J. D., Bucholz, K. K., Glowinski, A., Madden, P. A. F., Reich, W., & Heath, A. C. (2000). Social phobia in a population-based female adolescent twin sample: Co-morbidity and associated suicide-related symptoms. *Psychological Medicine, 30*(4), 797–804.

Nock, M. K., & Ferriter, C. (2005). Parent management of attendance and adherence in child and adolescent therapy: A conceptual and empirical review. *Clinical Child and Family Psychology Review, 8*(2), 149–166.

Owens, J. S., & Fabiano, G. A. (2011). School mental health programming for youth with ADHD: Addressing needs across the academic career. *School Mental Health, 3*(3), 111–116.

Piacentini, J., & Langley, A. K. (2004). Cognitive-behavioral therapy for children who have obsessive– compulsive disorder. *Journal of Clinical Psychology, 60*(11), 1181–1194.

Pine, D. S., Cohen, P., Gurley, D., Brook, J., & Ma, Y. (1998). The risk for early-adulthood anxiety and depressive disorders in adolescents with anxiety and depressive disorders. *Archives of General Psychiatry, 55*(1), 56–64.

Ranta, K., Kaltiala-Heino, R., Fröjd, S., & Marttunen, M. (2013). Peer victimization and social phobia: A follow-up study among adolescents. *Social Psychiatry and Psychiatric Epidemiology, 48*(4), 533–544.

Ranta, K., Kaltiala-Heino, R., Pelkonen, M., & Marttunen, M. (2009). Associations between peer victimization, self-reported depression and social phobia among adolescents: The role of comorbidity. *Journal of Adolescence, 32*(1), 77–93.

Rapee, R. M. (1998). *Overcoming shyness and social phobia: A step-by-step guide.* Northvale, NJ: Jason Aronson.

Rapee, R. M., & Heimberg, R. G. (1997). A cognitive-behavioral model of anxiety in social phobia. *Behaviour Research and Therapy, 35*(8), 741–756.

Rapee, R., Wignall, A., Spence, S., Lyneham, H., & Cobham, V. (2008). *Helping your anxious child: A step-by-step guide for parents.* Oakland, CA: New Harbinger.

Reese, S. (2010). A leading role for career guidance counselors. *Techniques: Connecting Education and Careers (J1), 85*(7), 16–19.

Rescorla, R. A., & Wagner, A. R. (1972). A theory of Pavlovian conditioning: Variations in the effectiveness of reinforcement and nonreinforcement. In A. H. Black & W. F. Prokasy (Eds.), *Classical conditioning II: Current research and theory* (pp. 64–99). New York: Appleton-Century-Crofts.

Ryan, J. L., & Masia Warner, C. (2012). Treating adolescents with social anxiety disorder in schools. *Child and Adolescent Psychiatric Clinics of North America, 21*(1), 105–118.

Ryan, R. M., & Kuczkowski, R. (1994). The imaginary audience, self-consciousness, and public individuation in adolescence. *Journal of Personality, 62*(2), 219–238.

Salkovskis, P. M. (1991). The importance of behaviour in the maintenance of anxiety and panic: A cognitive account. *Behavioural Psychotherapy, 19*(1), 6–19.

Salkovskis, P. M., Hackmann, A., Wells, A., Gelder, M. G., & Clark, D. M. (2007). Belief disconfirmation versus habituation approaches to situational exposure in panic disorder with agoraphobia: A pilot study. *Behaviour Research and Therapy, 45*(5), 877–885.

Schlenker, B. R., & Leary, M. R. (1985). Social anxiety and communication about the self. *Journal of Language and Social Psychology, 4*(3–4), 171–192.

Schoenwald, S. K., & Hoagwood, K. (2001). Effectiveness, transportability, and dissemination of interventions: What matters when? *Psychiatric Services, 52*(9), 1190–1197.

Selye, H. (1974). *Stress without distress.* Philadelphia: Lippincott.

Spence, S. H., Donovan, C., & Brechman-Toussaint, M. (1999). Social skills, social outcomes, and cognitive features of childhood social phobia. *Journal of Abnormal Psychology, 108*(2), 211–221.

Stein, M. B., & Kean, Y. M. (2000). Disability and quality of life in social phobia: Epidemiologic findings. *American Journal of Psychiatry, 157*(10), 1606–1613.

Storch, E. A., Brassard, M. R., & Masia-Warner, C. L. (2003). The relationship of peer victimization to social anxiety and loneliness in adolescence. *Child Study Journal, 33*(1), 1–19.

Storch, E. A., & Masia-Warner, C. (2004). The relationship of peer victimization to social anxiety and loneliness in adolescent females. *Journal of Adolescence, 27*(3), 351–362.

Stratakis, C. A., & Chrousos, G. P. (1995). Neuroendocrinology and pathophysiology of the stress system. *Annals of the New York Academy of Sciences, 771*(1), 1–18.

Strauss, C. C., Lease, C. A., Kazdin, A. E., Dulcan, M. K., & Last, C. G. (1989). Multimethod assessment of the social competence of children with anxiety disorders. *Journal of Clinical Child Psychology, 18*(2), 184–189.

Sulkowski, M. L., Joyce, D. K., & Storch, E. A. (2012). Treating childhood anxiety in schools: Service delivery in a response to intervention paradigm. *Journal of Child and Family Studies, 21*(6), 938–947.

Swedo, S. E., Rapoport, J. L., Leonard, H., Lenane, M., & Cheslow, D. (1989). Obsessive– compulsive disorder in children and adolescents: Clinical phenomenology of 70 consecutive cases. *Archives of General Psychiatry, 46*(4), 335–341.

Sweeney, C., Warner, C. M., Brice, C., Stewart, C., Ryan, J., Loeb, K. L., & McGrath, R. E. (2015). Identification of social anxiety in schools: The utility of a two-step screening process. *Contemporary School Psychology, 19*(4), 268–275.

Taylor, S., Woody, S., Koch, W. J., Mclean, P., Paterson, R. J., & Anderson, K. W. (1997). Cognitive restructuring in the treatment of social phobia efficacy and mode of action. *Behavior Modification, 21*(4), 487–511.

Thomas, S. E., Randall, C. L., & Carrigan, M. H. (2003). Drinking to cope in socially anxious individuals: A controlled study. *Alcoholism: Clinical and Experimental Research, 27*(12), 1937–1943.

Turner, S. M., Beidel, D. C., & Townsley, R. M. (1990). Social phobia: Relationship to shyness. *Behaviour Research and Therapy, 28*(6), 497–505.

Van Ameringen, M., Mancini, C., & Farvolden, P. (2003). The impact of anxiety disorders on educational achievement. *Journal of Anxiety Disorders, 17*(5), 561–571.

Vetter, N. C., Leipold, K., Kliegel, M., Phillips, L. H., & Altgassen, M. (2013). Ongoing development of social cognition in adolescence. *Child Neuropsychology, 19*(6), 615–629.

Weems, C. F., Berman, S. L., Silverman, W. K., & Saavedra, L. M. (2001). Cognitive errors in youth with anxiety disorders: The linkages between negative cognitive errors and anxious symptoms. *Cognitive Therapy and Research, 25*(5), 559–575.

Weems, C. F., Costa, N. M., Watts, S. E., Taylor, L. K., & Cannon, M. F. (2007). Cognitive errors, anxiety sensitivity, and anxiety control beliefs: Their unique and specific associations with childhood anxiety symptoms. *Behavior Modification, 31*(2), 174–201.

Weist, M. D., Paskewitz, D. A., Warner, B. S., & Flaherty, L. T. (1996). Treatment outcome of school-based mental health services for urban teenagers. *Community Mental Health Journal, 32*(2), 149–157.

Wittchen, H. U., Stein, M. B., & Kessler, R. C. (1999). Social fears and social phobia in a community sample of adolescents and young adults: Prevalence, risk factors and comorbidity. *Psychological Medicine, 29*(2), 309–323.

Woodward, L. J., & Fergusson, D. M. (2001). Life course outcomes of young people with anxiety disorders in adolescence. *Journal of the American Academy of Child and Adolescent Psychiatry, 40*(9), 1086–1093.

Yonkers, K. A., Bruce, S. E., Dyck, I. R., & Keller, M. B. (2003). Chronicity, relapse, and illness— course of panic disorder, social phobia, and generalized anxiety disorder: Findings in men and women from 8 years of follow-up. *Depression and Anxiety, 17*(3), 173–179.

Index

Note. *f* or *t* following a page number indicates a figure or a table.